RESIDENTIAL CARE

WELFARE AND SOCIETY
STUDIES IN WELFARE POLICY, PRACTICE AND THEORY

Series Editors:
Matthew Colton, Kevin Haines, Peter Raynor, Tim Stainton and Anthea Symonds
School of Social Sciences and International Development,
University of Wales Swansea

Welfare and Society is an exciting series from the University of Wales Swansea, School of Social Sciences and International Development in conjunction with Ashgate, concerned with all aspects of social welfare. The series publishes works of research, theory, history and practice from a wide range of contemporary applied social studies subjects such as Criminal Justice, Child Welfare, Community Care, Race and Ethnicity, Therapeutic and Intervention Techniques, Community Development and Social Policy. The series includes extended research reports of scholarly interest as well as works aimed at both the academic and professional communities.

Residential Care
Horizons for the New Century

Edited by

HANS GÖRAN ERIKSSON and TORILL TJELFLAAT
*The Regional Child Protection Research Unit, Norwegian University of
Science and Technology, Trondheim, Norway*

ASHGATE

Published by
Ashgate Publishing Limited
Gower House
Croft Road
Aldershot
Hants GU11 3HR
England

Ashgate Publishing Company
Suite 420
101 Cherry Street
Burlington, VT 05401-4405
USA

Ashgate website: http://www.ashgate.com

British Library Cataloguing in Publication Data
Residential care : horizons for the new century
   1.Children - Institutional care
   I.Eriksson, Hans Göran II. Tjelflaat, Torill
   362.7'3

Library of Congress Cataloging-in-Publication Data
Residential care : horizons for the new century / editors, Hans Göran Eriksson and Torill Tjelflaat.
     p. cm. -- (Welfare and society)
   Includes bibliographical references and index.
   ISBN 0-7546-4098-1
    1. Children--Institutional care. 2. Foster home care. I. Eriksson, Hans Göran. II.
Tjelflaat, Torill. III. Series.

HV862.R468 2004
362.73'3--dc22

2003070902

ISBN 0 7546 4098 1

Printed and bound in Great Britain by MPG Books Ltd, Bodmin, Cornwall.

Contents

List of Figures

List of Tables

List of Contributors

Helen Agathonos-Georgopoulou, **Kevin D. Browne** and **Jasmin Sarafidou**, Institute of Child Health 7, Fokidos str., 115 26 Athens, Greece, agatinst@otenet.gr.

James P. Anglin, Director and Associate Professor, School of Child and Youth Care, University of Victoria, PO Box 1700, Victoria, BC V8W 2Y2, Canada. janglin@uvic.ca.

Brian Ashley, Consultant, Ludvigsbergsgatan 10, 118 23 Stockholm, Sweden, brian.ashley@telia.com.

Hans Göran Eriksson (hans.g.eriksson@ahs.hist.no), PhD (MSW), Associate Professor, Sør-Trøndelag University College, Department of Social Work Programme, Ranheimsveien 10, 7004 Trondheim, Norway.

Rosa Heim, College für Familien Pädagogik, Gabelsbergerstr. 14, A-4600 Wels, Austria, colleg@sos-kinderdorf.at.

Ingrid Höjer, PhD (Ingrid.Hojer@socwork.gu.se) and **Monica Nordenfors**, Master of Social Work, PhD student (Monica.Nordenfors@socwork.gu.se), Department of Social Work, Göteborg University, Box 720, 405 30 Göteborg, Sweden.

Andrew Kendrick (andrew.kendrick@strath.ac.uk), **Richard Mitchell** (richard.mitchell@strath.ac.uk) and **Mark Smith** (m.smith.100@strath.ac.uk), Department of Social Work, University of Strathclyde, 76 Southbrae Drive, G13 1PP Glasgow, Scotland.

Erik J. Knorth, PhD (knorth@fsw.leidenuniv.nl), Associate Professor, Leiden University, Department of Education, PO Box 9555, NL-2300 RB Leiden, The Netherlands, **John P.M. Meijers**, MA, Director External Relations, Horizon Foundation, **Arianne Brouwer**, MA, Head Department of Research and Development, Horizon Foundation, **Eek Jansen**, MA, Child Psychologist, Horizon Foundation and **Hans Du Prie**, MSW, Director Care and Education, Horizon Foundation, Horizon Foundation, Institute for Child and Youth

Care and Special Education, PO Box 37056, NL-3005 LB Rotterdam, The Netherlands, centraalbureau@horizon-jeugdzorg.nl.

Clíona Murphy (clmurph@tcd.ie), Research Fellow, Children's Research Centre, Trinity College, 2 Dublin, Ireland.

Toyin Okitikpi (FRSA) (okitikt@sbu.ac.uk), London South Bank University, Faculty of Health and Social Care, Erlang House, 128 Blackfriars Road, London SE1 8EQ, UK.

Tarja Pösö (tarja.poso@uta.fi), University of Tampere, Department of Social Policy and Social Work, Pinninkatu 47, 33 014 Tampere, Finland.

Jane Prior (j.prior@strath.ac.uk), University of Strathclyde, Southbrae Drive, 913 1PP Glasgow, Scotland.

Torill Tjelflaat (torill.tjelflaat@allforskontnu.no), Director and Senior Researcher at the Regional Child Research Unit, Allforsk, Trondheim, Norway.

Arne Tveit (arne@mka.no) and **Bjørn Arnesen** (bjorn@mka.no), Midt-Norsk Kompetansesenter for Adferd, Jarleveien 4, 7041 Trondheim, Norway, www.mka.no.

Odilia van Manen-Rojnic (odilia.rojnic@pu.tel.hr), Nadomak Sunca, Oprtalj 21, 52428 Oprtalj, Croatia.

Acknowledgements

The publication of this book has been made possible through the cooperation of many. The Board of Directors for The Regional Child Protection Research Unit in Trondheim, Norway made the production of this book possible. The Board for the European Scientific Association for Residential and Foster Care for Children and Adolescents, EUSARF supported us from planning to completion of the 7th EUSARF congress in Trondheim, without which there would not have been a gathering with focus on residential and foster care in Trondheim, and no publication.

However, we are most grateful to the many children and young people around the world who have shared glimpses of their lives to the authors thereby providing them with insights, reflections and knowledge which they share in this book. The authors were contacted and invited to publish after the congress. A request, that for many put an extra burden on previous set schedule and tasks. We are greatly indebted to them for their contributions.

Hans Göran Eriksson
Torill Tjelflaat

Introduction

Hans Göran Eriksson

Placing children and young persons in residential care and foster care is ranking high on the political agenda and is also increasingly influenced through cultural and socioeconomic processes. New developments, phenomena and events challenge old images and opinions about what is the optimal care for these citizens. These processes show differences between continents, countries and even regions within countries. Residential and foster care for children and young persons has consequences for childcare in general. Certainly for those children who, as a result of moving out of their family home, against their own will or voluntary, to temporarily or permanently placements often due to lack of proper care.

Residential Care: Horizons for the New Century addresses many of the challenges which child and youth care confront at present. Institutions for children and young people have often been seen as an unsatisfactory alternative. Institutional care, however, is now increasingly oriented towards innovative thinking and methods, and there are many exciting developments at international level. In many countries, foster care is the preferred and most usually adopted alternative for placement outside the home, and it is beyond question that foster care has been professionalized in many of its aspects, in recent decades. As important as the actual generation of new and relevant knowledge, is dissemination of findings to those who can use them in the field and in policy development. The contributions presented here is hoped to give new insights and ideas that can help children and young people in need of care outside their own homes.

Part I: Challenges, Innovations and Education: Elements in Anti-oppressive Practice

Residential care and foster care should reflect anti-oppressive practice. The children and young persons are expected to meet caring adults whose training include morally informed practice. However, according to Prior (*Chapter 1*), there is little evidence of moral theory as a base for education of social workers, neither literature used in educating social workers in the UK. Prior questions the influence of technical rational approaches to practice and states that limiting social work to a technical occupation might be expedient for governments and managers driven by technical notions of efficiency and accountability. She argues for that until moral debate is established as a crucial element of social work education and practice technical and political accounts of social work will persist to dominate both the debate and practice.

While Prior describes the concerns for increasing moral debates in order to practice anti-oppressive, Knorth, Meijers Brower, Jensen and du Prie (*Chapter 2*) illustrate how anti-oppressive practice is carried out with success in The Netherlands. They refer to a development that is characterized as a move towards a more participatory, client empowering child and youth care practice. It broadly reminds of the old grandmother's rule: 'Catch the kids in doing something good, and let them know about it'! In the experiment at the Horizon Foundation client feedback, meaning '... that children and/or parents voice their opinion on the conduct of care givers or, in a broader context, on the care of the entire institution has become an indispensable building block to help realize a client centred child and youthcare'. However, it must not be an isolated method focusing only on staff behaviour but included to encompass all living and educational arrangements of the institution.

In contrast to Prior's concern with how focus on technical and managerial practice influence social work, Kendrick, Mitchell and Smith (*Chapter 3*) illustrate how an integrated residential model for practice with sexually aggressive young men with emphasizes on a safe, secure and nurturing environment has produced progress of the work. Through this approach the need for security and stability in the life of the young men through individual and personal focused change programmes has been successful.

To provide success for children and youth in care outside their own home does not just happens specifically when the external structure for practice does not define the profession. The SOS Children's Villages is such a structure. Heim (*Chapter 4*), describes and illustrate how by adapting a family life education model with particular focusing on the holistic processes of personal development adult carers are permitted to combine human kindness with the professional skills needed to shape the everyday childcare situation. Based on practical experience with focus on personality development, self-empowerment, self-reflection and knowledge assimilation the staff are helped and encouraged to establish conditions conducive to development in emotionally disturbed children and young adults.

Part II: Foster Care: Preparing For, Practising and Living in the Midst Of

The second part of this book is on foster care and starts with a contribution from Murphy (*Chapter 5*). Central to this contribution is the involvement of the child in the planning and preparation for placement in foster care. The role of the preparatory placement and the range of interventions and people involved in the preparation process is illuminated and discussed. Each process of preparation is customized for the child which demands creativity on all parts involving a unique blend of residential care and social work inputs in a whole, integrated service. The core in the process is to give the children the time they need to address issues about their own family, previous carers and how they deal with their issues. The bottom line is: Take the child seriously and involve the child both in the preparatory stage, the transition and during the early stages of the foster placement.

The contribution of van Manen-Rojnic (*Chapter 6*) is complementary to that of Murphy in the sense that the many case histories give strong evidence to the importance of listening to the lived lives of children in order to provide helpful placements. Created in the midst of a war, Nadomak Sunca, provide professional foster care within a family environment. With a plea for open adoption, well-organized and more professional foster care, and when necessary, modernized residential care in small units, van Manen-Rojnic gives voice to the children's stories. This challenges the reader to reflect upon and create a promising future for children who live in situations with minimal promise.

Being placed in a foster home is one thing, and living in a foster home as the biological child to the foster parents is another. Höjer (*Chapter 7*) gives a report of some first results from a study in Sweden on the experiences of children of foster carers. Children and young people usually show an understanding attitude towards the needs of foster children, and also towards their parents' strong wish to make the fostering task successful. This attitude and behaviour is expressed in the children's active part in the fostering assignment. Although they experience stress most foster carers seem to cope adequately, and to benefit in many ways from living with foster children. The 'empathy lesson' has been quite successful; these are children and young people with an unusually well developed capacity for caring and for understanding other people – siblings, parents and peers. However, they also have to pay a price for this 'empathy lesson'. They often have to accept less access to parental time and attention and sometimes also a noisy and chaotic atmosphere and need therefore to be acknowledged.

Part III: You Get It or You do Not: Mainstreaming in Education, Ethnic Origin and Competency Level

The theme in this section is inclusion and exclusion, and how demands for mainstreaming, the different ways beliefs, values and morals influences and affect the lives of children and youth in care. In the first contribution, Tveit and Arnesen (*Chapter 8*), highlight the transition period young persons from residential care experience when they arrive to a new municipal school. In order to fit into the mainstreaming challenges often void of care and support, help with the normalization is a key issue in order for the youngster to be included. Traditionally the school system has fallen short in providing adequate competence and sufficient support in fulfilling this task especially in regards to the special needs required for young people from residential care.

A phase model with a three level strategy with focus on the need for a mode of adaptation and a high level of acceptance serves as a useful transition process. Two major obstacles are recognized: 1) The widespread lack of recognition of other vocations than teachers, such as social workers, within the school system; and 2) The low consciousness amongst teachers for the need of mutual reflection and colleague guidance. Collaboration between teachers, support staff and residential care workers is crucial. In the daily work at school the different professionals must find methods of enhancing reflection and guidance from colleagues.

Anti-discriminatory practice is not an easy option. It is a difficult, complex and a dynamic approach that challenges organizations and practitioners. The expectation is not just about providing a tolerant and understanding environment, though this is very important. It is also about taking account of the views, feelings and experiences of ethnic minority children in care and encouraging an integrative, tolerant and equal opportunity social environment. These challenges in residential and foster care are the focus for Okitikpi in *Chapter 9*. He discusses the anti-discriminatory and anti-oppressive practice in working with children from ethnic minority backgrounds who are in care.

Children from minority ethnic backgrounds are also trying to make sense of their world in the midst of a socio-structural context that appears to be both hostile and unconcerned about their needs. Like their majority peers they are also trying to find solutions to such basic questions as; who am I, from where do I come, where do I belong and what is going to happen to me? These are fundamental questions that all humans are moved to ask irrespective of their gender, racial or ethnic background. These basic questions are not exclusive to, or reserved for the majority children. Ethnic minority children are also wrapped up in the search for self, a sense of identity and stability and fulfilment in a mainstream environment that sometimes appears unpredictable and incoherent.

The contribution of Ashley (*Chapter 10*) connects with the above. On the basis of his long experience with establishing and consulting on children's need for self-expressive play he expound on a special group, the 'Forgotten Group'. He argues the need for better provision for children's self-expressive play, an activity freely chosen by the child itself to meet needs which arise from within the child and directed towards goals chosen by the child.

In this chapter Ashley presents his case for important consideration also within the field of residential care. He also assumes that the role of the adult in children's play is to respond to the initiatives of the child and suggests the following essential principles which adults need to understand in order to provide appropriate support to children's play in the home and the community and institutions.

Principle 1: That all children and youth need space and time to develop self-directed play independently of the control of adults – even parents/parent substitutes or teachers. Principle 2: That play in the way it is defined in Principle 1 must be differentiated from play as it is otherwise generally understood and used in the educational world. Principle 3: That the role for adults such as parents, teachers and community workers in children's free play could be to create the external conditions around children and youth which are necessary to give them this opportunity for self-directed expression in play and leisure and for self-directed learning. Principle 4: That, due to institutional and social trends, the pre-adolescent stage of the 'Forgotten Group' presents special needs which are largely neglected in such provision.

These principles may present a significant and special problem for residential care. The underlying question is whether policy makers consider sufficiently the special need to apply these principles within residential care. The implication is that this question should be given special emphasis in the design, management and the programmes of residential care and in the selection and training of residential care workers.

Part IV: Research, A Useful Tool in Residential and Foster Care

The last part of this book, exemplifying research as a tool to discover new or alternative ventures in residential and foster care, starts with a contribution from Anglin (*Chapter 11*). Central to his contribution is the attempt to construct a theoretical framework for what makes a 'well-enough' functioning residential group care setting.

The study involving staffed group facilities was undertaken in a spirit of curiosity and with an appreciation of the importance of exploring the nature of residential life and work. This research inquiry emphasized the interactional rather than the structural elements of group home life and work, however structural aspects emerged where they had meaning and significance to the participants.

The research study of staffed group home life and work with children and youth was undertaken in order to construct a framework for understanding practice. The method utilized was grounded theory, and some of the major critiques of this method are also addressed. The resulting framework matrix for understanding group home life and work suggest that interactional dynamics, levels of group home operations, and basic psychosocial processes within the group home rests on assumptions and practice of reciprocity, coherence and consistency. The identified elements and dynamics will assist individuals, agencies, and government departments committed to providing good residential group home care to the young people who need it.

If a service such as group home care is to be utilized, Anglin argues that we need to know how, when and for whom it can best be used, and value it as a positive choice in these circumstances. A service that is not valued, or that is considered always to be an unsatisfactory or second-rate option will inevitably deteriorate, and will ultimately reflect these self-fulfilling expectations. Young people are asking for and deserve the best group care settings that we can provide.

In *Chapter 12* Agathonos-Georgopoulou, Browne and Sarafidou give a report of a follow-up study on abused children's behaviour in Greece. The study revealed high levels of behaviour problems scores among children with a history of abuse, much higher than the general population, while resembling those of clinical samples. Findings suggest that the treatment needs of the child should not be overlooked while concentrating on the multiple problems of the family. The implementation of the United Nations Convention on the Rights of the Child in child protection requires a reconsideration of the child from being an object of protection to being a subject of rights. This automatically entitles the child to all possible measures for treatment and rehabilitation as it is the child who should be the primary 'client' of the system.

The authors suggest that further research at international level should give priority to several issues. More research is needed on the various 'developmental careers' of abused and neglected children, namely, on the relation of early exposure to maltreatment with conduct disorders and on criminality in later life. With reference to Rutter's work on pathways from childhood to adulthood there is a need for an analysis of a quite complex set of linkages over time because this research suggests that antisocial personality disorder in adulthood is almost always preceded by conduct disorder in childhood, suggesting that continuity looking backwards is very strong.

Another area for further research is the issue of 'cost' as a result of a child's removal from home. More knowledge is needed not only about the 'cost' to the child but also to the family as whole, to the parents as individuals and to the siblings. Central to the evaluation of 'costs' is the concept of 'loss' and how it is transcribed to everyone involved. Furthermore, it would be interesting to see how this 'loss' is transcribed to the professionals involved and to the agency dynamics. Especially in the case of residential care for abused and neglected children, these dynamics among all partners involved, the parents, the child itself, staff and the state or the agency in a parental surrogate role, need a thorough consideration as research priority. Lastly, research emphasis should be given to both risk and protective factors together with interactions between them. The authors suggest that follow-up studies of abused children have a lot to contribute towards answering these questions while raising new ones.

In the final contribution on research issues, Pösö (*Chapter 13*) brings the attention to how the complexities of residential life pose a challenge to the analytic tools of the researcher. Her discussion is centred around the use of an ethnographic approach in a research project looking into the experiences of residential life. The study aimed to learn about young people's experiences of residential life in Finnish reformatory schools, and to understand them in relation to the biographies of the adolescents.

On the one hand, it is important to give the youngsters the chance to speak and to tell about their experiences in research where the research interview might offer a secure and confidential opportunity to speak about issues which have possibly not been given enough – or any – attention before. The researcher may function as a catalyst, possibly empowering the residents to see, among other things, as they learn that their personal views are of interest. On the other hand, the research may objectify the adolescents when, for example, presenting the results of the analysis. The research results may be used against them within the institution or in public debates.

Thus, the problems are always there when doing qualitative research. The researcher might get so much and so rich information that its misuse is possible as well. Empowering and critical aspects of qualitative research can offer, for example, a source for reflection for practitioners to evaluate their practices. Research in residential setting can include all those aspects, but Pösö's experience has been that there is always the possibility of harming and hurting as well. She suggests that the very nature of the residential setting is to be taken into account when conducting or assessing research in residential institutions.

A Final Note

The contributions from the authors unfold the complication and involvedness of residential and foster care. We need to remember that what residential care or foster care offers, for better or for worse, is a non-family and non-community life and it is in these apparent negatives rather than any approximation of their opposites that its value may lie. Alan Keith-Lucas (1979) outlines some major tasks that have to be carried out in regards to the child or youth entering living arrangements outside home. One of these is family clarification.

Without having any reference point to life outside the placement the young person will easily become a stranger both to the present place of living and to where he/she came from, and in addition to where the final placement once will be. The point being that the child/youth needs to gain some clarity in regards to which 'family' is the lifeline from and to the institution. This is what in social work with groups is called reference groups, the member's ties with the world outside the group. A central issue for both members of a group, as well as young persons placed in foster care of residential care.

The respect, liking, and wanting to belong to what one identify as one's reference group exert power for both negative and positive possibilities for change. Generally, the more the group is liked, the more the member will identify with it. Many children and youths enter the institutional living scenario due to the fact that their life space is either too full of temptation to handle adequately, or do not have enough resources and flexibility in meeting the demands of the environment and own needs, or is too punitive to the activities and behaviour the young person relies on.

Group work and group care should have that in common which we can call the network of skills, knowledge and talents that enables a person to interact with the environment. The ecological competence that is the person's capacities, skills and motivation and environmental qualities such as social networks, social supports, and demands or obstacles are one's ecological context. This is a shift from treating children and youth towards teaching them social skills, coping and mastery. As Henry Maier (1991) observes in his discussion of the developmental conception of human functioning:

Life is conceived as a process in which the human being is in a continuous search for stimulation, variation, and new experience rather than a homeostatic, balanced, stimuli – existence... most important, a non-homeostatic conception – challenges us to value people for their capacity to reach out and to develop more fully rather than for their low-risk striking for balance.

It is a non linear transformation from one stage to another of nurturing care where the basic pattern of care is to understand the child and youth in their development.

Residential Care: Horizons for the New Century is partly the closing chapter for the 7th EUSARF Congress in Trondheim 2002. The congress was a meeting place where connections between practitioners, politicians and researchers were established and nurtured on the bank of the Nidelven river. As the river slowly flows into the sea disseminating the richness of the many streams that feed into it above its estuary, may also the contributions in this book in a small way serve as tributaries with the same purpose within the field of residential and foster care for the new century.

References

Keith-Lucas, A. (1979), *Tasks and Alternatives for the Children's Institutions*, Chapel Hill, NC: Group Child Care Consultant Services.
Maier, H. (1991), 'Developmental Foundations of Child and Youth Care Work', in J. Beker and Z. Eisikovitz (eds), *Knowledge Utilization in Residential Child and Youth Care Practice*, Washington DC: Child Welfare League of America.

PART I
CHALLENGES, INNOVATIONS AND EDUCATION: ELEMENTS IN ANTI-OPPRESSIVE PRACTICE

Chapter 1

Anti-oppressive Practice: Why Bother?

Jane Prior

Social work has always been a contested concept. From the late nineteenth century when casework was seen as a method for working with applicants for charity, some organizations were keen to disassociate casework from moral welfare whilst other organizations tended to emphasize their work on what might be described as saving souls. Social casework became a scientifically rational account of how to help the poor. This scientifically rational account of 'helping' persisted in accounts of social work until the latter part of the twentieth century. The use of the notions of help and the helping process were central to social work discourse until service users and researchers challenged whether social work does in fact help. In the face of a crisis about the legitimacy of social work commentators[1] highlighted concern that social work in particular, and social welfare policy in general, was reflecting a move towards managerialism, technicism and anti-intellectualism. Any attempt to address difficulties inherent within conceptualizations of social work in the early twenty first century is therefore faced with the added dimensions of having to either justify or effectively deal with problems brought about through managerialism, technicisim and anti-intellectualism. This chapter takes as its starting point Lena Dominelli's (1997) claim that anti-oppressive practice is the new practice paradigm of social care work. It is questioned whether anti-oppressive practice is a technical, political or moral activity. The curriculum for social work education informs us that we should be anti-oppressive. Whilst it is not suggested in this chapter that we should be oppressive, it is argued that contrary to popular belief there is little evidence of moral theory in social work and substantial evidence of technicism. As such anti-oppressive practice looks more like a technical response to a problem posed by a drive for managerial efficiencies rather than a coherent and morally sustainable account of practice. It is questioned whether anti-oppressive practice could be a guiding principle for practice in an atmosphere of anti-intellectualism, technicism and managerialism.

The Contested Nature of Social Work

Social work is not the same as social service but wherever a social worker is employed there is some connection to what might be referred to as welfare. Social work may be considered to be a form of welfare service. Welfare can be defined as measures aiming to promote or increase the well-being of a person or group of people. However, as well as being positive, welfare and social policies can be negative. While the social democratic nature of the development of Britain's welfare system is clear the assumptions of equality and universal benefits are contested (Mishra, 1984). Part of the difficulty with sustaining welfare systems in Britain may be attributable to a particular form of liberalism. For example, despite the availability of some universal benefits, many British welfare services are selective and impose a means test. There are then different possible models of welfare in a liberal democracy, each with its own aims and objectives. In Britain, there are a range of possible models of social work as welfare. There seem to be three broad headings that cover social work aims and purpose. Payne refers to these as reflexive-therapeutic, socialist-collectivist, and individualist-reformist (Payne, 1997, pp. 4–5). Plant also discusses social work in terms therapy, reform and revolution (Plant, 1970, pp. 74–89). Social work is sometimes understood to be about clients changing their perceptions of themselves or others or society, providing means for material improvement and challenging systems that impoverish sections of society. It is also understood to be about controlling and changing behaviour deemed anti-social. Jones offers the following insight:

> [S]ocial work is a diverse and shifting activity, undertaken by various kinds of welfare worker, many of whom are currently employed by statutory local authority social services departments, others by voluntary and charitable agencies, still others being genuine volunteers offering social work through a wide range of community-based organizations and groups … [Social work practice] embraces a spectrum of activities along a wide continuum, with counselling and support at one end and statutory powers to remove liberties at the other … Service users, are in some respects equally diverse … This diversity of social work is one of its salient characteristics. For some clients, social work is an activity that brings solace and comfort at times of acute need; for others, it is an activity to be avoided because of the threat it poses to their liberty. (Jones, 1998, p. 34)

The literature seems to take one of three different perspectives on social work. Social work is either viewed as a technical, political or moral activity.

However, there are substantial problems with each perspective which render the notion of anti-oppressive practice vacuous and impotent.

There is an obvious tendency within liberalism to assume that social work is a technical activity. Politicians generate policies with particular aims and values and social workers implement these policies without consideration of ends and without regard to the values inherent within such policies. As such, social work can be viewed as technicist. Halliday makes the same point with regard to assumptions in policy and literature about teaching. He says:

> Technicism may be defined as the notion that good teaching is equivalent to efficient performance which achieves ends that are prescribed for teachers. (Halliday, 1999, p. 597)

On such an account of social work social workers are agents of the state who follow policy guidelines to the letter. Some versions of what social workers do encapsulate this perspective. With titles such as *Social Work Competencies: Core Knowledge, Values and Skills* (Vass, 1996) and *Competence in Social Work Practice* (O'Hagan, 1996) it is clear that there is a body of literature in which the focus is on the application and demonstration of a prescribed set of values for a competency based curriculum. Competency based curricula are examples of technicism (Carr, 1999). There are, of course, aspects of social work which are technical. For example, completing the correct paper work for an assessment of needs is a technical matter. That does not mean however that technicism should dominate curricula and practice in social work. The philosophical basis of social work cannot be a statement of professional values alongside a handbook of techniques.

Political accounts of social work suggest that social workers have a duty to bring about a better political system, whereas technical accounts simply seek to make the current one more efficient. Local authority social workers and those employed in Probation Departments/Criminal Justice teams are accountable to their local or central government employer. Legislation defines which social work services are statutorily required and which are permitted. Priorities within other areas of social policy may affect the demands placed on social workers. Social work and politics are obviously embedded for most social workers. In the early 1970s a radical political perspective on social work emerged. A group calling themselves 'Case Con' published literature and a manifesto based on a Marxist perspective.[2] For 'Case Con' social work practice should contribute towards a social revolution. The accusation levelled at social workers by 'Case Con' was that they were effectively maintenance engineers of a social system that reproduces capitalism and alienates the working classes through its dehumanizing effects. For these theorists it is the experience of alienation and dehumanization that create social problems. 'Case Con' argues that social workers should recognize the effects of capitalism on the working classes. Instead of treating the symptoms of alienation they should attempt to tackle the causes and empower clients to challenge the status quo and revolt against the social, economic and political structures which lead to their oppression. Two different perspectives emerged however on how such radical aims could be achieved through social work. Firstly, social workers could leave their employment in recognition that their role colludes with the maintenance of a capitalist oppressive system. In so doing a revolution is supposed to rise from the ensuing chaos. This is an interesting idea which suggests current social work is a means of quelling revolution – or at least it has that effect. In the second perspective social workers are envisaged as being responsible for educating, in political terms, their clients so that the clients will bring about a social revolution. Whatever weaknesses political accounts of social work may have they highlight the intimate relationship between politics and social work.

Saving the souls of the poor and demoralized is a common enough story in the nineteenth century for social work to be regarded as a moral crusade. Motives of organizations such as the Charitable Organization Society (COS), to remoralize the poor, support the perspective of social work as a moral activity. But this perspective is not without its difficulties. For example, in order to combat criticisms of being a moral crusade the COS, and other early pioneers of casework, advocated technical approaches to working with applicants to charity which would ensure uniformity of response. It is easy to see the attractions of this retreat to technicism. Given that it is possible to achieve technical know how without understanding general principles, it would seem to be possible for a social worker to be engaged in social casework at either a technical or principled level. What Carr asserts is that some occupations 'are primarily focused on moral rather than technical deliberation' (Carr, 1995, p. 323). Social work seems to be a clear example of an occupation that is essentially moral in nature – given the range of contexts within which social workers work. However, what the moral basis of social work might be is unclear. How is it that an occupation which is moral, political and technical and is at odds with a liberal democratic notion of keeping public and private spheres separate managed to not only survive but at times thrive? Conceptual analysis of the notion of social work as professional help reveals some interesting indications of an older practice paradigm.

Social Work as Helping: An Old Practice Paradigm

In an interesting chapter published in 1976 entitled 'The Changing Meaning of Social Work' Harrison makes repeated and clear references to social work as a 'helping process' (Harrison, 1976).[3] She concludes that:

> Since the term 'social work' was first invented it has undergone several changes of meaning. Yet all its meanings have been attempts to elucidate one thing, the relationship between man and society and its implications for the 'helping process'. (Harrison, 1976, p. 94)

Many organizations and individuals were involved in supporting this image of social work as a helping process around the turn of the twentieth century. For example, the COS and later the Councils of Social Service and Child Welfare Agencies viewed their endeavours as helping others whilst individuals like Helen Bosanquet, Margaret Sewell and later Elizabeth Macadem all supported the notion of social work as a helping process (Harrison, 1976, pp. 83–93).

Younghusband refers to social workers as helping people. She says:

> Social work [has] remained concerned with deprivation in all its manifestations, with misfits and the 'undeserving', and those who for many different reasons could not cope with the circumstances of their lives. Its consistent aim has been to discover how to help such people, though it has had very different ideas from time to time about how to do so. (Younghusband, 1981, p. 9)

A notion of befriending or being friends with those one is trying to help with welfare issues disappeared in the early part of the twentieth century when the term was thought to be too vague (Younghusband, 1981; Biestek, 1961). The profession of social work, as it was then being viewed, needed 'a more "scientific" and a more accurate word' (Biestek, 1961, p. 7). Instead of friendship Biestek refers to social workers needing to have 'controlled emotional involvement' which is defined as '[T]he caseworker's sensitivity to the client's feelings, an understanding of their meaning, and a purposeful, appropriate response to the client's feelings (Biestek, 1961, p. 50).

Biestek goes on to clarify that controlled emotional involvement is:

> [A] sharing in the client's feelings; not the sharing of a relative in another relative's grief, but the sharing of a warmly human professional person with fine sensitivities in the feeling of another human being who is in need of assistance. (Biestek, 1961, pp. 58–9)

It seems pertinent that Biestek has highlighted that a social worker, on his account, does not behave like a relative with a 'client'. In so doing he has been able to avoid using the terms befriending, friendship or care. He suggests instead that a professional is able to interact in some sort of way that is superior and better for the 'client'. For Biestek the qualities of a social worker spring from 'knowledge' (Biestek, 1961, p. 58) the 'purpose of the case ... [and[the worker's ongoing diagnostic thinking' (Biestek, 1961, p. 66). The qualities of a social worker do not spring from a particularity or contextualized relationship or understanding. This is a clear reference to the sort of rationality that modern theories rely upon. Friendship has been replaced by a scientific, technically rational enterprise of controlled emotional involvement referred to as the helping process.

The Younghusband Committee of 1959 suggests that social work help[4] includes supplying information, giving practical assistance or material help, bringing about environmental changes and reducing stress. In 'helping' individuals the method used is that of casework. The Younghusband Committee define casework thus:

> [A] personal service provided by qualified workers for individuals who require skilled assistance in resolving some material, emotional or character problem. It is a disciplined activity which requires a full appreciation of the needs of the client in his family and community setting. The caseworker seeks to perform this service on the basis of mutual trust and in such ways as will strengthen the client's own capacities to deal with his problems and to achieve a better adjustment with his environment. The services required of a caseworker cover many kinds of human need, ranging from relatively simple problems of material assistance to complex personal situations involving serious emotional disturbance or character defect, which may require prolonged assistance and the careful mobilisation of resources and of different professional skills. (Ministry of Health, 1959, p. 3)

Poverty and its effects on social and emotional well-being are still evident in mid-twentieth century understandings of what it is that social workers help with. However, to the repertoire of social work help are added services to those who have 'serious emotional disturbance or character defect'. The nature of the casework relationship is mutual trust and from this springs the abilities of service users to deal with their problems.

During the Second World War social work as a 'helping' profession was able to come into its own. The effects of family separations, bombings and homelessness, evacuation of children, women working full-time in industry to support the so-called 'war effort' in place of men and the proliferation of physical and psychiatric problems experienced by casualties of war all were seen to require welfare assistance from social workers. To the government it seemed there was no other service as well placed as social work to coordinate and respond to such a wide range of problems. The government's concern at that time was twofold. Firstly, people dealing with welfare issues should be trained and operating within a reasonably coherent social service structure and secondly, solutions must be found to dealing with the wide range of social and personal problems caused by the war (Department of Health, 1959). When the war ended and the newly formed Labour government put into place a framework for the welfare state to mushroom (Fraser, 1984): social work as a process of helping those in need of welfare support was established within statutes like the Children Act (1948) and the National Assistance Act (1948) (Walton, 1975).[5] *Indeed the National Assistance Act (1948) gave social workers freedom from what Walton refers to as 'a relief giving function'* (Walton, 1975: 202) *providing opportunities for social workers to concentrate on other social needs for which local authorities now had a duty to meet.*

During the first half of the twentieth century social work was able to assert itself as a helping profession within complex relationships and multifaceted stress related situations, as well as being a port of call for those needing financial and material assistance (Stevenson, 1976). So complete was the transformation from charitable relief of poverty to dealing with complex social problems that Richard Titmuss declared in 1968 that more social workers were needed to solve social problems. He writes, in support of his position:

> It is an interesting and often overlooked fact that, during the last twenty years, whenever the British people have identified and investigated a social problem there has followed a national call for more social work and more trained social workers. Consider, for one moment, the history of twenty years of Royal Commissions, central and local committees of inquiry, working parties, conferences and Government task forces concerned with: the mentally ill, the schizophrenic discharged from hospital, the mentally subnormal, the maladjusted child, the physically handicapped, the blind and the deaf, industrial rehabilitation and training, the elderly isolates and desolates, the chronically ill and bedridden, the long-stay patient in hospitals and other kinds of residential accommodation, neglected and deprived children, young delinquents and those brought before the juvenile court, youth employment, the after-care of prisoners, the prevention of venereal disease, and the after-care of those who have contracted it, the problems of prostitution, unmarried mothers, unsupported wives, marital breakdown and the role of the courts, drug

addiction, alcoholism, homeless families, immigrants from the Commonwealth and so on … In each and every case, when these committees have reported they have recommended the employment of more trained social workers. (Titmuss, 1968, pp. 85–6)

Much of what Titmuss (1968) refers to above as a social problem causes some difficulties in a contemporary context. What Titmuss (1968) does show though is the way in which governments turned to committees, working parties etc. to investigate a particular social issue and that these in turn recommended social workers could resolve the social problem. The allocation of welfare assistance was the main responsibility of the Department of Health and Social Security, and social workers only had limited financial and material resources under the terms of prevailing legislation. It must therefore be concluded that it is the process with which social work is associated that led to the conclusions of Committees and Working Parties to call for more social workers to solve the social problem. It is casework as a process that became associated with helping to solve social problems.

It is not that social casework solves private problems but that casework solves social problems. Quite how casework with an individual who has a mental health problem will solve a social problem created by mental ill-health amongst the population is not clear. However, the language Titmuss uses is a reflection of the process necessary to legitimate something, which by definition contradicts one of the crucial principles of liberalism – the intervention of the state in the private sphere. By referring to 'the physically handicapped' and 'the mentally ill' for example, the experiences of individuals who also happen to be ill or disabled become subverted to the collective. The collective experience is a legitimate area of concern for the state. Hence, social work can be legitimated as part of the state and the activities of social workers can cross the boundary to the private sphere by virtue of the assumed ability of trained social workers to solve social problems.

This was not however a signal that liberal principles of keeping public and private spheres separate should cease. When the Acts of the 1940s completed the picture of Britain as a welfare state, charities benefited financially. The fears of many charities however, were that once the state accepted responsibility for providing welfare charitable funding would be drastically reduced. Their fears were not ill founded. The 1870 Education Act made provision for free education for children and as a consequence many charity schools failed to survive. Parents realized they could have their child educated for free in a Board School and those giving to charity realized that the state had, in effect, rendered charitable giving to some education charities surplus to requirements (Whelan, 1996). Although the fears of many charities in the 1940s were that state welfare would drastically reduce voluntary gifts overall funding was not affected. Significantly though, 1940s welfare legislation did provoke a change in the funding arrangements for charitable concerns. Charities received large sums of money, in many instances far larger than they were used to raising themselves, to continue providing services they had originally established through Christian commitment to community service. In return, by contracting out services to the voluntary sector the state was able to provide services it was committed to through legislation at a greatly reduced cost of providing those services themselves, either through local or central government. In effect, the state provided the means for societal deficiencies to be addressed through public health, social security, housing, education and employment services. The voluntary sector was given the means to continue to attend to individual character deficiencies in the private sphere. The state could not be easily identifiable as intruding in the private sphere. Indeed, some charities told its supporters that they were not receiving state funding in order to allay fears that the charity had become an appendage to the state (Whelan, 1996). By the mid-twentieth century charities had begun to conform to technologies of discipline and, as such, had achieved a means of financial survival whilst apparently not having to compromise their Evangelical concerns for the saving of souls.

Social Work Help as Curing or Controlling Social Problems

What is not made clear in the literature or policy during the first half of the twentieth century is whether social work help should aim to help by curing individuals and groups or by controlling those who fall within a particular group and thereby cause a problem. For example, in considering juvenile delinquency and social work services the Seebohm Committee reporting in 1969 states:

> The size of the problem of juvenile delinquency and the numbers of children at risk of becoming delinquent are considerable and appear to be growing. The total costs in human happiness and to the community at large have never been calculated but must be high. We still do not know enough to be able to tackle effectively the range of problems labelled 'juvenile delinquency'. In particular, the persistent young offender who may become the adult offender

presents perplexing difficulties of identification and treatment ... whatever organisation is brought into being to implement the proposals in the White Paper, it should be prepared to adopt an experimental approach towards the problems of juvenile delinquency, and be prepared to try systematically and scientifically to evaluate different methods of care, treatment, education and training. (Seebohm, 1968, p. 272)

It could be argued that Seebohm and his fellow Committee members are most concerned to care for juvenile delinquents by offering them treatment, education and training. There is an assumption that there must be a way of reducing juvenile delinquency by curing this ill within individuals. It therefore follows that curing this social ill will reduce adult offending. There is also an overwhelming assumption that reducing delinquency is to be achieved by focusing on the individual offender. This sort of approach to understanding and resolving anti-social behaviour is commonly transmitted through psychology literature of the 1950s and 1960s into social work theory. For example, John Bowlby's *Maternal Care and Mental Health* published in 1952, signalled for Younghusband (1981) an opportunity for the newly formed children's departments to develop a theory of practice. Later Bowlby published *Child Care and the Growth of Love* (1965) texts on attachment and separation (1969; 1973 respectively) followed by *The Making and Breaking of Affectional Bonds* (1979). All of these texts reinforce the idea that children should not be separated from maternal care – but most especially that they should not be separated from their mothers. When Rutter published *Maternal Deprivation Reassessed* in 1972 Bowlby's theories were reinforced for a new generation of social workers.

Social work help solves a multitude of social problems. Or, at least, social work help is assumed to solve a multitude of social problems. Thus to claim status as a profession social work makes a claim to help in ways that others do not. Younghusband makes just such a claim:

> There are social diseases of delinquency, substandard family life and community disharmonies which will continue in varying degrees in every type of society until
> Man has entered in
His perfect city free from sin
> And the social worker's purpose is to lessen the tension of such personal and social disharmonies by applying a form of social therapy which is the essence of social work. (Younghusband, 1951, p. 3)

Social casework set itself the task of finding ways of preventing social problems and curing social ills and the ways they are experienced through a form of human interaction that became known as the casework relationship. This approach can be summarized to the effect of 'if human behaviour can be understood, then it can be changed'. However, that there is a possibility of controlling the problem by treating individuals is inherent within the position. This should not be surprising given the premise of modernity that there is coherence to life and definitive theories from which it is possible to establish answers to all our questions. Policy on social issues, attempts to establish that there is truth to be found and that this truth can be divined through 'systematic' and 'scientific' evaluation and experimentation. The tone of the rhetoric alludes to universalism and progressivism, so characteristic of scientific rationality.

Jones, who describes himself as a Marxist academic, views social problems as arising from unequal social and economic systems. As such social work is 'a reflection of a drive to develop strategies which manage some of the principle human casualties' (Jones, 1998, p. 42) of these inequalities. Jones is pessimistic about social works' ability to survive if it were perceived as a threat to an established social and economic order. Despite feeling sympathy for the perspective Jones adopts and his obvious commitment to wanting to eradicate poverty there is an explicit hopelessness and sense of nihilism about the nature and potential of social work within his analysis which closes off rather than opens possibilities. Jones argues that social work only survives because it is prepared to change 'its outer shape and appearance in keeping with the temper of the time' (Jones, 1998, p. 43) and 'because it appears to have some impact on the management and control of the disadvantaged and distressed' (Jones, 1998, p. 43). These suggestions have relevance but not necessarily for the reasons Jones endorses. Social work is concerned with working most clearly with those who are poor and less powerful. Many problems experienced by clients could be eradicated by improved social and economic circumstances. And when Jones highlights that throughout its short history, 'social work has been marked by suspicion and hostility ... [and] remains one of the few welfare activities that has at no time been the subject of working-class demands for expansion and development' (Jones, 1998, p. 38) he makes a strong point. Jones' focus of understanding is that state endorsed social work has the ability to control marginalized sections of society in a way that protects the status quo. Cohen (1985) makes a similar point when he refers to the authority of practitioners being conceived of in terms of social control. Donzelot (1979) has viewed social work as policing the family. An enduring feature of social work in modernity seems to be a preoccupation with subjectifying the other.

An examination of some further criticisms of social work in the latter part of the twentieth century, add to this perception.

Nineteen seventy saw the publication of an important text on the experience of social work clients – *The Client Speaks*. In this study Mayer and Timms interview clients from one voluntary sector organization regarding what they hoped and expected to gain from their use of the social work service and whether they consider that had indeed been helped. Mayer and Timms consider the experiences of clients seeking help with inter-personal relationships and those seeking material assistance. Mayer and Timms comment: 'As a rule, both sets of clients had certain views as to how their problems would be handled and each expected these to be shared by the worker' (Mayer and Timms, 1970, p. 129).

They continue to note:

> Those seeking interpersonal help expected the worker to base his actions on a unicasual-moralistic-suppressive approach to problem solving; those in search of material assistance took it for granted that the worker would consider material relief the only possible answer to their plight. Indeed, clients of both types were so certain that workers would see things as they did that on many occasions they felt it unnecessary to articulate their views and desires. (Mayer and Timms, 1970, pp. 129–30)

Mayer and Timms report significant sections of the study group being unable to understand the perspective adopted by workers in solving problems. This resulted in clients being, 'bewildered and frequently angered by the fact that the worker, rather than trying to 'help' them, dwelt on totally unrelated matters' (Mayer and Timms, 1970, p. 130). There was clear evidence that clients did not feel they were being helped and that the client's perceptions led to further difficulties for the establishment of a relationship that could be perceived as helpful.

Mayer and Timms (1970) make it clear that they do not see their research as definitive nor without weaknesses. However, that they did undertake a study of perceptions, expectations and reactions to social work service delivery signalled that the assumed helping nature of social work was open to critique. The social worker's stance as an expert, someone who knows, has been questioned.

Whether social work does help became the focus of a body of critique, which became firmly established in the 1970s and 1980s. A more damning critique of social work's ability to help was presented in 1980 when Brewer and Lait asked *Can Social Work Survive?* In their conclusion they make the point that they:

> [C]an find no convincing evidence that the intervention of social workers has prevented a single case of baby battering except where they have physically removed the child from the threatening environment (a course which they are frequently unwilling to undertake on account of their beliefs about the importance of the biological tie). As for old people, visits from social workers may be better than no visits at all, but the evidence is that the services needed are practical and can be provided by competent untrained officials, who are just as likely to be kindly, sympathetic people, and ... marginally more reliable. They may also be less resentful of practical tasks. (Brewer and Lait, 1980, p. 210)

If social work clients did not consistently appreciate that they were being helped and researchers were questioning evidence that social workers had the capacity to help the question of what it is social work and social workers do is open to question.

Contemporaneously to debates about the nature and validity of social work Plant (1970) challenged social workers and the academy to justify its moral foundations. He said:

> Unfortunately, in view of its unquestioned importance, the theory and practice of social casework has received very little attention from professional philosophers, and it is to be hoped that in the future a comparable amount of time and effort will be spent on analysis of casework concepts by the philosopher as is now spent on the philosophy of education. (Plant, 1970, p. 91)

Rather than the sustained debate that Plant called for, what there has been is a series of initiatives variously embedded in legislation, policies and guidelines. These initiatives refer to obviously moral concepts such as equality of opportunity, empowerment, anti-discrimination and, most recently, anti-oppressive practice. Closer examination of social work curricula shows how these concepts have become technicized both within the literature of service delivery and the overriding project to lessen expenditure on the welfare state.

The essay by Plant (1970) along with texts by Timms and Watson (1978), and Downie and Telfer (1980) are examples of philosophical debate about British social work and its moral basis.[6] A core issue addressed in the debate in the literature in the 1970s concerns the place for philosophical reflection in social work practice. Unsurprisingly perhaps, given the historical context in which debate took place, Kantianism features prominently. Kantianism dominated liberal thought in Britain and it may be seen to underpin Rawls' *Theory of Justice* (1971) widely acknowledged to be the cornerstone of liberal democratic thinking (Mulhall and Swift, 1996).

In his essay Plant argues that a Kantian notion of respect would provide the basis of a morally sensitive account of social work. Plant writes that the principle of respect is:

> [A] *presupposition* of morality if morality is taken as a rational enterprise. Respect for persons is not just a moral principle; on the contrary it is a presupposition of having a moral principle at all. (Plant, 1970, p. 20) (Original emphasis)

What Plant (1970) argues is that respect is owed to any person and is not dependent upon contingencies or roles undertaken by the person. In establishing a casework relationship, for example, a social worker cannot rely on their role to secure respect. Yet Plant highlights that respect is often presupposed in social work literature rather than argued for. He goes on to argue, correctly, that it is not morally justifiable to turn respect into a casework principle simply because in so doing, it might be technically useful. As Plant notes:

> That certain principles have been found to be useful in casework practice may explain why caseworkers now regard these principles as enshrining the basic values of their profession, but this does not, in itself, justify them. (Plant, 1970, p. 19)

He continues:

> The separation of values from facts, of normative from evaluative discourse, has led to the view that *qua* moral principles, principles such as respect for persons and client self-direction merely express a conviction on the part of the caseworker, a conviction which can be neither proved nor disproved. (Plant, 1970, p. 19)

Unfortunately, proponents of anti-oppressive practice do not seem to have taken this point into consideration when declaring that anti-oppressive practice should be adopted. In the absence of philosophically informed debate social workers are being prescribed a set of values and, laudable as they might be, they are, in Plant's words, 'merely' an expression of a conviction on the part of the worker.

Rather than helping clients social workers have been accused of controlling, marginalizing, subjectifying and oppressing clients. It is perhaps not surprising that in more recent years social work has been viewed less coherently and it is now difficult, if not impossible, to find a definition of social work that includes a notion of helping to solve social problems. There is academic and policy debate about what work should statutorily fall to social workers but the language and rhetoric have turned away from notions of helping people. For example, Davies (1994) argues that social work should be concerned with securing resources and passing on information that the client may find helpful. In this respect Davies attempts to resolve the sort of issues raised by Mayer and Timms (1970) when client's voices are not heard and neatly side-steps the difficulty of whether or not social work helps by placing emphasis on what clients might find helpful. In this model social workers are brokers, and work on behalf of clients. This approach to defining social work begs the question though regarding what is special about social work that requires training and professional status. These functions of brokerage and information resources might be equally well achieved by welfare rights workers, librarians, community education workers, citizen's advice bureaux, for example.

Social policy with regard to social work and people with disabilities, mental health issues, or older adults now tends to rely on notions of brokerage as reflected in the National Health and Community Care Act, 1990. Indeed, social work departments are charged within this legislation with the responsibility for coordinating the development of community care planning, a role previously given to health authorities in England and Wales and health boards in Scotland. In this legislation it is services that will meet needs not social workers. Between the late 1960s and 1990 policy has changed focus from the onus on social workers as a professional group to solve social problems of adults to social work departments identifying services that can meet needs of clients. Parton makes a similar point:

> No longer are social workers constituted as caseworkers drawing on their therapeutic skills in human relationships, but as care managers assessing need and risk and operationalizing packages of care. (Parton, 1996, p. 12)

Social work, it could be argued, has become subject to a watering down of its uniqueness. For example, occupational therapists are deemed suitably qualified to fulfil community care social work posts. The point is that it is not that occupational therapists cannot undertake the role of coordinating a community care package or an assessment of needs under the terms of community care legislation. Rather that the uniqueness of social workers skills and abilities to help with particular problems is no longer so clearly espoused in policy.[7]

The word 'help' has been effectively erased from the vocabulary of social workers who subscribe to the 'new practice paradigm', the focus instead being improving quality of life and the implementation of social justice. Social work as help or as a helping process seemed to be unsatisfactory for clients and certainly did not solve the sorts of social problems it was thought capable of achieving. What then of what Dominelli refers to as the 'new practice paradigm'? Is the new practice paradigm able to deal with issues of controlling clients, marginalizing individuals and groups, subjectifying and oppressing clients from a morally coherent basis? These questions require attention.

Dominelli asserts that:

> Anti-oppressive practice, insofar as it is preoccupied with the implementation of social justice, is intimately bound up with notions of improving the quality of life or well-being of individuals, groups and communities. The concern lends it a holistic mantle which encompasses all aspects of social life – culture, institutions, legal framework, political system, socio-economic infrastructure and interpersonal relationships which both create and are created by social reality. (Dominelli, 1998, pp. 5–6)

In making reference to paradigmatic shifts Dominelli is resting, one assumes, on the work of Kuhn, although no reference to any perspective is made. Kuhn asserts that there has to be a limit to the number of ideas that can be consistently held within culture at any one time once a paradigmatic shift has occurred (Kuhn, 1970). To use a fairly commonly used example consider whether or not a member of a contemporary western society could hold a view that the earth is flat and engage in other aspects of culture. It is understood that the earth is spherical and not flat. Therefore, a person holding a view of the earth as flat would have quite severe difficulties relating that concept to other phenomena like gravity, space travel, the universe as a collection of planets and space. What Dominelli seems to be saying is that now a shift in thinking has occurred about social work needing to be anti-oppressive other shifts in thinking will follow until the paradigm is, for want of a better expression, complete.

What this new paradigmatic shift entails is interesting. Parton (1996) Clarke (1996) Webb (1996) and Jones (1996) are all concerned that what is being reflected in social work, and social welfare policy in general, is a move towards to managerialism, technicism and anti-intellectualism. These are not entirely new phenomena in social work since evidence of their presence in ideas about social work began to appear in policy with the White Paper on

Community Care in 1989. However, that literature on anti-discrimination and anti-oppressive practice made its debut around about the same time may not be purely coincidental. For example, Dominelli in 1988 published *Anti-racist Social Work* and a year later, with Elaine McLeod, *Feminist Social Work*. In the second edition of *Anti-racist Social Work* Dominelli highlights the nature of change in social work's legitimacy during the 1990s.

> [S]ocial work is both in a state of flux and under attack. Pressure for change is emanating from privatisation measures; managerial imperatives aimed at improving efficiency and coping with a situation of dwindling resources; legislative requirements, particularly in relation to child care, community care, mental health and social security; increasing public scrutiny of social work, especially around child abuse; consumer demands for more sensitive, unstigmatised and less oppressive services; and social workers' own emerging activism as they organise collectively to defend their rights as workers and improve the services they provide. (Dominelli, 1997, p. 6)

On the face of it Dominelli (1997) is not putting anti-oppressive practice in opposition to managerialism and technicism but a little later she does just this. She says:

> Without suggesting that there are easy solutions, I argue that we need not feel helpless in the face of the challenge before us. Our feelings of powerlessness and inability to change things can be countered if white social work educators and practitioners accept the importance of struggling against racism and take up the issue of transforming social work education and practice to promote people's welfare and empower users. (Dominelli, 1997, p. 6)

What Dominelli (1997) presents as the challenge before (white) social workers is to address the range and depth of racism that permeates social welfare services and service delivery. However, in so doing, she suggests other difficulties of social work practice (balancing care and control, managerialism, and dwindling resources) can be put into perspective and transformed through anti-oppressive practice. This does not sound like a paradigmatic shift but the emergence of a new dichotomy, anti-oppressive practice against managerialism and the realities that this encapsulates. And what better to combat managerialism and technicism than something as indisputable as anti-oppressive practice? Dominelli's (1997) suggestion that if social workers practice in anti-oppressive ways they will be able to provide good service seems to completely ignore the fact that service managers have different priorities and perspectives within the technicist and managerial regime that dominate service provision. So whilst individual social workers might be able to practice in non-discriminatory and non-subjectifying ways they are firmly enmeshed in a system which demands technical competence and managerial accountability. Far from resolving the moral dilemmas and moral unsustainability of modern social work anti-oppressive practice is dangerously close to exacerbating the philosophical ineptitude of social work.

Summary

Anti-oppressive practice, laudable as this is as a value, does not provide moral resources upon which practitioners can draw. Indeed, the proliferation of literature seems to be preventing analysis of power/knowledge rather than opening up possibilities for morally informed practice since anti-oppressive practice has to be subscribed to rather than arrived at through rigorous moral debate. That a new paradigm could be created from a morally unsustainable perspective has to be questioned. Unfortunately, the academy seems unwilling or unable to do so. Until moral debate is established as a crucial element of social work education and practice technical and political accounts of social work will persist to dominate debate, often in opposition to one another, and will limit the possibilities of social work as a morally coherent activity.

Whilst limiting social work to a technical occupation might be expedient for governments and managers driven by technical notions of efficiency and accountability, social workers who wish to challenge politically orchestrated forms of oppression will find their practices rendered impotent in the face of technicism without recourse to morally sustainable accounts of practice. What is required is more debate about moral theory in social work and less prescription to values like anti-oppressive practice. Unfortunately, the social worker who wishes to practice in a morally sensitive way has little in the way of literature upon which to draw. It is a responsibility of the academy to address this need. It may then be possible to establish why anti-oppressive practice can be a morally coherent guiding principle and therefore why we should bother about anti-oppressive practice.

Notes

1   See, for example, Parton, 1996, pp. 9–11; Clarke, 1996, pp. 44–9 and 55; Webb, 1996, pp. 178–83; Jones, 1996, pp. 198–9.

2   See, for example, the collection of chapters in Bailey and Brake, 1975.
3   See especially pp. 83–7.
4   The Younghusband Committee define social work thus: 'The process of helping people, with the aid of appropriate social services, to resolve or mitigate a wide range of personal and social problems which they are unable to meet successfully without such help' (Younghusband, 1959: 15, p. 3).
5   See especially pp. 196–208.
6   There are some texts that fall into this category that examine the philosophical framework of social work in the USA, for example, the comprehensive exposition by Reamer, 1993. The work of Reamer, for example, provides a useful and thorough introduction to political and moral philosophy, logic, epistemology, and aesthetics which have all been contextualized for the reader interested in social work. There is limited space here however, I would argue that a philosophical framework for social work must also be culturally and historically located if it is to inform anti-oppressive practice and theory.
7   Parton (1996, p. 12) makes a similar point saying that the skills that used to 'key to social work' are now more likely to be associated with counselling, which would be bought in as a specialist service for a care package if needed.

References

Bailey, M and Brake, M (eds) (1975), *Radical Social Work*, London: Arnold.
Biestek, F (1961), *The Casework Relationship*, London: George Allen and Unwin.
Bowlby, J (1952), *Maternal Care and Mental Health: A Report on Behalf of the World Health Organisation as a Contribution to the United Nations Programme for Homeless Children*, WHO.
Bowlby, J. (1965), *Child Care and the Growth of Love*, 2nd edn, Harmondsworth: Penguin.
Bowlby, J. (1969), *Attachment and Loss, Vol. 1: Attachment*, London: Hogarth Press.
Bowlby, J. (1973), *Attachment and Loss, Vol. 2: Separation, Anxiety and Anger*, London: Hogarth Press.
Bowlby, J. (1979), *The Making and Breaking of Affectional Bonds*, London: Routledge.
Brewer, C. and Lait, J. (1980), *Can Social Work Survive?*, London: Temple Smith.
Carr, D. (1995), 'Is Understanding Professional Knowledge of Teachers a Theory-Practice Problem?', *Journal of Philosophy of Education*, Vol. 29: 3.
Carr, D. (1999), 'Professional Education and Professional Ethics', *Journal of Applied Philosophy*, Vol. 16: 1.
Clarke, J. (1996), 'After Social Work?', in N. Parton (ed.), *Social Theory, Social Change and Social Work*, London: Routledge.
Cohen, S. (1985), *Visions of Social Control*, Cambridge: Polity Press.
Davies, M. (1994), *The Essential Social Worker: Introduction to Professional Practice in the 1990s*, 3rd edn, London: Arena.
Dominelli, L. (1997), *Anti Racist Social Work*, 2nd edn, Basingstoke: Macmillan.
Dominelli, L. (1998), 'Anti-oppressive Practice in Context', in R. Adams, L. Dominelli and M. Payne (eds), *Social Work: Themes, Issues and Critical Debates*, Basingstoke: Macmillan.
Donzelot, J. (1979), *The Policing of the Family*, New York: Pantheon.
Downie, R.S. and Telfor, E. (1980), *Caring and Curing*, London: Methuen.

Fraser, D. (1984), *The Evolution of the British Welfare State*, Basingstoke: Macmillan.

Harrison, E. (1976), 'The Changing Meaning of Social Work', in A.H. Halsey (ed.), *Traditions of Social Policy: Essays in Honour of Violet Butler*, Oxford: Basil Blackwell.

Halliday, J. (1999), 'Technicism, Reflective Practice and Authenticity in Teacher Education', *Teacher and Teacher Education*, Vol. 14, 6, pp. 597–605.

Jones, C. (1996), 'Social Work and Society', in R. Adams, L. Dominelli and M. Payne (eds), *Social Work: Themes, Issues and Critical Debates*, Basingstoke: Macmillan.

Jones, C. (1998), 'British Social Work and Anti-Intellectualism', in N. Parton (ed.), *Social Theory, Social Change and Social Work*, London: Routledge.

Kuhn, T.S. (1970), *The Structure of Scientific Revolutions*, Chicago and London: University of Chicago Press.

Mayer, J.E. and Timms, N. (1970), *The Client Speaks: Working Class Impressions of Casework*, London: Routledge and Kegan Paul.

Mishra, R. (1984), *The Welfare State in Crisis: Social Thought and Social Change*, Brighton: Harvester.

Mulhall, S. and Swift, A. (1996), *Liberals and Communitarians*, 2nd edn, Oxford: Basil Blackwell.

O'Hagan, K (Ed.), *Competence in Social Work Practice*, London: Jessica Kingsley.

Parton, N. (1996), 'Social Theory, social change and social work: an introduction', in N. Parton (ed.), *Social Theory, Social Change and Social Work*, London: Routledge.

Payne, M. (1997), *Modern Social Work Theory*, 2nd edn, Basingstoke: Macmillan.

Plant, M. (1970), *Social and Moral Theory in Social Work*, London: Routledge and Kegan Paul.

Rawls, J. (1971), *A Theory of Justice*, New York and Chichester: Columbia University Press.

Reamer, F.G. (1993), *The Philosophical Foundations of Social Work*, New York: Columbia University Press.

Seebohm, F. (1968), *Report of the Commission on Local Authority and Allied Personal Social Services*, London: HMSO.

Stevenson, O. (1976), 'The Development of Social Work Education', in A.H. Halsey (ed.), *Traditions in Social Policy*, Oxford: Basil Blackwell.

Timms, N. and Watson, D. (1978), *Philosophy in Social Work*, London: Routledge and Kegan Paul.

Titmuss, R. (1968), *Commitment to Welfare*, London: George Allen and Unwin.

Vass, A. (ed.) (1996), *Social Work Competencies: Core Knowledge, Values and Skills*, London: Sage.

Walton, R.G. (1975), *Women in Social Work*, London: Routledge and Kegan Paul.

Webb, D. (1996), 'Regulation for Radicals: The State, CCETSW and the Academy', in N. Parton (ed.), *Social Theory, Social Change and Social Work*, London: Routledge.

Whelan, R. (1996), *The Corrosion of Charity: From Moral Renewal to Contract Culture*, London: Institute of Economic Affairs.

Younghusband, E. (1951), *Social Work in Britain*, Edinburgh: T. and A. Constable.

Younghusband, E. (1959), *Report of the Working Party on Social Workers in Local Authority Health and Welfare Services*, London: HMSO.

Younghusband, E. (1981), *The Newest Profession: A Short History of Social Work*, Sutton, Surrey: IPC Business Press Ltd.

Chapter 2

Changing the Horizon: Client Feedback as a Driving Force behind Innovations in Residential Child and Youth Care

Erik J. Knorth, John P.M. Meijers, Arianne Brouwer, Eek Jansen
and Hans Du Prie

Introduction

> The one thing that I would have liked to see is more consultation (or just a good long talk about the state of things) between the family worker and the group workers. But also a positive comment: they are all doing their stinkin' (pardon my French) best. (Brouwer, 2001, p. 22)

This remark from a parent, quoted from a client feedback study in one of the largest organizations for child and youth care in The Netherlands – the Horizon Foundation – is illustrative for the attempts of this institute to listen actively to what clients (youth and parents/caretakers) have to say about the help they receive. Making use of client feedback is a significant way to shape a client-oriented assistance process (Jumelet, de Ruyter and Kayser, 1999). It is part of a development that is going on in the Netherlands, but also in other European countries like Belgium, France, Germany and the United Kingdom; a development that can be characterized as a move towards a more *participatory, client empowering* child and youth care practice. It means that youths and parents have an active role in the helping process, that the emphasis is on the their strengths rather than on their deficits, that they have their own responsibility concerning the implementation and the success of the applied interventions, and that their evaluation of and feedback on the process is recognized as being unusual valuable (Knorth, Van der Bergh and Verheij, 2002).

In this context, Horizon can be seen as a typical case standing in the front line of innovation. The institute underwent a crucial development for the past five years in both philosophy and practice: it evolved in approach to a demand- or client-oriented organization (Du Prie, 1999a; Prakken, 2002). In this chapter, we shall sketch the outline of this development. Next, the results of a recent pilot study with client feedback data concerning some residential units of Horizon will be discussed: what do children and parents think of the support and treatment they receive? First of all, we will pay attention to the theme of client feedback in child and youth care in a more general sense.

Client Feedback

Client feedback means, simply put, '… that children and/or parents voice their opinion on the conduct of care givers or, in a broader context, on the care offer of the entire institution. Their comments can subsequently be used at the evaluation of the own conduct of the institution and her staff' (Jumelet et al., 1999). Clients can give their feedback when invited – also designated as 'client consultation' – but of course also uninvited. In The Netherlands, systematic client consultation is regarded as an important instrument on quality care (Van IJzendoorn, 1997). The data emanating from the application of a client feedback system, can be put to use – depending on the design and made agreements – on various levels:

- on the micro level of individual clients and care givers;
- on the meso level of a group of clients (residential group, unit) and care givers (team);
- on the macro level of the entire institution (management, policy makers, youth council).

An example of the gathering of client feedback data at the level of an institution as a whole (macro level) can be found in a research project in two locations of the Youth Care Bureau Amsterdam (Konijn, 2003). Since some time the Youth Care Bureau is the central 'gate' to child and youth care facilities in the Netherlands. The Bureau offers support and guidance in case of 'simple' psychosocial problems. At the same time it is a referral and allocation agency for more complicated problems that call for intensive support and treatment programs like family treatment, individual psychotherapy, day treatment, family foster care or residential treatment. The research team employed a so-called *Child and Youth Care Thermometer*, a short written questionnaire based on the Patient Experience Survey (Zastowny, Stratmann, Adams and Fox, 1995). Well over 350 clients (73 per cent parents; 27 per cent youths) returned questionnaires (response rate 28 per cent). The mean contentment score, expressed in a report mark, amounts to 6.6. The contentment of the clients, related to intervention characteristics, proves to be predicted best by: 1) the quality of the professional support as experienced by the parents; 2) the outcomes of the interventions; and 3) the level of involvement and participation of clients during the intervention and referral process. This latter outcome can be considered as empirical support for the participation paradigm in the child and youth care field as mentioned before. Comparable results were shown in a research project with 100 children treated in German ambulatory services (Lenz, 2001).

In interpreting the collected client feedback data and addressing the question which implications they have for every day practice, the following issues should be observed. First, studies after the best known type of feedback, client satisfaction, revealed usually a large degree of satisfaction among the respondents (Lemmens and Donker, 1990; Welling, 2002). In connection, the extent of differing in assessment, especially with children, is often limited. Therefore, results should be judged by 'strict, high standards'. Second, the results are susceptible to the manner the data were obtained. For example, compared to open interviews, the use of standardized, written questionnaires is less favourable because the response is often lower, the questions could easily lead to misperceptions (no additional questions can be asked), and respondents – mostly children – are more inclined to give socially desirable answers (cf. Jumelet et al., 1999). It is therefore advisable to collect feedback from clients using various, complementary methods. Third, usually little is known about the validity and reliability aspects of the used instruments in obtaining client feedback (Hennessy, 1999). Caution at the interpretation of results is called for; data should not be viewed as 'objective conclusive facts', but as information on subjective perceptions and experiences, which could incite further investigation and action within an organization.

With these short comments in mind, we are of the opinion that systematically collected client feedback can play an important role to keep an organization 'sharp'. It also issues a grave message to children and parents: 'We as an organization highly value your opinion on our work.' To illustrate this further, we present some results from a recent client feedback study within the Horizon Foundation.

The Case of Horizon

The Horizon Foundation is a multifunctional organization for child and youth care in the western part of The Netherlands (the province of South-Holland), intended for children and families with severe conduct and educational problems, living in urban environments like Rotterdam and The Hague, and the more rural areas skirting these cities. The organization offers various types of assistance, mainly focusing on *residential* types of help: Horizon has a capacity for more than 240 children and youth, to be admitted in residential units (see Table 2.1).

Table 2.1   Capacity Horizon Services, related to three main locations

Type of service	Capacity			Total	
	Alphen a/d Rijn	Rotterdam	Oostvoorne*		
Residential care	106	85	53	244	(67.4%)
Day treatment	20	10	73	103	(28.4%)
External project**	10	5	–	15	(4.2%)
Total	136	100	126	362	(100%)

*   Oostvoorne, Hellevoetsluis, Hoogvliet.
**   Project Family, Experiential Education.

Source: Horizon (2002).

Furthermore, Horizon disposes of (partially domestic) special schooling facilities at each location. There are more than 330 full-time jobs in the organization, 180 of which within the residential groups for pedagogical workers (Horizon Foundation, 2002).

In addition to residential placement and day treatment, Horizon offers increasingly outpatient counselling to youth and parents, especially before and after an admission. In 2001, rather more than 200 families made use of this so-called *placement counselling* (Du Prie, 1999b; Horizon Foundation, 2002). Placement counselling (abbreviated: PC) fits within the more client centred policy of Horizon. This development started some five years ago. A brief review follows.

Developments

Phase 1: Listening – Clients as Informers

For many years Horizon acknowledged that quite some placements came untimely – thus undesired – to an end. At the Horizon location of Alphen aan den Rijn it annually involved 40–45 per cent of the children (Prakken, 2002) – a percentage though which we know can be found in other Dutch institutions as well (see e.g. Scholte, 1997).

It was decided to investigate how clients perceive the help they receive. Using the results as a basis, Horizon hoped to be able to attune the care to the ideas of children and parents, and thus reduce the percentage of untimely termination.

The results of the first, qualitative study – obtained by semi-structured interviews with 60 admitted children and young persons (Meerdink, 1997, 1999) – were deemed 'shocking' by Du Prie, director of Horizon:

> Almost none of the interviewed young persons saw a relation between the problems they had and the treatment they received in the institution. Also, actually none of them had any idea how long they were to stay. The group worker was not regarded as a care giver, but rather as someone to be on one's guard against. The children found their support mainly with their fellow group mates. (Prakken, 2002, p. 17).

Also with the parents Du Prie observed – partly based on a survey by the Inspectorate of Youth Care and Protection (Inspectie JHVJB, 1996) – quite some discontentment:

> Parents appeared to be dissatisfied with the quality of care giving, and the changes in behaviour in their children resulting from that. What's more, they absolutely did not consider themselves 'shareholders' in the problem. This became obvious in every day reality; we had the idea parents withdrew from the care giving process. (Prakken, 2002, p. 17).

Simultaneously – and perhaps somewhat paradoxally given the aforementioned – a problem surfaced with which Horizon as well as the whole child and youth care system in the Netherlands has been wrestling for considerable time: the *waiting list* problem. Children and their parents had to, and still have to wait for many months before a placement could be effectuated. It may be clear that this is pernicious for the motivation of clients and badly enhances the risk of pulling out or ad hoc solutions. Clients were very, very dissatisfied about it.

Studies revealed that many placement agencies applied a so-called 'full spread strategy' in order to tackle this problem (cf. Knorth and Dubbeldam, 1999): children were put forward for treatment simultaneously with as many institutions as possible to increase the chance of a 'fast' placement – wherever. The fact that the children were unable to discern the connection between their problem and the treatment they received – as mentioned above – is undoubtedly partly a result of this procedure. The received feedback prompted Horizon to take action.

Phase 2: Involving – Clients as Participants

In a first attempt to address the waiting list problem – in a report evocatively described as the problem of 'the carpenter without tools' (Bureau WESP, 1994) – Horizon developed in cooperation with the Utrecht Academy for Professional Education a new working method that – equally evocative – was entitled 'Help that cuts ice' (Rijnhove Foundation, 1997; Ravelli, 1998), but that in the meantime largely is known as *Placement Counselling* (Du Prie, 1999a).

Placement Counselling implies that clients on the waiting list are already offered help, emphatically not to prevent placement in care (such as intended with family preservation programmes, see Whittaker, 1997), but to enhance the chances of a successful residential placement. Aims are (cf. Ravelli, 1998):

- to establish a close cooperation with child and parents;
- to activate the parental responsibility for the child;
- to come to an agreement with both the child and the parents as to the goals of the placement;
- to come to an agreement about the way these goals could be achieved.

Underlying principles are to work *family oriented* and *demand oriented*. From the knowledge that parents and children can have their absolute own ideas about nature, background and due approach of problems (cf. Kromhout et al., 2000; Sonuga-Barke and Balding, 1993; Szajnberg and Weiner, 1996), extensive attention is given their perception and opinions on the matter, and in close cooperation with them a plan for help is drawn up.

From the side of the institution the aim is to make the members of the client system *sharers* in the help course at hand as much as possible, and to involve them in all relevant decisions and agreements. Besides these 'participation goals', aims connected with the actual placement are distinguished (cf. Ravelli, 1998):

- to prevent the problem from aggravating (for instance, using crisis management);
- to prepare for the actual placement (getting acquainted, etc.);
- to counsel the separation between child and parents;
- (occasionally) to start specific treatment activities (such as part taking in a project of experiential education in France to stimulate the young person's motivation for help).

For the implementation of the PC-module, extra family counsellors and activity therapists were hired. From studies, of which the report is under preparation, the conclusion can seemingly be drawn that the 'drop out' of clients during the waiting period can be reduced significantly by PC (Stikkelman, in preparation).

Phase 3: Sharing Responsibility – Clients as Partners

The PC method, which initially started as an experiment, had an enormous impact within the organization, in particular as to the position the young persons and the parents occupied within the care giving process. In terms of the so-called 'participation ladder' by Arnstein and Hart (see Knorth, Van den Bergh and Verheij, 2002, p. 9) a process had started: from informing and counselling of clients to involving and having them participate in decisions about the form of the placement and the care plan. This process, which is closely connected to the management's policy to make Horizon a demand oriented institution, is presently attempting to take a next step on this ladder – sometimes called 'beyond participation' – by entering into a *partnership* with children and parents, at which point the responsibility for the form and the course of the helping process emphatically also is with the client (cf. Figure 2.1). In this context one can also speak of *dialogue centred* care giving (De Winter, 2002).

A father phrases the current method as follows:

> No parent would like to see his child admitted here, but it is my last stalk of straw. If things go wrong here, I'm at my wits end. I have to say, she has been here for four months now [in Horizon] and it seems to take a turn for the better. Unlike with the crisis centre, she cannot do as she pleases and as a father I

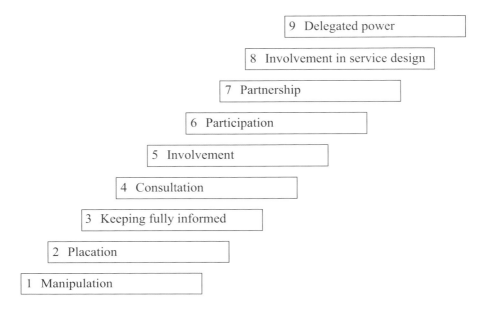

Figure 2.1   Participation ladder

Source: Adapted by Thoburn et al. (1995).

> am not being put at the sideline. The care givers strictly observe my rules and involve me in everything. Myself, I have learned to be more diplomatic with my daughter. But I would be afraid to say now that she is going to make it. (Prakken, 2002, p. 24)

The consequence of this client centred method of working is that the organization has to become much more *flexible* in the offering of care, support and treatment; for the starting point is the request for help from child and parents, and not the (already set) offer from the residential institution. An example: when, from the context of the request for help, it is desirable that a child attends a residential unit for three days a week instead of five, then this should be made possible (cf. Naayer, 2002).

In the described development it also fits that the organization keeps an open ear for feedback from clients; indeed, client feedback is regarded an indispensable source of reflection on the quality of given care. Actually, this is the state of affairs within Horizon. This theme will now be elaborated.

Client Feedback Study Horizon

Design

It involves a pilot study as to the usefulness of a client feedback system (CFS), developed in the province of South-Holland for the child and youth care system (PSJ, 2001; Welling, 2002).

The system consists of various questionnaires for young individuals and parents who make use of outpatient care, day care and treatment, or residential care. The clients receive the questionnaires two weeks after the start of the care, at by-evaluations and at the conclusion of the care giving process. Some 30 statements are presented with the request to indicate to what extent one agrees with these statements (5-point scale).

Also, the list contains a more general query about the client's satisfaction as to the received help – to be indicated by means of a report mark – and a few open queries, where suggestions for improvement of care giving can be made. The list comprises six main themes, among other things based on previous study on the opinions of children about, in their view, important quality criteria (Van Beek et al., 1999):

- the treatment and approach by care givers;
- the information the clients have at their disposal;
- the professionalism of the care givers;
- the results of the care process;
- the continuity of care (in a both methodical and personnel sense);
- the accommodation of the institution, i.e. unit.

Within Horizon, five units participated in the study (Brouwer, 2001). The response amongst the young individuals (± 50 per cent), but even more amongst parents (± 35 per cent) is most certainly capable of improvement. We present a selection of the results.

Results

In Table 2.2, the degree of general contentment of children and parents per unit, by means of a report mark, is noted. Moreover, in the rightmost column is displayed how many clients are dissatisfied (here a strict norm of a mark smaller than or equalling 6 – on a 10-point scale – is applied).

Table 2.2   Level of general contentment of parents (N=52) and children (N=39) on the care process in five Horizon units (average report marks)

Unit	No.	Parents (no.)	Report mark Children (no.)	P + C	% with a report mark ≤ 6
A	14	7.2 (7)	7.8 (7)	7.6	21%
B	11	7.4 (5)	7.8 (6)	7.5	36%
C	22	7.5 (11)	7.9 (11)	7.7	18%
D	29	7.5 (22)	7.1 (7)	7.4	17%
E	15	7.4 (7)	8.8 (8)	8.1	7%

Note: A = Bergse Bos – young; B = Bergse Bos – old; C = Rijnhove – young;
          D = Rijnhove – old; E = Rijnhove – day treatment.

We see that on average the clients mark a 7-plus, so in general they are quite content. Young individuals are on average somewhat more satisfied than parents, but the spreading amongst them is wider. Looking at the rightmost column, we see that in unit B a third of the respondents is dissatisfied. Remarkable is that the mark for general contentment remains the same over the several moments of evaluation: a few weeks after the start, midway and at the conclusion of the care process – both with the youth as with the parents. Apparently, the tone has been set in an early stage.

Table 2.3 shows on all points positive scores with the itemization of the six various aspects of the care giving process under scrutiny. The only aspect (with a strict norm of a score smaller than 4) that leads to a relatively negative opinion in young individuals, is the category 'continuity': children are, both midway and at the conclusion of a residential stay, unhappy with matters such as:

- still being with the same mentor as at the start;
- in case of an emergency, immediate availability of the care giver;
- continued dealings with one and the same team;
- the consistent and logical application of rules and agreements by staff.

The overviews do not show the situation on unit level. For workers in the field this level (and the level below, that of the living group) is the most interesting and informative. We confine ourselves in this context to a reproduction of the unit scores of children, midway their stay. In Table 2.4, some results are presented.

Table 2.3 **Average contentment of parents (N=52) and children (N=39), related to 6 aspects of the care giving process by Horizon (5-point scale), midway and at conclusion of the residential placement**

| | Midway | | At conclusion | |
Aspect of care	Parents	Children	Parents	Children
1 Treatment	4.5	4.2	4.5	4.2
2 Information	4.2	4.2	–	–
3 Professionalism	4.4	4.5	4.4	4.3
4 Results	4.4	4.8	4.4	4.7
5 Continuity	4.4	**3.6**	4.3	**3.6**
6 Accommodation	4.5	4.6	4.5	4.6

Scores < 4: bold.

Table 2.4 **Average contentment of children (N=39), related to six aspects of the care giving process in five Horizon units (5-point scale), midway in the residential placement**

| | Units | | | | | |
Aspect of care	A (N=7)	B (N=6)	C (N=11)	D (N=7)	E (N=8)	Total (N=39)
1 Treatment	4.0	**3.9**	4.2	4.5	4.3	4.2
2 Information	4.7	**3.9**	4.2	4.1	**3.9**	4.2
3 Professionalism	4.6	4.4	4.5	4.2	4.6	4.5
4 Results	4.5	4.9	4.8	4.7	4.9	4.8
5 Continuity	**3.9***	**2.5**	**3.9**	**3.0**	4.1	**3.6**
6 Accommodation	4.8	4.8	4.8	4.5	4.0	4.6

* Scores < 4 : bold. A = Bergse Bos – young; B = Bergse Bos – old; C = Rijnhove – young; D = Rijnhove – old; E = Rijnhove – day treatment.

The table confirms the finding that the category 'continuity' generates a point of (mild) criticism in almost every unit (not in unit E). Furthermore we recognize differences between the units. The children in the units B and E are of the opinion that providing more information about several items of the care giving system would be advisable. In unit B also the approach by the group workers should be the focus of attention. Items such as 'having time for me', 'listen closely to me', 'take me serious' and 'approach me in a positive way' are not fully endorsed by everyone. Using additional open queries, this is further elucidated.

In addition to the feedback data collected by means of the CFS-lists, in a number of units semi-structured interviews were held with children (Jansen, Hoefnagels and Vanuxem, 2001a, 2001b). These yielded important additional suggestions.

Conclusions

In accordance with a recently published study by Jansen and Feltzer (2002) on the perceptions of children of their stay in an institution, we too at Horizon find in the client feedback study that positive opinions on the received help and care from young individuals and parents clearly predominate: the overall opinion generates a mark between 7 and 8 on a 10-point scale. At the same time we saw that, in relation with the separate units, some critical remarks are being made: In almost every unit the continuity of care is a target of criticism, in some units attention is being drawn for a better dissemination of information and in one unit there is some disgruntlement about the approach by the residential workers.

With these issues the team sets to work, with the result that in a number of groups the theme 'mentor talks' is being put on the agenda of the team meeting. For the study shows that a number of children have the experience that these mentor talks do not take place regularly. So the question arises: is there indeed too little continuity on this point or is it that the young individuals do not perceive the conversations they have to be mentor talks (cf. Jansen et al., 2001b, p. 64)?

The overall and general positive perception of help received though does not mean that all emotional and behavioural problems, which were the direct cause of the placement, have vanished at the conclusion of the stay. In the Horizon study this has not (yet) been researched, but from other studies (Smit, 1993; Jansen et al., 1998), including the just mentioned study by Jansen and Feltzer (2002), we know that the problems children and families are wrestling with, cannot be solved in an instant. Whoever thinks this is the case is selling illusions.

As a pilot, the study can be considered a success, but additional study as to the used questionnaires is in order. When data are collected on a large scale and the percentage of non-respondents is reduced, it can be verified if the used six-categories system acquires empirical support (for example by means of principal components analysis). Also the reliability aspect (for instance, the homogeneity of the scales) deserves further investigation.

It is argued that systematic client feedback is an indispensable building block at the realization of client centred child and youth care: it continually confronts the organization with the customer's perspective. Needless to say that it should not be a method 'on an island'; working with a client feedback system is most effective if it is part of a participatory approach in all living and educational arrangements of the institution (Jumelet et al., 1999).

A final remark. The quality of an institution as self-learning organization (Van IJzendoorn, 1997) can be enhanced, not only through collecting client feedback, but also the *feedback from workers*. How could workers in the field take their clients seriously if they themselves are not taken seriously? In this connection for example a reference can be made to a study on the opinions of group workers at Horizon on the validity and usefulness of treatment planning. The results are reported back to the organization, as well as made available to a larger public (Jongejan et al., 2001; Knorth and Smit, 2002).

References

Bart, H. and Dijkstra, P. (2000), 'Cliëntenfeedback: Van instrumentontwikkeling tot managementrapportage', *Nederlands Tijdschrift voor Jeugdzorg*, Vol. 4 (3), pp. 22–9.

Brouwer, A. (2001), *Eindverslag pilot cliëntenfeedback bij Horizon*, Alphen aan den Rijn: Horizon Foundation.

Bureau WESP (1994), *Een timmerman zonder gereedschap. Plaatsingen en indicatiestellingen in drie bovenregionale internaten in Zuid-Holland*, Voorhout: Author.

De Winter, M. (2002), 'The Century of the Participating Child', in E.J. Knorth, P. M. Van den Bergh and F. Verheij (eds), *Professionalization and Participation in Child and Youth Care*, Aldershot/Burlington,VT: Ashgate Publishing, pp. 49–62.

Du Prie, H. (1999a), Vraaggericht werken als cement voor kwaliteitsverbetering, In H. Jumelet and C. Teunis (eds), *Kwaliteit in uitvoering: Kwaliteitszorg in de jeugdzorg*, Utrecht: SWP Publishers, pp. 224–36.

Du Prie, H. (1999b), 'Plaatsingsbegeleiding: Van experiment tot organisatiebrede inzet', *Nederlands Tijdschrift voor Jeugdzorg*, Vol. 3 (5), pp. 20–24.

Hennessy, E. (1999), 'Children as Service Evaluators', *Child Psychology and Psychiatry Review*, Vol. 4 (4), pp. 153–61.

Horizon Foundation (2002), *Jaarverslag 2001*, Rotterdam: Author.

Inspectie JHVJB (1996), *Kwaliteit Van het Hulpverleningsproces in de Jeugdhulpverlening: Deel 3*, Rijswijk: Author.

Jansen, E., Hoefnagels, G. and Vanuxem, B. (2001a), *Onderzoek naar beleving en mening Van jongeren uit de leefgroep 'De Sperwer' over de hulpverlening*, Alphen aan den Rijn: Horizon Foundation.

Jansen, E., Hoefnagels, G. and Vanuxem, B. (2001b), *Onderzoek naar beleving en mening Van jongeren uit het zorgprogramma 'Tussen Wal en Schip' over de hulpverlening*, Alphen aan den Rijn: Horizon Foundation.

Jansen, M.G. and Feltzer, M. J. A. (2002), 'Follow-up en belevingsonderzoek bij jeugdigen uit een behandelingstehuis,' *Tijdschrift voor Orthopedagogiek*, Vol. 41 (6), pp. 332–45.

Jansen, M.G., Schüller, C.M.L., Oud, J.H.L. and Arends, C. (1996), 'Outcome Research in Residential Child Care: Behavioral Changes of Treatment Completers and Treatment Non-completers', *International Journal of Child and Family Welfare*, Vol. 1 (1), pp. 40–56.

Jongejan, C., Smit, M. and Knorth, E.J. (2001), *Hulpverleningsplanning in de praktijk: Het perspectief Van de groepsleiding*, Amsterdam: SWP Publishers.

Jumelet, H., De Ruyter, D. and Kayser, T. (1999), *Gebruikmaken Van cliëntenfeedback in de jeugdzorg*, Utrecht: NIZW Publishers.

Jumelet, H., Jurrius, K. and Bruggeman, D.A.G. (2002), *Maar het gaat wel over mij! Kwaliteit Van de jeugdzorgketen in cliëntenperspectief*, Deeltraject 5 Van de LPJ Monitor 2002, Amsterdam: Alexander Foundation.

Knorth, E.J. (1990), *Ingenomen met opname? Ervaringen Van jongeren met de opname in een tehuis*, 2nd edn., Leiden/Amersfoort: Leiden University/Kwiek Press (KLOP Series, 2).

Knorth, E.J. and Dubbeldam, J.W.E. (1999), 'In Search of a Place in Residential Care', in H.E. Colla, Th. Gabriel, S. Millham, S. Müller-Teusler and M. Winkler (eds), *Handbook Residential Care and Foster Care in Europe*, Neuwied/Kriftel: Luchterhand Verlag, pp. 675–81.

Knorth, E.J. and Smit, M. (2002), 'The Role of Residential Child and Youth Care Workers in Care Planning: An Exploratory Study', in E.J. Knorth, P.M. Van den Bergh and F. Verheij (eds), *Professionalization and Participation in Child and Youth Care*, Aldershot/Burlington, VT: Ashgate Publishing, pp. 107–19.

Knorth, E.J., Van den Bergh, P.M. and Verheij, F. (2002), 'Professionalization and Participation in Child and Youth Care: Two Sides of One Coin?', in E.J. Knorth, P.M. Van den Bergh and F. Verheij (eds), *Professionalization and Participation in Child and Youth Care*, Aldershot/Burlington, VT: Ashgate Publishing, pp. 1–23.

Konijn, C. (2003), 'De Jeugdzorg Thermometer: Waardering Van Bureau Jeugdzorg door cliënten in de agglomeratie Amsterdam', Utrecht: NIZW (unpublished manuscript).

Kromhout, M., Eldering, L. and Knorth, E.J. (2000), 'Cultural Differences in Residential Child and Youth Care: Analyzing Perspectives', *Child and Youth Care Forum*, Vol. 29 (6), pp. 359–72.

Lemmens, F. and Donker, M. (1990), *Kwaliteitsbeoordeling door cliënten: Een metastudie naar tevredenheidsonderzoek in de geestelijke gezondheidszorg*, Utrecht: NcGv.

Lenz, A. (2001), *Partizipation von Kindern in Beratung und Therapie: Entwicklungen, Befunde und Handlungsperspektiven*, Weinheim/München: Juventa Verlag.

Meerdink, J. (1997), *Weet u wanneer ik wegga? Kinderen over hun beleving Van en mening over de jeugdhulpverlening*, Voorhout: Bureau WESP.

Meerdink, J. (1999), *Weet u waarom ik hier ben? Kinderen en jongeren over de kwaliteit Van het primaire proces Van de (semi)residentiële hulpverlening*, Utrecht: SWP Publishers.

Naayer, P. M. H. (2002), Better With Home: The case of Amstelstad Youth Care in Amsterdam', in P.M. Van den Bergh, E.J. Knorth, F. Verheij and D.C. Lane (eds), *Changing Care: Enhancing Professional Quality and Client Involvement in Child and Youth Care Services*, Amsterdam: SWP Publishers, pp. 157–68.

Peters, F., Trede, W. and Winkler, M. (eds) (1998), *Integrierte Erziehungshilfen: Qualifizierung der Jugendhilfe durch Flexibilisierung und Integration*, Frankfurt am Main: IGfH Verlag.

Prakken, J. (2002), 'Horizon: het einde Van het beddenpaleis'', in J. Prakken et al. (eds), *Van tribune naar speelveld: Vraaggericht werken in de praktijk*, Utrecht: NIZW Publishers, pp. 15–26.

PSJ (Provinciale Samenwerking Jeugdzorg) (2001), *Cliëntfeedbacksysteem voor ouders en jeugdigen*, Rotterdam: Author.

Ravelli, A.J. (1998), *Hulp die hout snijdt 1: Plaatsingsbegeleiding, contouren Van een nieuwe methodiek*, Utrecht: Utrecht Academy for Professional Education, Department of Social Pedagogical Care.

Rijnhove Foundation (1997), *De verruiming Van het residentiële aanbod in hulpverlening-strajecten: 'Hulp die hout snijdt'*, Alphen a/d Rijn: Author.

Scholte, E.M. (1997), 'Effectiviteit Van centra voor opvoeding, verzorging en scholing; uitvaller en blijvers', in J.R.M. Gerris (ed.), *Jongerenproblematiek: Hulpverlening en gezinsonderzoek*, Assen: Van Gorcum, pp. 40–58.

Smit, M. (1993), *Aan alles komt een eind. Een onderzoek naar beëindiging Van tehuishulpverlening*, PhD dissertation, Leiden University.

Sonuga-Barke, E.J.S. and Balding, J. (1993), 'British Parents' Beliefs about the Causes of Three Forms of Childhood Psychological Disturbances', *Journal of Abnormal Child Psychology*, Vol. 21, pp. 367–76.

Stikkelman, S. (in preparation), *Plaatsingsuitval na Zorgtoewijzing in de Jeugdzorg* [working title], MA thesis. Leiden: Leiden University, Department of Education.

Szajnberg, N.M. and Weiner, A. (1996), 'The Child's Conception of Psychiatric Care', *Child Psychiatry and Human Development*, Vol. 26, pp. 247–54.

Thoburn, J., Lewis, A. and Shemmings, D. (1995), *Paternalism or Partnership? Family Involvement in the Child Protection Process*, London: HMSO.

Van Beek, F. (1999), *'Dat ik niet alleen hun werk ben': Trends in kinderkwaliteitscriteria over de (semi)residentiële hulpverlening*, Amsterdam: SWP Publishers.

Van IJzendoorn, M. (1997), *Kwaliteit zonder kapsones: Een denkkader voor kwaliteitszorg in de welzijnssector*, Utrecht: NIZW Publishers.

Welling, M. (2000), 'Vraaggericht werken in de jeugdhulpverlening', *Nederlands Tijdschrift voor Jeugdzorg*, Vol. 4 (6), pp. 28–32.

Welling, M. (2002), 'Een cliëntenfeedbacksysteem voor de jeugdzorg', *Nederlands Tijdschrift voor Jeugdzorg*, Vol. 6 (2), pp. 82–5.

Whittaker, J. K. (1997), 'Intensive Family Preservation Work with High-risk Families: Critical Challenges for Research, Clinical Intervention and Policy', in W. Hellinckx, M.J. Colton and M. Williams (eds), *International Perspectives on Family Support*, Aldershot: Arena, pp. 124–39.

Zastowny, T.R., Stratmann, W.C., Adams, E.H. and Fox, M.L. (1995), 'Patient Satisfaction and Experience with Services and Quality of Care', *Quality Management in Health Care*, Vol. 3.

Chapter 3

The Development of a Residential Unit Working with Sexually Aggressive Young Men

Andrew Kendrick, Richard Mitchell and Mark Smith

Introduction

> Well it's helping me anyway and I probably, if I wasnae in here I'd probably
> be some place else I didnae want to be. These folk come to my rescue ... All
> I can say is they have done all the best they can. And it is time to move on.
> (young man)

In this chapter, we will report on the first three years in the development of a residential unit for sexually aggressive young men. Sexual offending and the sexual abuse of children has been the focus of recent government policy and legislation. There has also been increasing attention focused on the issue of children and young people who are sexually aggressive. However, research knowledge and the development of services for young people who are sexually aggressive lags behind that for adult sex abusers.

Research evidence has shown that many adult sex offenders begin their sexually abusive behaviour in adolescence. It is also argued that identification of sexually aggressive behaviour, and intervention at an early stage is important as children and young people are more tractable and their behaviour is easier to change (Expert Panel on Sex Offending, 2002; O'Callaghan and Print, 1994). It is vital then to address the development of services for children and young people who are sexually aggressive.

The Context for the Development

There is a growing consensus that between roughly a quarter and a third of sexual abuse is perpetrated by children and young people (Expert Panel on Sex Offending, 2002; Grubin, 1998; Masson and Erooga, 1999; Ryan, 1997). Fisher and Beech (1999), however, contrasted recent developments for adolescents with those for adults: 'the availability of assessment and treatment is … largely dependent on local developments, and these do not constitute a coherent service that requires a framework of resources and policies' (Fisher and Beech, 1999). Farmer and Pollock (1998), in their study of sexually abused and abusing children in substitute care, found that little work focused on the abusing behaviour.

This was also highlighted in an inspection of the management of sex offender cases in the community in eight local authorities in Scotland which included 46 cases of children and young people who had committed sexual offences or displayed sexually aggressive behaviour (Social Work Services Inspectorate, 2000). Most of the authorities inspected had no local strategy or guidelines for staff in children's services working with sexually aggressive young people. None of the authorities were able to consistently demonstrate satisfactory management of risk from sexual aggression by young people, although some cases were well-managed and demonstrated a high standard of social work practice. The supervision and management of the cases of children and young people who are sexually aggressive has yet to reach the general standard of the adult cases (Social Work Services Inspectorate, 2000).

The report *A Commitment to Protect* concluded that 'young people's sexual offending must be more effectively addressed at an early stage if their progression to more serious offending in adulthood is to be prevented' (Social Work Services Inspectorate, 1997) and called for strategic collaboration and a national oversight of all work with sex offenders in Scotland. The Scottish Executive, therefore, established the 'Expert Panel on Sex Offending' in 1998 (Expert Panel on Sex Offending, 2002). It developed a strategic approach which focused on four themes for protecting children and young people:

i)   developing personal safety programmes to protect children and young people from all forms of abuse;
ii) early identification of and intervention with young people demonstrating sexually aggressive behaviour through the promotion of safe and healthy relationships;
iii) reviewing existing legislation and measures which protect children and young people from sex offenders outside the home;
iv) developing proposals to involve local people positively in community safety.

The Expert Panel confirmed that while some good collaborative and flexible practice in the assessment and treatment of children and young people was taking place, it tended to be on an ad hoc basis and that there was little skilled specialist provision for children and young people who are sexually aggressive. It therefore called for the development of a national strategy of current assessment and intervention programmes. Services should include access to robust and comprehensive risk and needs assessment, and offence-specific personal change programmes should be available both in the community, and in secure and non-secure residential settings. All children and young people identified as at risk of sex offending or who are displaying sexually aggressive behaviour should have access to an appropriate personal change programme (Expert Panel on Sex Offending, 2002).

These recommendations have been accepted by the Scottish Executive and the Education Department and the Social Work Services Inspectorate will be responsible for developing this part of the strategy on sex offending in Scotland (Scottish Executive, 2002).

It has been suggested that there is now a good deal of consensus on specialized interventions with sexually aggressive young people with treatment goals including:

> increasing offender accountability; assisting offenders to understand and interrupt the thoughts, feelings, and behaviours that maintain sexual offending; reducing deviant sexual arousal, if present; developing healthy attitudes towards sex and relationships; and reducing the offenders' personal trauma, if present. (Worling and Curwen, 2000)

Research in the UK and the United States 'lends support to personal change programmes which use a range of methods based on a core of cognitive-behavioural work' (Social Work Services Inspectorate, 1997; Vennard, Sugg, and Hedderman, 1997). Cognitive-behavioural interventions focus on changing patterns of deviant arousal, correcting distorted thinking, and increasing social competence (Beckett, 1994; Ryan and Lane, 1997). Diversionary strategies and coping skills to stop reoccurrence of sexually aggressive behaviour are identified through relapse prevention work (O'Callaghan and Print, 1994; Pithers, Kashima, Cumming, and Beal, 1988; Richardson and Graham, 1997).

Longo, however, has also stressed that a more holistic approach needs to be taken with children and young people, rather than to focus solely on their sexually aggressive behaviour.

Holistic treatment means treating the whole person not just a particular problem ... When we see the whole person as a person with many facets, many of which are damaged parts, then we are better able to understand the nature of what we must treat and the complexities of doing so. (Longo, 2002, p, 229; see also Morrison, 2001)

There are a number of serious issues concerning work with sexually aggressive children and young people in residential and foster care. There has been a great deal of concern about the danger of children and young people being abused by other young people in residential and foster care. Sexually aggressive children and young people have frequently experienced discontinuity of care which can involve placement in residential care, foster care, or special education settings. Some children and young people will be living in these settings before their sexually aggressive behaviour is known and will abuse other children and young people in these settings (Barter, forthcoming; Green and Masson, 2002; Kendrick, 1997; Lindsay, 1999b).

In addition, children and young people will frequently be placed in residential or foster care following discovery of their sexually aggressive behaviour. There is, however, a shortage of appropriate resources and placements for this group of children and young people. Young people's sexually aggressive behaviour may be minimized or ignored in order to get placements (Bankes, Daniels, and Quartly, 1999). In *Managing the Risk* (Social Work Services Inspectorate, 2000), 24 of the 46 young people were looked after away from home and most of these were in residential settings. It is essential that if a young person is known to have a history of sexual aggression, decisions about placement must be based on careful assessment of the risks, agreed protection plans and appropriate levels of supervision (Epps, 1999; Social Work Services Inspectorate, 2000). Such placements have important implications for placement policies, staffing levels, training and supervision of staff. There are also significant issues in relation to building design and structure, peer group characteristics, behaviour management and control, communication and decision-making, and confidentiality (Centre for Residential Child Care, 1995; Epps, 1997a, 1997b; Skinner, 1992). The issue of through-care and integration back into the community is also a particular problem with sexually aggressive young people placed away from home (Greer, 1997; Hird, 1997). Epps, however, states that one of the 'advantages of working in a residential context is that it allows for greater control over the environmental and situational variables that contribute to sexually abusive behaviour' (Epps, 1997a, p. 45).

History to the Development of the Unit

The unit is part of Geilsland School which offers a residential care service for young men aged between 15 and 18 and operates as a Scotland-wide resource. It is managed by the Church of Scotland's Board of Social Responsibility; although it is non-denominational in its intake and staffing. Through the 1990s, Geilsland School steadily developed its work with sexually aggressive young men. In April 1999, one-third of the young men in the school were specifically identified as sexually aggressive at the point of referral. At this time, these young men were placed across all three of the residential units in the school. Work with this group of young men was carried out in conjunction with specialist community-based services for sexually aggressive young people and with appropriate external support, in particular involving a consultant psychologist with expertise in the field of sexual aggression.

During 1998, an extensive consultation exercise took place to consider the potential benefits of establishing a unit which would focus on work with sexually aggressive young men. A number of potential benefits were considered which included: identifying this work more clearly as an area of special provision; having more scope to support dedicated programmes of intervention such as relapse prevention and groupwork; being able to organize the daily life and regime of the unit round the needs of this particular group; reducing the risk to other residents; and concentrating staff resources more effectively (Geilsland School, 1998). Following the consultation, the decision was made to run a three-year pilot project to provide 'an integrated programme of care and intervention' with the overall aim 'to directly address the issue of sexual aggression whilst at the same time continuing to meet the holistic care needs of each young person' (Geilsland School, 2000). Funding from the Social Work Services Inspectorate of the Scottish Executive supported the development of this work.

The unit can accommodate nine young men in eight core places and one bedsit used for young men preparing to move on from the unit. The staffing resource was intended to provide a higher ratio of staff than applied in the other units of the school.

The criteria for admission to the unit are:

- conviction for a sexual offence or formal identification of involvement in sexual aggression;
- acknowledgement by young person of problem;
- willingness to participate in focused programme (Geilsland, 2000).

There has been a clear commitment to openness with the young men about the reason why they are all in the unit:

> Without compromising the confidentiality surrounding individual circumstances there is openness within the Unit regarding the fact that all the young people have common problem with sexual aggression. This acknowledgement is an important starting point in terms of encouraging young people to take responsibility for their behaviour and to believe that it can be worked on and changed. (Geilsland, 2000)

The unit set out to provide a non-abusive environment for the young men, a safe and secure placement was considered a core aim of the unit (Centre for Residential Child Care, 1995; Epps, 1999). Within this core context of 'a safe and developmentally appropriate environment', the stated aims of the programme are to:

> Help the young person to avoid or reduce the risk of behaving in an abusive manner.
> Reduce the seriousness of the abusive behaviour.
> Encourage an increase in appropriate social interaction through understanding and being offered the opportunity to learn new skills and enhance those already required.
> Develop appropriate links with family and help the family understand the behaviour of their son.
> Assess risk in terms of planning for future placements/return to the community. (Geilsland School, 2000)

The Research

The research was commissioned by Geilsland School and has aimed to provide a 'process evaluation' of the development of the work in the focused unit over the period of the pilot up until June 2002. The research has focused on: safe caring in working with sexually aggressive young males in a residential context; outcomes for young people; development of personal change programmes (e.g. risk assessment, relapse prevention, group work); confidentiality and individual's rights; staff development and training issues; and inter-agency relationships. An interim report focused on the first year of the unit's operation (Kendrick and Mair, 2002) and this chapter draws from this report and initial analysis of data collected during the final two years of the pilot period.

Given the sensitive nature of the subject area, detailed discussions took place about consent, confidentiality, and procedures in the event of further suspicions of abuse raised by the research in general and interviews with the young men in particular (Alderson, 1995; Cleaver and Freeman, 1995). This information was gone through with the young men by key workers and the researcher.

Data collection consisted of four main methods. Relevant school and unit documents were reviewed and information collected from the case files of the young men in the unit. Semi-structured interviews were carried out with school and unit staff over the period of the research. Telephone interviews have taken place with the young men's social workers where possible. In addition, a number of young men were interviewed about their experience of living in the unit and undertaking work on their sexual aggression. In the first phase of the research structured questionnaires were completed for 13 of the young men in the unit and these focused on aspects of the young men's attitudes and behaviour at referral to the unit; progress in the placement in relation to attitudes and behaviour; and achievement of aims and objectives. Fieldwork at Geilsland School allowed observation of school events; group work; staff team meetings; and unit meetings involving the young men. It also allowed time to be spent in the unit at different times of day, for example, mealtimes, recreation times, and night-time; an opportunity to chat with young men and staff informally.

The Young Men

During the first three years of the pilot, 30 sexually aggressive young men were placed in the unit. One young man, however, withdrew co-operation from the programme and very shortly moved out of the unit. Information in this chapter therefore relates to 29 young men. Nine of the young men were 15 years old when they moved in to the unit, 18 were 16 and the remaining two young men were 17 years old.

The young men had carried out a range of sexually aggressive acts which including inappropriate touching; indecent exposure; stalking; indecent assault of children or adult women; rape of younger children; and mutilation of animals involving a sexual element. The number of known victims ranged from one to over twenty. The victims of the abuse included family members (siblings, step-siblings and cousins); younger children (both male and female) in the community; other children and young people in residential, foster care or day school settings; female staff in residential settings; and adult women.

The young men frequently had complex histories of sexually aggressive behaviour. A significant number also had histories of involvement in the care system going back to early childhood. Many of the young men had been in residential and/or foster care before their sexually aggressive behaviour came to light and most of these had abused victims in previous residential or foster care placements or in special educational establishments (Barter, forthcoming; Gibbs and Sinclair, 2000; Kendrick, 1997). Only a quarter of the young men came into the unit directly from their home community.

Almost half of the young men in the unit had moderate to significant learning difficulties (O'Callaghan, 1999) and all of these had attended special educational provision. Many of these had attended special educational provision since primary age and about half had experienced residential special schools or residential care because of their challenging behaviour. Most of the other young men, however, had exhibited problem behaviour in education, having been excluded from school, truanted or having involvement with educational psychological services (Masson and Erooga, 1999; Vizard, Monck, and Misch, 1995).

The young men's case histories also highlighted significant issues of trauma and disruption in their lives (Mulholland and McIntee, 1999; Social Work Services Inspectorate, 2000; Way, 2002). This reinforced the focus on their holistic care needs and the need to provide stability and security as the basis for individual work.

Two of the criteria for inclusion in the programme were: conviction for a sexual offence or formal identification of involvement in sexual aggression; and, acknowledgement by young person of a problem. There were, however, still major issues in terms of the young men's acceptance of responsibility and the levels of their denial at the time of their referral to the programme. Most of the young men, even if they accepted their offence, accepted no, or little, responsibility and minimized their sexually aggressive behaviour. The young men were considered to have very poor awareness of victim issues; very poor levels of understanding of the distinction between consensual and coercive relationships; very poor understanding of their own sexually aggressive behaviour; and poor levels of knowledge of sex and sexuality. Most of the young men had low self esteem and tended to have poor assertiveness skills, poor personal and social skills and poor anger management skills.

The Development of the Unit

The high profile nature of the developments in the unit, including the involvement of the Scottish Executive and an external evaluation, meant that staff felt a great deal of anxiety at the start. There was concern about the reaction of the young men to being told that the unit would be focusing work on sexual aggression. However, to a large extent, this proved unfounded and there appeared to be a visible sense of relief for some of the young men.

> … and then they come and telt me it was for sex offenders and I went 'Ah well, at least I'm not the only one'. That put a big bit off of me because now I ken it's not just me, the whole unit's part of it. So it took a lot off of me, kind of calmed me down a bit. (Young man)

A concern that the creation of the unit might lead to scapegoating of residents by other young men in the school also proved, for the most part, to be unfounded. Having the focused unit appears to have afforded the group a degree of normality, acceptance and protection.

Integrated Model of Work

The unit aimed to develop an integrated model of working with sexually aggressive young men. Residential staff were to be involved, with appropriate support, in all aspects of the work, both in the day-to-day care of the young men and in the programmes focusing on their sexually aggressive behaviour. This, however, has not been an easy aim to achieve and there have been a number of issues which have affected its successful implementation. The two main issues have concerned the work-load issues for residential staff in the unit and the impact of staff changes. At the end of the three year pilot, only one of the original staff members was still in the unit. This obviously affects the ongoing development of knowledge and skills in the staff group, especially given the general difficulties of recruiting residential staff with the appropriate levels of qualifications and skills.

The Core Programme

The initial aim was to establish a culture and ethos which was consonant with the work of the unit (Brown, Bullock, Hobson, and Little, 1998; Lindsay,

1999a). Over the period of the pilot, meeting the core task of providing a safe and secure environment has been seen as one of the most successful aspects in the development of the work. Staff feel that the unit has been successful in providing appropriate levels of care and support.

> I think the kind of messages we are trying to get across, the ethos and the culture, and the way people treat each other, reiterated day-in and day-out. And that's the most important thing. (Staff member)

> Safe boundaries, I think that is something that is reinforced every single day as to what is going on and why we are asking them to behave in a certain way. It is for their safety, it is for the other boys' safety, it is for ours … We are very clear. (Staff member)

Local authority social workers interviewed were mostly positive about the care provided and one commented on the 'very high standard' of care.

> I think they did a pretty good job, given [young man's] extremely difficult behaviour, they did an extremely good job …. (Social worker)

> I think it has been really quite successful because [young man] before he went to [the] Unit had a variety of residential placements which had broken down and hadn't been particularly positive for him either … he was displaying quite aggressive behaviour as well towards staff and they found him very, very difficult to manage. Since he has come to [the unit] he has been very, very settled I would say. (Social worker)

Although there are high levels of supervision in the unit (Epps, 1999), Geilsland is an open setting. School staff, however, considered that there had been relatively little absconding from the unit. Similarly, staff considered that drugs and alcohol had not been a major issue in the unit.

Bullying was considered to be a concern over the period of the pilot (Barter, forthcoming; Gibbs and Sinclair, 2000; Kendrick, 1997). The mixed abilities in the group were seen to contribute to this. It was acknowledged as a problem and was consistently confronted within the unit.

> Bullying is always an issue … on a regular Monday afternoon meeting with the boys and it comes up every single week, the bullying, the name calling … There is a lot of talk, there is not a lot of physical bullying but there is a lot of name calling, it is addressed all the time but it seems to be around all the time. (Staff member)

Notwithstanding this, unit ground rules stated that 'swearing and sexualized talk or gestures will not be acceptable'. An external consultant who was requested by the Board of Social Responsibility to provide an independent view of the culture of Geilsland highlighted that the general atmosphere in the unit was much calmer than the rest of the school and that 'the absence of swearing may have made a significant contribution to that' (confidential report, 2000).

Over the pilot period there have been a number of incidents of sexually aggressive behaviour. Some of these have involved the sexually aggressive behaviour targeted at female members of staff. This has taken two main forms; verbal abuse and inappropriate touching. There have also been a number of incidents of a sexual nature between the young men in the unit.

> ... I think again when this has arisen, we have been able to rehearse those issues, go through those issues with the young people, with the social work department, the police and try and arrive at as good an understanding of what the dynamic of particular episodes had been. We've also learnt how vigilant you have to be ... (Staff member)

Consistency of approach in regard to safe caring and stability has to be worked at over time and this was recognized by staff. The development of the core programme, however, has also focused on the holistic care needs of each young man and on providing a nurturing experience. Getting the balance right between the emphasis on safe care and providing an environment within which the young men can thrive has been an important aspect of the core programme.

Individual Programmes of Work

In the first phase of the study, individual work with the young men was carried out either by the consultant psychologist or the unit manager in conjunction with a residential care worker (in male-female pairs). There was a separation, however, in the role of key-worker and individual worker; the key-worker focusing on the core task of care and support and the individual worker focusing on direct work related to sexually aggressive behaviour. Individual work begins with a six-week programme of assessment, after which a longer-term plan of work is drawn up (although staff did consider that the planning of individual work should be more rigorously formalized). In the first phase, it was generally considered that too great a load of direct work fell on the consultant psychologist and the unit manager.

However, changes in staff and a reduction in the time commitment of the consultant psychologist (due to factors external to the unit) meant that over the pilot period, there have been major difficulties in developing consistency in the development of individual programmes of work.

> I think the development of the individual and group work programmes has been more ..., we've had bits where we have had a good run at that and where there has been consistency of staff and input and we have been able to develop. There are points where we appear almost to have had to go back to square one and start again on those programmes because of changes of personnel and so on or because of other things that were impacting on the unit at particular points in time. (Staff member)

Involved staff felt that there was also an issue relating to the consistency of the individual sessions with the young men. Too often, it was felt, weekly sessions did not take place, either because of staffing issues or because the young men were not available. Other factors, the length of time of the legislative process for example, also affected the work. It was apparent that for some of the young men, this process could be highly disruptive to the work they were doing in the unit because of the levels of anxiety created by court appearances (Scottish Executive, 2000).

However, in relation to some of the young men, the positive effect of the work was identified by social workers.

> When he was working in the sex offender programme there was lots of work on how to plan for not re-offending and it appears to have been successful. (Social worker)

> I'm 100 per cent convinced he did benefit from the Programme and that has contributed to his not re-offending ... I have no doubt that he took something with him from the Programme that has helped him this way. (Social worker)

An important aspect of the individual work with the young men which was recognized to be an area for concern in the first phase of the research, related to the provision of assessment reports and written feedback.

> I think we are quite good in assessment, we assess everything constantly. What we have to be better at is formalising that. Actually writing reports ... and part of that is about actually finding the time to do that ... I think we are quite good at assessing the risk that somebody might pose, or what would be safe

> for somebody to do. But actually writing that down is the bit that, I certainly think, we are not so good at. (Staff member)

This was the main area of criticism made by the social workers interviewed.

> Since we have no indication of his treatment plan, or any therapy that took place while he was in Geilsland, we have to tell the court that we assume he did nothing. And we start over again. This ... is a real problem. (Social worker)

Group Work

As was seen from the unit ground rules, attendance at group work is not optional. Cognitive skills group work takes place in weekly sessions. Issues which have been addressed in group work have included: problem solving; social skills; anger management; values and beliefs; power and control; men and violence; consequences of behaviour; self-awareness. The decision at the outset was that offence specific group work would not be appropriate. In addition to the cognitive skills group, task centred and time-limited groups have been run for smaller groups of young men focusing on sex education and social skills (Taylor, 1997) during the first phase of the research. These, however, had lapsed and towards the end of the pilot, plans were under way to re-introduce sex education input.

Over the period of the pilot, there was an issue of keeping group work going throughout the year, due largely to staff holidays during the summer. Generally, however, the group work was felt to be effectively run, although staff did acknowledge that there was scope to develop it further.

> The guys themselves talk. They are quite good about saying, 'We did that in group work'. They are working quite well; they are taking it on board ... It's amazing, they ... take part. You know, at first it was, 'I don't want to do it'. Now they are up for it and they take part. (Staff member)

> I certainly hear people referring to [group work and individual work]. Again, it is probably something that they could do better but I have regularly heard staff saying 'Remember we talked about that at Group Work'. (Staff member)

> So I've got a lot out of group work and it has helped me a lot. And the stuff I'm doing in group work at the moment contrasts with my individual work, so I know what to say in my group work and I know what to say in my individual work, because the two are helping each other, know what I mean. (Young man)

Family Work

Acknowledging the importance of work with families (Burnham, Moss, deBelle, and Jamieson, 1999; Morrison, 2001), one of the stated aims of the programme is to: develop appropriate links with family and help the family understand the behaviour of their son. While there have been instances of positive work with families, it is very costly in terms of staff time when the young men's families live at a considerable distance from the unit and there are issues of access to the families of these young men because of their reactions to the sexually abusive behaviour. This was felt to be an aim which had been achieved to a very limited extent.

> We haven't really got into a lot of direct family work or focused structured family work but I think there [are] really good relationships being struck up with parents and grannies, because the boys are accepted, they begin to have a better understanding of things, so I think there is a lot of value for boys who might not be going home but still having contact with their families. (Staff member)

The lack of structured family work impacts on the progress of individual work and on the planning for the young men's return to the community. Accordingly it is recognized as an important area for future development and at the end of the pilot period, there were plans to employ a family support worker to progress this work.

Issues of the Integrated Model

One of the main benefits of the integrated model of work is the way in which the work done with the young men in direct individual work and group work could be reinforced by discussion and work within the unit on a day by day basis. Similarly, issues arising in the unit, such as bullying or instances of sexually aggressive behaviour could be confronted openly and linked to work in individual sessions or in group work.

> I think it is good, you know, if you are speaking to a guy in individual work and things are getting passed on, and you add that to group work and you add that to the culture … (Staff member)

However, this integration has also led to a high degree of stress on staff due to the intensive nature of the direct work on top of the expectations of the core task of caring and support. Following the first phase of the research, staffing levels were increased but, given the turn-over of staff in the unit, this has continued to be a major issue in the work of the unit.

> … what we under-estimated was the pressures of multi-tasking that that entails, so we were asking staff to be involved in the daily routines of the unit, looking after the young people and at the same time delivering individual programmes, taking part in group work and so on. So some of that multi-tasking was really very demanding and something we are having to think carefully about as to whether that is the best way to deliver … of whether it might be worthwhile having some dedicated staffing within the overall complement of the team. (Staff member)

Conclusion

There has been major progress in the development of work in the unit over the pilot period. In particular, the development of the core ethos of the unit has, to a large degree, produced positive results in ensuring an open, supportive and non-abusive environment for the direct work on sexually aggressive behaviour. This has led to the unit providing secure and stable placements to many young men whose behaviour is extremely difficult.

While there has also been significant progress in the development of group work and individual programmes of work for the young men, staff have recognized that this has not taken the 'linear' track that might have been expected. Significant issues have been identified in relation to staff resources for the work in the unit. The staff team has been stretched, even with increased staffing levels, in covering the range of tasks expected of them. The intensive nature of direct work with sexually aggressive young men is an important additional factor. Issues identified in the first phase of the research, concerning the extent of specialist input in the direct work focused on sexually aggressive behaviour have been exacerbated by staff turnover in the unit.

The positive features of the integrated model of work developed in the focused programme have been identified. Central to this has been the development of the 'core programme' which emphasizes a safe, secure and nurturing environment. The focus on sexual aggression is balanced by addressing the range of needs of the young men in a holistic way. The experience of the unit highlights the need for security and stability in the life of these young men in order to address their sexual aggression through individual personal change programmes. As Farmer and Pollock state, '… the *context* in which therapeutic help was offered seemed to be of considerable importance' (Farmer and Pollock, 1998, p. 182).

References

Alderson, P. (1995), *Listening to Children: Children, Ethics and Social Research*, Ilford: Barnardos.

Bankes, N., Daniels, K. and Quartly, C. (1999), 'Placement Provision and Placement Decisions: Resources and Processes', in M. Erooga and H. Masson (eds), *Children and Young People who Sexually Abuse Others: Challenges and Responses*, London: Routledge, pp. 51–66.

Barter, C. (forthcoming), 'Peer Abuse in Residential Child Care', *Scottish Journal of Residential Child Care*, Vol. 2 (2).

Beckett, R. (1994), 'Cognitive-behavioural Treatment of Sex Offenders', in T. Morrison, M. Erooga and R. Beckett (eds), *Sexual Offending Against Children: Assessment and Treatment of Male Abusers*, London: Routledge, pp. 80–101.

Brown, E., Bullock, R., Hobson, C. and Little, M. (1998), *Making Residential Care Work: Structure and Culture in Children's Homes*, Aldershot: Ashgate Publishing.

Burnham, J., Moss, J., deBelle, J. and Jamieson, R. (1999), 'Working with Families of Young Sexual Abusers: Assessment and Intervention Issues', in M. Erooga and H. Masson (eds), *Children and Young People who Sexually Abuse Others: Challenges and Responses*, London: Routledge, (pp. 146– 67).

Centre for Residential Child Care (1995), *Guidance for Residential Workers Caring for Young People who have been Sexually Abused and Those who Abuse Others*, Glasgow: Centre for Residential Child Care.

Cleaver, H. and Freeman, P. (1995), *Parental Perspectives in Cases of Suspected Child Abuse*, London: HMSO.

Epps, K. (1997a), Managing Risk', in M. Hoghughi, S. Bhate and F. Graham (eds), *Working with Sexually Abusive Adolescents*, London: Sage, pp. 35–51.

Epps, K. (1997b), Pointers for Carers', in M.C. Calder, H. Hanks and K. Epps (eds), *Juveniles and Children who Sexually Abuse: A Guide to Risk Assessment*, Lyme Regis: Russell House, pp. 99–109.

Epps, K. (1999), 'Looking after Young Sexual Abusers: Child Protection, Risk Management and Risk Reduction', in M. Erooga and H. Masson (eds), *Children and Young People who Sexually Abuse Others: Challenges and Responses*, London: Routledge, pp. 67–85.

Expert Panel on Sex Offending (2002), *Reducing the Risk: Improving the Response to Sex Offending*, Edinburgh: Scottish Executive.

Fisher, D. and Beech, A.R. (1999), 'Current Practice in Britain with Sexual Offenders', *Journal of Interpersonal Violence*, Vol. 14 (3), pp. 240–56.

Geilsland School (1998), *Developing the Service for Sexually Aggressive Young People*, internal document.

Geilsland School (2000), *Focused Care and Work with Sexually Aggressive Young People*, internal document.

Gibbs, I. and Sinclair, I. (2000), 'Bullying, Sexual Harassment and Happiness in Residential Children's Homes', *Child Abuse Review*, Vol. 9, pp. 247–56.

Green, L. and Masson, H. (2002), 'Adolescents who Sexually Abuse and Residential Accommodation: Issues of Risk and Vulnerability', *British Journal of Social Work*, Vol. 32, pp. 149– 68.

Greer, W.C. (1997), 'Aftercare: Community Integration following Institutional Treatment', in G. Ryan and S. Lane (eds), *Juvenile Sexual Offending: Causes, Consequences and Correction*, 2nd edn, San Francisco: Jossey-Bass, pp. 417–30.

Grubin, D. (1998), *Sex Offending Against Children: Understanding the Risk*, London: Home Office.

Hird, J. (1997), 'Working in Context', in M. Hoghughi, S. Bhate and F. Graham (eds), *Working with Sexually Abusive Adolescents*, London: Sage, pp. 177–95.

Kendrick, A. (1997), 'Safeguarding Children Living Away from Home from Abuse: A Literature Review', in R. Kent (ed.), *Children's Safeguards Review*, Edinburgh: The Stationery Office, pp. 143–275.

Kendrick, A. and Mair, R. (2002), 'Developing Focused Care: A Residential Unit for Sexually Aggressive Young Men', in M.C. Calder (ed.), *Young People who Sexually Abuse: Building the Evidence Base for your Practice*, Lyme Regis: Russell House Publishing, pp. 112–24.

Lindsay, M. (1999a), 'Dilemmas and Potential Work with Sexually Abusive Young People in Residential Settings', in M.C. Calder (ed.), *Young People who Sexually Abuse: Building the Evidence Base for your Practice*, Lyme Regis: Russell House Publishing, pp. 281–93.

Lindsay, M. (1999b), 'The Neglected Priority: Sexual Abuse in the Context of Residential Child Care', *Child Abuse Review*, Vol. 8, pp. 405–18.

Masson, H. and Erooga, M. (1999), 'Children and Young People who Sexually Abuse Others: Incidence, Characteristics and Causation', in M. Erooga and H. Masson (eds), *Children and Young People who Sexually Abuse Others: Challenges and Responses*, London: Routledge, pp. 1–18.

Morrison, T. (2001), 'Surveying the Terrain: Current Issues in the Prevention and Management of Sexually Abusive Behaviour by Males', *The Journal of Sexual Aggression*, Vol. 7 (1), pp. 19–39.

Mulholland, S.J. and McIntee, J. (1999), 'The Significance of Trauma in Problematic Sexual Behaviour', in M.C. Calder (ed.), *Young People who Sexually Abuse: Building the Evidence Base for your Practice*, Lyme Regis: Russell House Publishing, pp. 266–79.

O'Callaghan, D. and Print, B. (1994), 'Adolescent Sexual Abusers: Research, Assessment and Treatment', in T. Morrison, M. Erooga and R. Beckett (eds), *Sexual Offending Against Children: Assessment and Treatment of Male Abusers*, London: Routledge, pp. 146–77.

Pithers, W.D., Kashima, K.M., Cumming, G.F. and Beal, L.S. (1988), 'Relapse Prevention: A Method of Enhancing Maintenance of Change in Sex Offenders', in A. Salter (ed.), *Treating Child Sex Offenders and Victims*, Newbury Park: Sage Publications.

Richardson, G. and Graham, F. (1997), 'Relapse Prevention', in M. Hoghughi, S.R. Bhate and F. Graham (eds), *Working with Sexually Abusive Adolescents*, London: Sage, pp. 162–76.

Ryan, G. (1997), 'Incidence and Prevalence of Sexual Offences Committed by Juveniles', in G. Ryan and S. Lane (eds), *Juvenile Sexual Offending: Causes, Consequences and Correction*, 2nd edn, San Francisco: Jossey-Bass, pp. 10–16.

Ryan, G. and Lane, S. (eds) (1997), *Juvenile Sexual Offending: Causes, Consequences and Correction*, 2nd edn, San Francisco: Jossey-Bass.

Scottish Executive (2002), *Analysis of External Consultation on and the Scottish Executive's Response to, 'Reducing the Risk: Improving the Response to Sex Offending', the Report of the Expert Panel on Sex Offending*, Edinburgh: Scottish Executive.

Skinner, A. (1992), *Another Kind of Home: A Review of Residential Child Care*, Edinburgh: Scottish Office.

Social Work Services Inspectorate (1997), *A Commitment to Protect – Supervising Sex Offenders: Proposals for More Effective Management*, Edinburgh: The Stationery Office.

Social Work Services Inspectorate (2000), *Managing the Risk: An Inspection of the Management of Sex Offender Cases in the Community*, Edinburgh: Scottish Executive.

Taylor, J.L. (1997), Educational Approaches to Treatment', in M. Hoghughi, S. Bhate and F. Graham (eds), *Working with Sexually Abusive Adolescents*, London: Sage, pp. 114–27.

Vennard, J., Sugg, D. and Hedderman, C. (1997), 'The Use of Cognitive-behavioural Approaches with Offenders: Messages from Research', in *Changing Offenders' Attitudes and Behaviour: What Works?*, London: Home Office.

Vizard, E., Monck, E. and Misch, P. (1995), 'Child and Adolescent Sex Abuse Perpetrators: A Review of the Research Literature', *Journal of Child Psychology and Psychiatry*, Vol. 36 (5), pp. 731–56.

Way, I. (2002), 'Childhood Maltreatment Histories of Male Adolescents with Sexual Offending Behaviours: A Review of the Literature', in M.C. Calder (ed.), *Young People who Sexually Abuse: Building the Evidence Base for your Practice*, Lyme Regis: Russell House Publishing, pp. 26–55.

Worling, J.R. and Curwen, T. (2000), 'Adolescent Sexual Offender Recidivism: Success of Specialized Treatment and Implications for Risk Prediction', *Child Abuse and Neglect*, Vol. 24 (7), pp. 965–82.

Chapter 4

Family Life Educator Training as the Key to Effective Family Development Work

Rosa Heim

Since 1999 the Colleg für FamilienPädagogik (Family Life Education College) has been running an innovative course for training educational staff and carers. The aim of the course is to communicate the knowledge and skills required for working in a complex field of interaction to establish conditions conducive to development in emotionally disturbed children and young adults. This specific model was developed by SOS Children's Villages to provide the training and trigger the learning processes needed by adults working in professional out-of-home care communities with children and young adults. The relevant core competence constitutes the professional self-image of the family life educator and is the qualification needed for a field of education in which not an external structure but the performance of the tasks involved defines the profession. This article presents the theoretical background and describes a training model that we believe offers the key to effective family development work.

Professional Self-image in Family Life Education

Posch and Putzhuber (2001, p. 203) give a clear picture of the distinctive features of professional self-image in the child care sector and also of the related problems. Daily involvement with an out-of-home care community that differs little from the everyday world of other families makes it much more difficult to maintain a clear distinction between the private and the professional spheres, and thus to appreciate and communicate the specific quality of the profession. There are few artefacts or props, such as a dress code, a specific setting or typical spatial components, which would serve as a signal for the professional activity involved. The greater the everyday character of the work, as in the case of out-of-home care communities, the less the professional role will be supported by the working environment and the less likely it is that a professional self-image will receive external confirmation, with the risk of fading awareness.

A professional self-image depends on repeated social confirmation within the professional communication processes. In pedagogical processes, such as in the fields of education and caring, however, the immediate beneficiaries are children and young adults. They are hardly in a position to call for the services of the adults themselves and indeed are socially dependent on these adults. Creating a professional self-image and anchoring it in people's awareness is only possible if this basic understanding can be maintained in a continual dialogue with the employer and client. In a sector in which the everyday quality dominates, instruments are therefore needed to provide regular support for professionalism, which otherwise will gradually be lost. Nor is it enough to seek professionalism solely through a training process.

As there are no externalities to identify the professional activity involved, such as a specific location or clearly defined hours of work, professionalism in out-of-home care communities remains largely concealed from the outside observer. On the subject of professionalization in the social sector, Thiersch (1998, p. 265) accordingly focuses on inner factors. Professionalism in the social sphere is communicated through a specific approach, a special language and methods which are typically assigned to the field. This would seem to suggest that, in view of the strong affinity of such professional activity to everyday situations compared with other fields of education, professionals working in out-of-home care are even more dependent on a clearly defined professional self-image.

In the field of family life education as a profession, we therefore operate with concepts combining the holistic involvement of the adult working in an educational setting with a commitment to reflection on the social activity involved. The term 'education' itself indicates that the work differs from unreflected everyday actions; it implies a conscious and targeted form of activity. The term 'family' defines the field of work as a social activity in a shared life-world. In professional out-of-home care communities the degree of autonomy at the level of action, the diversity of interactional relationships that affect the care provided, and the complexity of the task involved are all highly pronounced. The distinctions vis-à-vis other systems of care are blurred and depend on which professional role is adopted in which system.

In the process of developing our innovative training model, Posch and Träger (1999, p. 11) made the first attempt to define family life education as a profession:

> In this context family life education relates to co-existence and educational work in out-of-home care for children and youngsters in families with adults

living and working as significant others. The latter shape the interpersonal relationships through their private and professional activities and professional reflection. Family life education operates between the three poles of the original family, the new family and the organizational structure.

Specific Approaches in Family Life Education

Adding Being to the Role of the Educator/Carer

In most professional contexts, private activities are basically treated as a disturbance in the professional process, but in professional out-of-home care communities the private lives of the adults constitute an essential addition to the opportunities provided to the children and young adults for learning and building relationships. Pedagogical work cannot be defined merely in terms of the professional tasks involved; it also includes the personality of the respective adult. As they all live together, the children and young adults are able to observe how the educators shape their personal lives according to their own satisfaction and how they themselves master the challenges of everyday life. They are given a direct insight into the ways in which the adults manage their private relationships, how they perceive and satisfy their own needs, and how they resolve private problems and conflicts. As any situation in which different people of different ages live together will always involve a variety of problems and challenges, there is no need to artificially create opportunities for social learning in the context of family life education; they derive from day-to-day coexistence and constitute an immediate experience with direct impacts for the children and young adults. In family life education, an awareness is thus created of one's personal role model as an individual human being.

Authenticity

In the family life education approach, the distinction between the private person and the professional person is no longer made. The individual as a whole with all the elements of his or her past is involved in the educational process. His/her way of thinking (ideas and attitudes), feeling and acting have a direct impact on the world of the child or young adult. In this holistic view, it cannot be meaningful to merely assume an exemplary style of behaviour in direct contact with the child or to seek to create a better picture of oneself in some way unless the qualities involved have really been developed and are lived and internalized. Authenticity, i.e. the genuine character of the interpersonal contact, is accordingly a key concept in family life education. This view has nothing to do with the creation of a new ideal adult and educationalist, as normative aspirations are always in some way detrimental to human development. What is important is the ability to know oneself in all the facets of one's personality and to act in the spirit of authenticity. Effective pedagogical support always presupposes authenticity and the willingness to accept oneself as one is. This is in keeping with the principle that in educational processes only what the educators/carers are capable of themselves can be communicated to others.

The Autonomy of the Individual

In family life education, the human being is seen as an autonomous individual. This view implies that real learning processes cannot be directly triggered in the child or young adult. In all pedagogical work, it is therefore important to preserve the child's freedom to make his or her own decisions. All behaviour on the part of a child makes sense and it is up to the child to decide whether he/she wishes to change that behaviour and is open to new behavioural patterns. The task of the educator can only be to create the right conditions for new learning processes. The educator's scope for action is limited to shaping his or her relationship with the child and the environment and to setting an example. A family life educator wishing to bring about change must always start with him/herself. For the child or young adult, new opportunities for development can only take the form of a changed environment, i.e. a change in the way the adult behaves towards him or her.

The Perception of Emotion as a Tool

Emotion and professionalism are by no means mutually exclusive in family life education. The emotional side of the adult is seen as a central pillar of the process as it is needed to lend expression to the adult's needs and personal state and thus signal the subjective condition of the educator or carer. Both positive and negative emotionality show how the adults experience the reality of their world and the relational structures involved. For the educator/carer, the emotional level is also a key indicator for assessing the psychological state of the child or young adult, with negative emotions seen as an expression of unresolved relational conflicts or situations requiring clarification. However, the emotional level can also be destructive or an obstacle to development in interpersonal relationships. For that reason a sensitive approach to one's own feelings is always important in family life education.

Process-based Thinking

In family life education, educational activity is defined as a process. Only where the adult relates continuously to the child/young adult can a process be initiated in the first place and lead to a positive outcome. It is also a precondition for the process of reflection on the adult's pedagogical effectiveness. Processes also presuppose a clear definition of the pedagogical goals required to guide them, although the child/young adult must not merely be seen in terms of those goals. Through regular reflection it is possible to match the educational processes with greater accuracy to the child's or young adult's subjective condition and point of departure. In our model, the children/young adults are involved – to a degree commensurate with their age – in the definition of the next developmental steps. This increases the perceptivity of the educator/carer with regard to the relational situation, the point of departure for the child and the impacts of his/her work. At the same time it ensures that the adults themselves are involved in a continuous process of learning and change in their interaction with the children/youngsters.

Room for Development

In family life education we need to be aware that processes of change require time and space, and a good educator/carer is one who sees the need to allow room for progress to be made within the development processes, who has confidence in the child's capacity for development, and knows that the learning process can be fostered but not dictated. That presupposes the view that – given a supportive environment and due attention to his or her individual needs – every child is capable of positive development and change.

The Unique Quality of every Human Being

A good educator focuses on the unique quality of both the child or young adult and the adult his/herself. Every person is seen as a unique human being with individual qualities that have developed in the course of that person's life. A holistic view of the individual is essential if the child is to be seen in the fullness of his or her personality and assessed from a variety of perspectives.

This in turn presupposes a system in which the educators and carers working in the field of family life education are not judged by one standard yardstick either, but are treated as unique individuals with the competence to support positive developmental processes.

Key Qualifications for Family Life Educators

The following key qualifications relate to basic abilities that distinguish professional work in out-of-home care communities from unreflected everyday activities. The central qualifications of a family life educator relate to the ability to shape interactional relationships within the field of action, and the life-world and the environment of the child or young adult, and to make effective use of available resources. The availability of the personnel, and the social and material resources to cope with the tasks involved in a defined caring situation and the resulting burdens is a *sine qua non*. It is the responsibility of the employer to make them available or give access to them. In the following I will discuss those key qualifications in family life education that in my opinion are germane to successful relationship-building by educators and carers in out-of-home communities.

Self-empowerment

The complexity of the tasks involved in family life education calls for a high degree of self-empowerment and organizational ability. The daily routines of the life-world need to be developed and continually adapted according to the needs of the children/youngsters and the relevant social structures. Independent working is called for in the deployment of one's own resources and the resources of others. Family life educators must therefore be able to identify the tasks as they present themselves in this life-world and to prioritize as necessary. At the same time they are free to choose the most appropriate method in the execution of the tasks. With holistic life-worlds increasingly disappearing, professional life becoming more and more specialized and social structures quickly changing, this ability can no longer be taken for granted. The key qualification presupposes intrinsic motivation. Only a system of inner meaning constitutes a reliable factor for sound pedagogical work in this life-world.

Appropriate Relationship-building

Family life educators learn to build strong relationships of trust with the children in their care and to give each relationship a degree of closeness or distance that is appropriate to the child's biography. A positive relationship between the adult and the child is a prerequisite for effective working in any pedagogical and social context. Children who are already bonded to a primary significant other are encouraged to maintain that emotional bond within the professional childcare relationship so that no conflict of loyalty can arise. Family life educators learn to match the intensity of their relationship to the needs of the child – from providing an anchor in a sound and familiar relationship to offering support when and as required or letting go altogether – and to modify that relationship in response to the development process. In a shared life-world and shared experience of everyday life, the degree of mutual dependence is high and reinforces mutual influence within the relationship.

Accessing the World of the Child

Another key qualification is the ability to gain access to the world of the child at both the cognitive and the emotional level so as to comprehend his/her emotional situation in out-of-home care. The meaning of seemingly inappropriate behaviour on the part of children or young adults in their new life-world can only be derived from its significance in the context of their past lives. Once that has been recognized, educators/carers can better support the process of reorientation, i.e. the development of more appropriate behaviour on the part of the child in the new life-world. In his article on professional family life education, Klaus Wolf calls this skill 'deciphering the child's experience of life' (Jugendhilfe, 1998 p. 37). It is a qualification that is hard for outsiders to see and hence appreciate.

Avoiding Emotional Transfer

What we do, how we seem to be and how we react to others can only be understood in the context of our own unique experience in life. Educators/ carers transfer their experiences in life to the children they work with. Children in out-of-home care for their part often display inappropriate behaviour towards adults as a result of the burden of their traumatic experiences in their original families. In order to cut through this emotional Gordian knot, educators/carers need to develop a professional awareness for these transfer and projection mechanisms. In this context Klaus Wolf speaks of an 'anti-transfer check' (Jugendhilfe, 1998, p. 36ff). Through the process of self-reflection and self-knowledge, family life educators acquire the ability to recognize the contribution of their own and the child's biographies in their relationship and to unravel the emotional knots.

Helping the Child to Process the Past

The children's earlier experiences in their original families should not be simply forgotten, suppressed or made taboo. From the security of their new world, it is usually easier for the children and young adults to look back and evaluate or re-assess much of their past. Family life educators learn to talk to the children/youngsters about their experiences, to support them and help them avoid problematical or idealized fantasies (Ryan and Walker, 1997, p. 15). The techniques employed vary from playful communication to writing one's life story. A good educator or carer will be touched by the child's fate but will not identify with it, so as to be free to help the child process his or her past experiences.

Building a Positive Role for the Child's Natural Parents

As the child's first significant others, the parents play a unique role in the development of personal identity. For that reason, a further key competence for educators and carers must be the ability to access – at the cognitive and emotional levels – the situation and the behaviour of the child's natural parents as well as of the child him/herself. This enables them to develop a positive approach to the parents and to appreciate their contribution to the life of the child. This occurs independently of the actual style of contact maintained with the child's natural parents. Where the childcare mandate and the situation of the natural parents permit, they are always involved in the pedagogical process.

Exploiting the Life-world as a Place of Learning in Appropriate Developmental Steps

Another key qualification of the family life educator is the ability to shape the child's everyday life in his/her new world to create learning opportunities conducive to further development. In other words, family life educators seek to create an environment for learning. The shared life-world is an ideal point of departure for such learning processes. There are enough opportunities for learning to be generated in shaping both the child's everyday world and the relationships that exist in that framework. The involvement of the child at a level appropriate to his/her maturity and flexible rules for interpersonal relationships that are appropriate to the situation are signs of a positive environment.

Systems Thinking

Family life educators develop the ability to see relationships as a network in which individuals have a mutual influence. This means that all behaviour is also perceived in terms of its effects on the whole relational fabric. Family life educators take note of the actions of the individuals within the system and of their own actions with regard to their impacts on the system. They learn to recognize the effect of the individual on the system as well as the effects of the system on the individual, and to take any measures needed in support of the system.

Definition of Appropriate Goals

Defining the goals of the learning process has an influence on social behaviour in the given situation. The ability to define appropriate goals helps avoid stressful experiences for both parties and enhances the child's scope for learning. Inappropriate learning goals quickly lead to a situation where all the blame for failure is placed on the child or the adult falls victim to destructive self-criticism.

Competence Development in Family Life Education

The innovative course in family life education we developed in 1999 is a model for matching training to the above professional self-image so as to enhance the competence of family life educators in a complex life-world with all its uncertainties and provide them with a reliable basis for professional working.

The Role Model of the Training Course for Promoting Personal Development

The key to the design of an appropriate training course is the view that people can only learn what they experience themselves with in the framework of the training process. For that reason training must be targeted at a holistic process of experience and learning that relates to the personal needs of the individual trainee and also takes account of the learning environment, and the personal and professional make-up of the trainer. All interaction in the framework of the training process has a model function with regard to relationship-building, conflict-solving and personal development in a given learning context.

To do justice to his basic approach, it was decided to avoid a school-curriculum style of training and instead to give trainees responsibility for steering their own personal development process on the road to becoming family life educators. Within a given framework the trainees themselves can therefore determine the length of the training period in accordance with their personal situations (three year minimum, six year maximum). The training facility is responsible only for initiating the learning process, providing support along the way, and guaranteeing the standards set. However, targeted learning opportunities in the framework of the training programme are considered necessary as a source of systematic support for each individual learning process.

Three Central Platforms for Learning in Family Life Education

The learning processes in family life educator training are initiated via three different channels. That establishes a meaningful mix of theory and practice and ensures that the experience and knowledge acquired is fully assimilated by the trainees. The three platforms for learning are:

a) practical experience: learning by doing;
b) coaching and counselling; and
c) seminars.

a) *Practical experience: learning by doing* The main point of departure for a learning processes in the field of family life education is practical experience in working with emotionally traumatized children and youngsters in out-of-home care. It takes this personal work experience for trainees to develop a realistic basis for relating to the tasks involved and developing their abilities in line with current practice. Relevant past experience is therefore a precondition for training in family life education. In order to add the necessary degree of diversity to the trainees' practical experience and thus equip them to distinguish between different approaches in the field, a programme of internships (four times four weeks) was integrated in the course. They make varying demands and cover different fields, such as family-based out-of-home care, socio-educational child-care, and the role of the child welfare authorities. The trainees are supported in the learning process by local experts, who enter into a process of reflection with them.

b) Coaching and counselling　Coaching and counselling serve as a source of reflection at the meta level on the skills and knowledge acquired through the training processes. They are designed to promote complete assimilation of the learning experience and consolidate the newly acquired personal competence. This learning process can be tailored to meet the individual needs of the trainees. It comprises a minimum of 44 units reinforced by a process of reflection on the practical experience involved in the framework of the seminars (81 units).

c) Seminars　All the seminars relate to the subject of practical work with emotionally traumatized children and youngsters. They are designed to promote both cognitive and emotional access to the tasks involved as well as the power of self-reflection and the ability to take effective action in the practical situation. In-depth involvement with a subject over a period of time triggers related activities on the part of the trainees and promotes social learning processes. Training in seminar form encourages the trainees to focus on the subject and the shared learning process at the same time. The subjects of the seminars are treated holistically as far as possible, with each subject requiring a different approach. In order to maintain an appropriate balance, the focus of the seminars is varied in the course of the programme. By providing this diversity of focus and linking the course contents, we ensure that trainees finally acquire a complete picture reflecting a variety of approaches and perspectives. The family life education training course includes a total of 28 one-week seminars on the following subjects:

- understanding development processes;
- basics of pedagogics and applied pedagogics;
- the family of origin;
- relationship-building in family-based childcare systems;
- living and working with emotionally traumatized children/young adults;
- disorders – diagnosis and therapy;
- fundamentals of medicine;
- self-experience and self-competence;
- social competence;

- home economics;
- quality assurance;
- basics of law.

The support process for trainees in the framework of our course in family life education, an individually targeted learning process is initiated with every trainee and supported by the training facility over and beyond the formal channels of learning. As the point of departure for this personal development process, a joint evaluation is performed of the trainee's existing qualifications as an educator/carer working with children and young adults. Subsequent assessments are performed at regular intervals in order to evaluate progress made and any other changes with regard to the situation of the individual trainee. This kind of process strengthens the trainees' powers of self-observation with regard to their capabilities, needs and wishes and thus promotes self-empowerment and the ability to promote self-empowerment in the children.

Interpersonal Course Assessment

The goal of the course is to empower trainees to foster personal development in emotionally traumatized children and young adults. We therefore selected a form of trainee assessment that corresponds to the style of evaluation employed in the childcare process, i.e. avoiding a system of numerical scores or grades and focusing instead on a communicative process for the joint assessment of the competence acquired in family life education. Final assessment is based on a combination of self-evaluation, reports from the practicals, a short thesis and a full report on the trainee's experience with one of the children worked with. These assessment items are additionally correlated with observations made in the course of the training process and with the process itself before a final protocol is drawn up. The evaluation process involves several people, offering a plurality of views and avoiding dependence on any one person. The different personalities and developmental processes of the trainees result in a high degree of individuality in the competence acquired as educators and carers at the end of the course. Given the fact that family life educators consider their own individuality and a continuous process of personal development as basic to their professionalism, this system offers optimum conditions for professional work with children.

Conclusion

Family life education constitutes a model for the introduction of suitable professional self-image for people living and working holistically in professionally managed out-of-home care communities. The aim is to define and develop specific expertise in family life education as an independent profession by focusing in particular on the holistic processes of personal development. The system permits the adults working in professionally managed out-of-home care communities to combine human kindness with the professional skills needed to shape the everyday childcare situation and the communicative processes involved in effective support of the children and their development. The result is not a new ideal of the modern educator but simply carers and educators capable of working as human beings with their individual strengths and weaknesses on a truly professional basis. The training processes in family life education are geared to this professional self-image and to that extent differ from traditional training models in social pedagogy. Competence in family life education is based on practical experience and focuses on personality development, self-empowerment, self-reflection and knowledge assimilation.

References

Kupffer, H. (1999), 'Sozialpädagogik und Familienpädagogik', unpublished manuscript.

Lauermann, K. (1998), *Sozialpädagogische Berufsbildung. Genese-Gegenwart – Zukunftsperspektiven*, Studienverlag Innsbruck.

Nave-Herz, R. (1994), *Familie Heute. Wandel der Familienstrukturen und Folgen für die Erziehung*, Darmstadt: Wissenschaftliche Buchgesellschaft.

Posch, C. and Putzhuber, H. (2001), 'Professionelle Familienerziehung im Spannungsfeld von Herkunftssystem, Pflegefamiliensystem und Jugendwohlfahrt', in *Der österreichische Amtsvormund. Fachzeitschrift für Kindschaftsrecht, Familienrecht und Jugendwohlfahrt*, 33. Jahrgang, Folge 162.

Ryan, T. and Walker, R. (1997), *Wo gehöre ich hin? Biografiearbeit mit Kindern und Jugendlichen*, Weinheim and Basel: Beltz Edition Sozial.

Schneewind, K. (1998), 'Familienentwicklung', in R. Oerter and L. Montada (eds), *Entwicklungspsychologie. Ein Lehrbuch*, 4th edn, Weinheim: Beltz, Psychologie-VerlagsUnion.

SOS-Kinderdorf Österreich (1997), *Ausbildung der SOS-Kinderdorf-Mütter zur Familienpädagogin. Lehrplan des Collegs für FamilienPädagogik/Fachbereich Pädagogik*, Innsbruck: SOS-Kinderdorf.

Thiersch, H. (1992), *Lebensweltorientierte Soziale Arbeit. Aufgaben der Praxis im sozialen Wandel. Edition Soziale Arbeit*, Weinheim and Münich: Juventa Verlag.

Wolf, K. (1998), 'Professionelle Familienerziehung: Professionalität oder Harmonie?', *Jugendhilfe*, Vol. 36.

PART II
FOSTER CARE: PREPARING FOR, PRACTISING AND LIVING IN THE MIDST OF

Chapter 5

Preparing Children for Foster Care: Exploring the Role and Value of a Preparatory Residential Placement

Clíona Murphy

Introduction

This chapter highlights the role and value of a preparatory residential placement for children entering foster care, with particular reference to a new and innovative fostering service in Ireland. The Lisdeel Family Placement Initiative (LFPI) was set up as a response to the perceived deficiencies in the provision of foster care by the Irish state. The service has been piloted over a three year period[1] and this chapter is based on findings from a formative evaluation of the service that took place over two and a half years. Children referred to the Initiative remain in the residential unit for approximately one year while a wide range of services are combined to prepare the child for fostering. This chapter looks first at the role of the preparatory placement and documents the range of interventions and people involved in the preparation process for the first ten children referred. The chapter also identifies the unique and creative ways in which this work has been carried out and finally, explores the value of the preparatory placement through the perspectives of the various stakeholders; the children's birth and extended families, and the service providers.

Background and Context

The Lisdeel Family Placement Initiative

The Daughters of Charity, a religious order, established Lisdeel House in 1995. It is a residential unit located in a detached six-bedroom house situated on a main road and looks the same as the rest of the houses in the neighbourhood. Initially, the house was used to provide a short-term emergency unit for children aged 6 to

12. The children there are cared for by two residential childcare workers at any one time. A manager and team leader also work in the unit during the day.

Late in 1995, the first year of its operation, the assessment unit became blocked as children placed there were unable to return home and the state provider of family support and child care services; the area health board, was unable to provide appropriate onward placements for the children, in either residential or foster care. All but one of the children in Lisdeel at that time had been assessed as needing foster care.

A working group was set up to address why children were not moving on from Lisdeel House and to try identify a way forward. Arising from the recommendation of the working group, the Lisdeel Family Placement Initiative was set up in May, 1999 and is based in an office extension to Lisdeel House. Lisdeel House is for the sole use of the LFPI. The aims of the service can be set out as follows:

1   to provide foster care, or relative care, for children who are assessed as in need of placement by Lisdeel House;
2   to provide all necessary support, financial and otherwise, to enable foster carers to care for the children placed with their family;
3   to prepare children to benefit from their placement;
4   to reduce the risk of placement breakdown by aiming for a placement experience which meets the needs of both child and carer;
5   to explore and test alternative models for enhancing the delivery of fostering services;
6   to work in partnership with the area health board (AHB) to secure stable, successful foster placements for children in the care of the AHB.

All children referred to the LFPI are referred by AHB social workers and come from a particular community care geographical area of the health board. Reasons for the children coming into the care of the health board include parental addiction to drugs or alcohol, abandonment, parental imprisonment and neglect. They are all in the 5–12 age range, although there is some leeway at either end of the age range where children are part of a sibling group. Children must have good potential to be placed in foster care following interventions in Lisdeel House, and referrers must have ruled out the option of returning home, at the point if referral. The service prioritizes sibling groups, and there were four sibling groups among the first ten children referred. The first five children stayed in the residential placement for a period of about a year and the next three for about 20 months.

The Evaluation

This chapter arose out of a formative evaluation of the LFPI that took place over a two and a half year period and focuses on one aspect of that evaluation. Data for the evaluation was gathered through the methods of qualitative interviewing, focus group interview and participant-observation. The data used for this chapter then is largely based on interviews with a range of the key stakeholders involved in the evaluation. They include interviews with all the LFPI staff (one resource worker and three social workers), three members of residential staff, with nine foster carers, eight birth and extended family members, six senior managers from the service, three area health board social workers, and a focus group with residential staff who are key workers. Given the young ages of the children interviewed and the limited data elicited, their perspectives are not included in this chapter.

The Role of the Preparatory Placement

In essence, the role of the preparatory placement is to assess need, to address behavioural and emotional issues, to provide a period of stability and, ultimately, to prepare children to live with foster carers.

The role of the placement incorporates a number of key elements. Firstly, a comprehensive needs assessment is conducted including assessment of social, emotional, educational, and health needs. The placement also serves to provide a period of stability, and provides routine and boundaries. For example, the first two children placed in Lisdeel House were siblings, aged 5 and 6, who had nine moves in the year before they came to Lisdeel House. In his discussion of the functions of residential care Hill (2000) outlines the five main functions as identified in the Wagner Report of 1998. Two of those functions are identified as preparation for placement and keeping sibling groups together, which are also two key functions of Lisdeel House. The need to provide children with a period of stability was a function further identified by Berridge (1985) who warns us not to underestimate the damaging effects of fostering breakdown and continuous movement on children, which were described as often leaving children 'emotionally shattered'. The preparatory placement is also used to find out more about the children's past and the key people involved in their lives. Birth and extended family are considered to be a resource to the children and every effort is made to involve those family members that are important to the children. Cooperation between the various service providers and carers involved with a child, in addition to linking with parents, has been described as essential in making a placement work (Berridge, 1985; Triseliotis et al., 2000). A key element of the placement that differs from many other residential placements is that there is ongoing talk about fostering; it is a live theme in the House and for the children. Work on behaviour and social skills is another key element of the preparatory placement. Staff spoke about how they are mindful that it is a family that the children are moving on to live with, and that behaviours that a residential team are able to handle may be very difficult to manage in a family setting. While in the unit, children are linked with outside activities and sports. As the foster families are recruited in the area surrounding the residential unit, it is anticipated that children will be able to continue with their sports and activities when they move to a family. Where it is an assessed need of the child, s/he is introduced to a friendship family, whose role in the preparation process will be detailed later in this chapter.

The Preparatory Work

There are a number of people involved in carrying out the preparatory work with the children.

The Key Worker Role

Each child is allocated a key worker who meets with the child before they come to Lisdeel House and who then acts as the key person with responsibility for the child. Key workers take on the responsibility for the physical care of their key child (clothes, appointments) and for liaising with the child's family, teacher, social worker and any other significant adult in the child's life. Key workers also organize access, attend all meetings relating to the child and monitor the child's care plan. Key workers spend 'special time' with their key child, the purpose of which is to provide an opportunity to build up trust with an adult, to build up friendship, and to give the child time to express how they think and feel without having to compete for attention with other children. Staff perceived the time as having many aspects including the social, therapeutic and emotional. Lisdeel House has now developed a working document entitled 'Special Work Programme' and it outlines subject areas to be covered between key worker and child, followed by a list of ideas for exploring each subject. The format includes getting to know Lisdeel and key worker, starting the 'all about me' book/life story book, starting special work, feelings work and preparation for fostering.

The Residential Team

Although the key worker is the person with the main responsibility for a child, all residential staff are involved in preparing children for fostering. This is seen as important in ensuring that the information given to children is consistent and provides continuity. The involvement of the whole team is also important as key workers and residential staff continue to play a role during the child's move to foster care and in the early stages of the placement itself.

The Role of LFPI Staff

Although the main role of the LFPI workers concerns recruitment and preparation of carers, and the support of carers to foster, the LFPI staff themselves play a key role in the preparation of children for fostering. It is a unique feature of the service that the children have direct access to the people whose job it is to find, prepare and support the families who will care for them and the fact that the main office of the LFPI is located in Lisdeel House facilitates this role. The staff spoke about how the children are curious about foster families in general and often ask what do they look like, as if they all look like a particular thing! Curiosity as to how a family becomes a foster family is also a common query:

> … how do the family become a foster family, how long it takes … I think in some ways it helps their self-esteem that they know all that goes into it, that it's not just like a family appears one day and they say, you can foster … (LFPI social worker 3)

The children also worried. They worried about what would happen if they went to a family and the family did not like them. They worried whether they would be able to see their own family and continue to go to the same school. Some children worried about whether they would be left on their own, once placed. One member of LFPI staff stated that she thought it helped the children in Lisdeel that the staff talk about children who have left, so that the children in Lisdeel know staff will have some contact with them when they move, that they are not forgotten about once they leave Lisdeel House. Children are also reminded that their key worker will visit them, for a limited time, when they move. Fostering social workers talked about how they intervened with one child's worries about fostering:

(Residential) staff have been saying over the last while that Michael has been losing the notion and the sense of security that there will be a foster placement for him. We agreed to set up some time to meet Michael and talk to him about the ongoing process of finding a family for him and also to make sure that he's welcomed in here when we are here and to keep him abreast of what we are doing around finding families so a foster family can become his focus again. (LFPI social worker 1)

There was also the idea to invite foster parents in to have a chat with him about why they do fostering, as another child was saying they only do it for the money…. (LFPI social worker 2)

The Role of Area Health Board Social Workers

Health board social workers are the social workers given responsibility for children in the care of the state. Three health board social workers described their own role in relation to the preparation of placements as working with the children and their families around issues concerning the child's care. In relation to the child, social workers said that they had the job of ensuring the children are safe, that their placement is meeting their needs, of liaising with the children about what they want, hearing their concerns and listening to their fears. Social workers also attended reviews of the child's care, usually with a social work team leader, where available. In relation to the child's family, social workers have a crucial and ongoing role – giving information to, involving and supporting families with regard to plans for their child's care. Social workers also arrange and facilitate access with the child and their families. Social workers talked about the role of the preparatory placement in terms of how it could address the children's needs (some of which were basic, e.g. provision of regular meals). All of the social workers identified the children in their care as having 'huge issues' about being rejected or abandoned by parents and previous carers. The need for a period of stability, security and routine was identified as needed by all of the children. Most of the children placed in Lisdeel House, especially those in the older age range, exhibited aggressive and/or sexualized behaviours and social work referrers hoped that the placement would address these behaviours.

Developing Key Interventions

There are two aspects of the preparatory placement that have been particularly developed, and these are work with behaviour and social skills, and work with birth and extended families.

Behaviour and Social Skills

Over the past year, there has been an increase in the kinds and incidences of challenging behaviours presented by children. Staff work with behaviour and social skills in consideration of how they might impact in a family environment, as it is a family that the children are moving forward to live with. This aspect of the role was also described in terms of preventing placement breakdown. The example of bed-wetting or a child refusing to shower was given by one worker who stated that although a foster carer may not find this a big problem initially, it was often these kinds of behaviour that can eventually became very wearing in a placement. New and different ways of working are continually developed by the team, as the children admitted to Lisdeel present with differences of age, with different experiences of loss and grief, and with different experiences of families. For example, staff use TV work and children's storybooks to work with the youngest children admitted. As there is no deadline by which children have to be out of the placement, the placement has the capacity to deal with previously unidentified and unanticipated behaviours that arise.

Involving Children's Families

Another key aspect of the work that has been further developed over the past year is work involving the children's families. The work emerges from the ethos that children's birth and extended families are of vital importance to each child, particularly with regard to helping children understand why they can't live with their family, and in giving the child permission to be fostered. One member of the LFPI staff gave an example of how she observed the residential staff working in this way. She spoke about how one of two siblings recently admitted to Lisdeel House would run home to his parents. After this had happened a few times, the staff asked the child to let them know when he wanted to go so that they could bring him for a short time.

> He hasn't run since. He can phone when he wants to phone. And that is part of the huge openness and acknowledgement of family. Even though the family are very chaotic and have huge problems. There is a great awareness of the importance of family for those kids. In the beginning they would have phoned their mum to say goodnight. Very thoughtful stuff like that. (LFPI social worker 2)

There's a huge acceptance of the importance of family. (LFPI social worker 1)

Families' Perspectives on their Involvement

Eight members of the birth and extended families of children placed in Lisdeel House were interviewed in the evaluation; two family members were interviewed twice – before and after their child relative was placed with a family. Family members were asked as to whether and how they were made feel welcome in Lisdeel House. Relatives spoke about being welcomed in the House through invitation to and attendance at children's parties, collecting the children from school, phoning the child's school, and having dinner or a sandwich in the House. Another relative said that staff had invited her to use the kitchen to cook with the children if she wanted.

All of those interviewed had access to their child relative in Lisdeel House and only one relative was unhappy with the nature of her access to the children. Five interviewees spoke about how Lisdeel House supported them around access. Supports for access included Lisdeel staff giving lifts to parents and relatives, bringing the children to access, and paying for taxis where staff were unable to give lifts. This facilitation of access was appreciated by those who spoke about it.

The data showed that all but one relative attended reviews and meetings about the child in Lisdeel. Those who could not attend as often as they would like said that the child's key worker rings them after reviews to update them on what happened. Information about the child was usually given to relatives in the form of a phone call with the House Manager or the child's key worker and half of the interviewees spoke at length about how good the level of contact was.

> … they always keep in touch with me – let me know what is going on and if he is in bad humour … (Family 4)

Five interviewees spoke about how they supported staff in dealing with the child's upset and challenging behaviours. One parent spoke about how he talks to his child about why he is in Lisdeel, his behaviour there and encourages the child to work with staff.

> I can only try support them in dealing with his behaviour. (Family 1)

Four other interviewees spoke about how Lisdeel House rings them sometimes when the child's behaviour there is very disruptive or the child is upset and distressed. Relatives said they would speak to the child on the phone, try to calm them down and encourage the child to work with staff. One couple said that one or both of them call to the House on these occasions to help calm the children. Sometimes the children themselves will ring. Another relative said that Lisdeel have asked her to take the child for overnight access if the children in the House are acting out. That relative also spoke about conversations that she has had with staff about how they can best manage the child's behaviour together.

Considering the reports by parents and relatives about how they are involved by Lisdeel, it would seem that Lisdeel works in a way that tries hard to involve those who care about the child, in decisions about how best to care for the child. In the main, relatives were clear about how staff were dealing with challenging behaviours and what the plans for the child were. It is apparent that both staff and the children's families strive to support each other in being clear and consistent in their care of the children. The nature of the involvement of relatives then would seem to involve a sharing of decisions and caring of the child on a day-to-day basis.

Unique Features of the Preparation Process

There are two unique features of the preparatory work that have greatly facilitated the preparation process to date, namely the co-location of fostering and residential services and the use of friendship families.

Co-location of Residential and Fostering Services

The co-location of Lisdeel House and the LFPI has been identified as a key factor in facilitating the communication and joint work between the LFPI and Lisdeel House. Berridge's (1985) study of children's homes repeatedly highlights the interrelationship, and the importance of, continuity between residential and fostering services. Both fostering and residential staff explained that when the children arrive in Lisdeel House they are told that they are welcome to call to the LFPI office. They can ask questions or hang around and draw pictures, if they like. Formal meetings are also arranged. The access by children and their families to LFPI staff was built into the service from the outset and one fostering social worker said:

> We always thought it was good to be available because if a child has a question or they have a worry about it [fostering], they have it that day. (LFPI social worker 3)

One of the benefits of this way of working is that the children can avail of the option of talking to the fostering workers in their own time:

> We don't push the fostering at the kids at all, we have it according to their pace, of where they're at. (LFPI social worker 3)

Another benefit is the facilitation of consistency and clarity for all involved: children, their families and service providers. Residential and fostering staff speak to each other about questions or concerns that individual children have had about fostering and inform each other of the answers that they gave. Sharing of information from both sides of the preparation processes was viewed as very useful. One worker spoke about how children usually start raising questions about fostering in the context of the direct work with their key worker, who in turn can talk to fostering staff about the child's queries or concerns. The key worker may also sit in on some of the sessions with the child and LFPI staff, as issues or questions from the session may then come up that night or later on. Fostering staff also stated that, when they met with a child, they would inform staff or key workers as to what was happening either in advance or after. Consistency in approach then was described as a strength of this way of working:

> Here all interaction with the kids is in kind of a planned way and there is always more than one person to pull the other person back into the plan, this is how we decided we were going to work with this child. (LFPI social worker 1)

> While it's all done on a very casual, informal basis, it's a huge part of the fabric of how this place works. (LFPI social worker 2)

Friendship/Respite Families

A second unique feature is the use of friendship/respite families. A friendship/respite family is a family that has been assessed as respite carers by the Initiative and one that commits to giving children some experience of routinized family life as part of the children's process of preparation for fostering. Families who act as friendship families pre-placement also give a commitment to act as respite families post-placement to those same children, in an effort to reduce the children's experience of loss and change. It is also anticipated that if a foster placement breaks down that the child will be placed with their respite family, where possible, until another long-term placement can be made.

Children are introduced to a friendship family while resident in Lisdeel House and levels of contact vary depending on the child's needs. A friendship/respite family can be a child's relatives.

Staff spoke about the benefits of giving children the experience of 'normal'/routinized family life. One residential staff member stated that the time a child spends with their friendship family allows the child to see that it is usual to have boundaries and rules and times to go to bed in families and that this may help the children understand why Lisdeel House and family homes also set rules and boundaries. Friendship families have also been used as respite for children while in Lisdeel House.

LFPI build in the support of respite care early on by introducing children to their friendship family. Children sometimes visit their respite family once placed so as to keep this contact and familiarity up. Planned respite has been used for three of the children placed, and one child who is currently in Lisdeel House. Respite families have been prepared to respond to the needs of a wider variety of children, and to respond in emergency situations although to date there has been no need for families to respond to emergencies.

Value of the Preparatory Placement

The value of the preparatory placement is considered firstly by looking at the placements made at the point of final data collection for the evaluation, and secondly by examining the perspectives of family members, AHB social workers and foster carers.

Placements Made to Date

The first five children placed experienced smooth transitions from Lisdeel House to the foster family. It is also of key importance that none of the children or carers have had the need for any crises or emergency interventions, with stability a feature of all the placements made so far. The lengths of the foster placements made by June 2002 were 23 months (two siblings), 13 months, and 10 months (two siblings) respectively.

Family Members' Perspectives on the Value of the Preparatory Placement

All family members interviewed said that the placement had benefited their child in some way, although there were mixed reports of some children's progress in the preparatory placement. The main benefits described were in the areas of social skills and behaviour. Relatives of two brothers in Lisdeel House had glowing reports about their children's progress. The placement there was described as 'of immense benefit' and as 'the best place for them'. The relatives spoke about how the children had changed a lot over the past year in Lisdeel House. The children were described as very helpful when on access in the relatives' house, cleaning up dishes and toys after themselves, etc., and as having quietened down. One of the children, who had previously used lose his temper at times and, who threatened his relatives with knives, no longer did this. In school, the children's behaviour and progress had improved and the siblings did not fight with each other as often as they used to.

Two aunts spoke of how it was of huge importance to their extended family that their nephews were looked after in the safe and secure environment of Lisdeel House. It was reported that the move itself to Lisdeel was positive as it allowed the two siblings to be together, and the children were described as happy being together and of help to each other. The children had been cared for separately by their two aunts before moving to Lisdeel House. Previous to their move to Lisdeel, the children were described as 'very wild' and unable to sit still. The children were found to be calmer and better behaved now. The children's speech was also reported to have improved greatly as had their manners. The eldest child now shared his sweets, which was a big shift, as when he was living with his aunt, he would get very upset and cry if asked to share. The children now had no problems with sleeping or eating and had got into a set routine. They were also reported to have put on weight. However, three interviewees reported deterioration in their two children's progress after a period of time in Lisdeel House. One parent had concerns that his child was 'mixing with other kids with a lot more problems than him' and was swearing a lot more than in his previous placement. That child's progress was described as a mixture of doing okay and then getting worse. Another parent described her child as 'fed up with that place' and this view was (F-3, F-1) also held by one of the extended family members who stated that 'the longer [the child] is there, the more damage is done'. Both the child's parent and aunt expressed concern that the child came to Lisdeel House for six months to be placed with a foster family and was still there after 18 months, while other children have come and moved out into families. Both hoped that the child would soon be able to move into a family but expressed concern that the child's deteriorating behaviour would impact on this happening.

Area Health Board Social Workers' Perspectives on the Value of the Preparatory Placement

Three area health board social workers were interviewed about their views on the value of the preparatory placement. One social worker spoke of her satisfaction with how children on her caseload in Lisdeel House were progressing:

> I am very happy with the three children who are there. I am confident that they are progressing as well as they possibly can in that unit. (AHB social worker 2)

Social workers also considered the preparatory placement as positive in terms of how Lisdeel worked with birth and extended families. They talked about how there was time to work through the plan for the child with relatives so they understood what was to happen and were then able to answer the child's questions. One child in particular was described as very anxious that all the important people in his life were cooperating. The child's social worker talked about the benefits for the child, as he prepared to move, of seeing his mother meeting his friendship family and seeing that everyone is supporting the plans for him. According to social workers, a lot of families knew little about the concepts of residential care and fostering, and through their contact with Lisdeel House and the LFPI they were able to find out more and ask questions about fostering. For example, one social worker described how a relative thought that foster carers could walk in off the street and be given children to look after without any assessment or training. Discussion of relatives' concerns can and does happen informally while family members are in the House on access, or at meetings.

Foster Carers' Perspectives on the Value of the Preparatory Placement

Residential staff in Lisdeel House are involved in supporting the child in their placement for the first six weeks. They also play a role in supporting foster carers. Before children move to their placement, the key worker meets with the carers to talk to them about the child. Written information is also compiled by the key workers to give to carers. In addition, a 24-hour service is also provided where carers can ring Lisdeel House at any time. These kinds of supports to carers and children can only be provided because the children and staff have lived and worked together in Lisdeel House. The fact that the staff in Lisdeel House had experience of living with the children and could offer support from this perspective was described by two carers as 'brilliant' and carers stated that Lisdeel House were very involved in advising them on how to deal with the children in the earlier stages of the placement. To summarize, invaluable information on the child's daily routines, likes and dislikes, and other such details gathered during the preparatory placement have proved helpful and useful to foster carers.

Working at the Child's Pace

One valuable element of the preparatory placement, as described by residential staff, is the capacity of the placement to deal with unanticipated and previously unidentified needs and behaviours. Residential staff shared the view that referrers were often not aware of the depth of upset children had about previous placement breakdowns and rejection by birth parents. In a focus group, residential staff expressed the view that they thought it better that the challenging behaviours and violence showed up in Lisdeel House rather than in a foster placement. It was thought that some of the behaviours that have emerged were likely to have led to a breakdown if they occurred in a foster placement. In one instance, the placement committee decided to extend the placement of two children in Lisdeel House by six months rather than risk the breakdown of the placement.

AHB social workers also talked about the importance of making time available to work with the child's families to prepare them for the child's move. A lot of work is done with children and parents about the role of Lisdeel House and reassuring parents that their role will not change as children move out of Lisdeel House and on to a family. There was also value in the fact that the move was not immediate, allowing time for issues for children and their families to be raised and worked on.

Senior managers in the service spoke about the 'huge investment of time' needed to work with children's experiences of loss, grief, abandonment and rejection. They also spoke about the importance of having all in agreement as to what is best for the child, so that the child is not put in a position where they have to chose between carers. The huge loyalty that children have to their parents was acknowledged.

Summary

The evaluation shows that the process of preparing children in Lisdeel House for foster care is creative and customized for each child. Lisdeel staff work at the child's own pace and are continuously learning and trying out new ideas such as the use of friendship families. Preparation of children for fostering involves a unique blend of residential care and social work inputs in a whole, integrated service. Co-location of the fostering and residential services allows children and their families to access services at their own pace and increases clarity and consistency of information for all.

There is recognition of, and action regarding, the importance of involving children's families in their care and decisions about their care. Time is spent with relatives in reaching an understanding so that the child sees all his carers working together and providing consistent information. Children are given the time they need to address issues about their own family, previous carers and how they deal with their issues. Furthermore, the preparatory placement also extends its role and value to supporting the child's transition to, and the early stages of, the foster placement.

Notes

1   At the launch of the evaluation report on the service in November 2002 it was announced that the service no longer has pilot status and is to be funded as a mainstream service.

References

Berridge, D. (1985), *Children's Homes*, London: Basil Blackwell.

Hill, M. (2000), 'The Residential Child Care Context', in M. Chakrabarti and M. Hill (eds), *Residential Child Care: International Perspectives on Links with Families and Peers*, London: Jessica Kingsley.

Murphy, C. (2003), 'The Role of a Residential Placement in Preparing Children for Placement with a Foster Family', *Scottish Journal of Residential Child Care*, Vol. 2 (1), February/March, pp. 27–38.

Murphy, C. and Gilligan, R. (2002), *Building Family Placements: An Evaluation of the Lisdeel Family Placement Initiative*, Dublin: Daughters of Charity.

Wagner, G. (1988), *Residential Care: A Positive Choice*, London: HMSO.

Chapter 6

Nadomak Sunca:
Alternative Foster Care in Croatia

Odilia van Manen-Rojnic

David, a 9 year-old boy, expresses the wishes and needs he and many other children hope to have met at Nadomak Sunca:

Wind!
Tell me where to go
Tell me the way home
I am completely confused
And lost
Bring me to the dreams
Of the fairies and the fireflies
So I can see the stars
And the moon
Bring me to the house, to bed
So I can dream.

Nadomak Sunca is a humanitarian organization, created to provide professional foster care within a family environment. The organization is not religiously or politically orientated and it welcomes children from all ethnic and cultural backgrounds. Nadomak Sunca was established in 1994, when Croatia was in the midst of war, and is based in the little Istrian town of Oprtalj. Since then, four foster parent couples have come to live there, in large family houses, renovated by the organization with the help of many volunteers. Each couple has taken 6–8 foster children into their family and they raise them together with their birth children. The care parents are all full-time mums and dads, and some of them also have professional backgrounds as psychologists, pedagogues or therapists. The couples are employed by the organization and are also directly contracted to the Centres for Social Welfare, making them fully responsible for the children. Nadomak Sunca is not an institution but a group of organized foster parents. The help of young volunteers from different parts of Europe has always been an important element of the functioning of the organization.

The children fostered within Nadomak Sunca feel accepted, no matter what kind of problems they bring with them and they know that they can stay 'forever'. Although they keep their own surname and bare the legal status of a foster child, the children feel that their situation is stable an very similar to that of adopted children. Contact with their birth parents is maintained, if the situation allows this.

The Children of Nadomak Sunca

The children, fostered by Nadomak Sunca families, often have certain characteristics in common. For instance:

- they have a history of several placements, which were mostly unsuccessful. They are no longer welcome in institutions or in ordinary foster care, usually due to behavioural problems. Sometimes, a disciplinary youth institution would be the only option left besides placement at Nadomak Sunca;
- they are a second or even third generation of a family within a socially weak surrounding which sometimes displays socially unacceptable behaviour. The economic problems caused by the war and post-war situation are often the final blows that cause such families to fall apart and let the parents to give up on their responsibility for the children;
- they come from families where siblings have often been separated before, due to their stay in orphanages. The large capacity of Nadomak Sunca families allows them to be reunited;
- they might have been young enough to have a chance of being adopted, but their birth parents have refused to give up consent. Instead, these children find permanent security, attachment and a loving surrounding (which are most essential for young children) in a Nadomak Sunca family;
- they have in the past been discriminated against or bullied because of being different (due to ethnic background or nationality or because of being an 'orphanage' child) and are now received into an atmosphere of tolerance and full acceptance.

The foster parents of Nadomak Sunca do not select children on their case history or behaviour diagnosis. Usually, the only selection criterion is age. In principle new children can be taken in until the age of 12, with some exceptions. Consideration is given to ensure that each family has a balanced age and gender. Nadomak Sunca cannot offer care for children with exceptional mental or physical disabilities.

So, on one side, the aim of Nadomak Sunca is to destigmatize children who have had problematic pasts and to provide them the opportunity to restart their lives in a normal family together with children from a non-problematic backgrounds. On the other side, the Nadomak Sunca team has experience and expertise in dealing with most of their problems. If necessary, external therapists can be consulted. Once the house parents take responsibility for a child, they will not give up on it. When things get hard to handle, help can always be found.

Programme Featured at Nadomak Sunca

Acceptance Phase

When new children arrive to Nadomak Sunca, they often do not fully realize what is going on. They are hardly prepared for this big change in their lives and their first reaction is to behave well. They try to adapt as quickly as possible to the new situation. Because of their past experiences, they usually have excellent adaptation skills, and rapidly calculate that the Nadomak Sunca option has a good chance of success. But soon, little cracks start to show in the wonderful behaviour of these newcomers. Having been abandoned usually already more than once, they are taken over by anxiety and fear that this pattern will be continued. Anxiety can express itself in many ways. From clear bodily reactions as perspiration, vomiting or bed-wetting to behaviour disorders such as aggression, kleptomania, ADHD or depression. These symptoms usually stay for some months up to one year. At their most fierce, they can drive both the child and the foster parents to desperation. The greatest danger in this phase is that the symptoms are not recognized as being caused by the underlying and all-consuming anxiety. Unprepared and unsupervised foster parents are likely to give up in this phase and the child's self-fulfilling prophecy – that in the end they will always be rejected – becomes again a reality.

To help a child with anxiety during the adaptation phase, we take care that the surrounding of the newcomer is calm and reassuring. Their room is light and tidy. Activities are limited and there is a clear daily schedule. Television watching is only allowed at certain times. Children greatly enjoy being pampered with a calming bath or a relaxing massage treatment. They often feel reassured when listening to stories or fairy tales that have a happy ending.

When anxiety calms down and the child starts to feel safe, the trial period for him and his care parents is still is not over. Foster children will now start exploring the boundaries of their new situation, testing their parents whether their love for them is really unconditional. How far can I go? How naughty can I be? And, because the self-image of these children is quite negative in general, there is still the underlying question: will they send me away when they find out how I really am? This kind of behaviour, which is acted out differently by every child, asks for understanding and patience. Because these times can be very challenging, psychological support for the care parents can be crucial for the successful outcome of the fostering process.

Therapy

Our experience showed us that it usually takes a child 12 to 18 months to get accustomed to, and fully accept, its care family and the whole new situation. This new state, in which the child feels completely safe, loved and accepted, opens the possibility for therapy. Every child that has come to live with Nadomak Sunca has been suffering from some kind of trauma. Very often they have been abused, they have been abandoned and neglected over a longer period of time or they have witnessed scenes, which have caused profound psychological shock. As a mechanism necessary for survival, most of these experiences have until now been safely locked away, somewhere in the child's subconscious. In a safe surrounding, children could start showing signs that this negative baggage is beginning to bother them. Intuitively they feel that they have to start coping with things that could otherwise negatively influence their development.

In our opinion, therapy can take the form of anything that enables and stimulates a child to express itself in a way suitable to its psychological potential and stage of development. This can be offered through such artistic activity as drawing and painting, workshops of creative writing, music, dancing, acting – as long as the child feels free to work according to his own needs and tempo and guidance exists which provides understanding and a safe atmosphere.

The Nadomak Sunca children sing regularly in the children's choir or on 'guitar evenings', where mainly folk and popular songs are sung. Many children learn to play an instrument (violin, guitar or piano) and on regular occasions they can show their progress through performing in public. These experiences of success greatly enhance their self-esteem and confidence. A few times a year, artistic workshops are organized for the children, run by guests, usually followed by a performance or exhibition. On our farm, children have the opportunity to learn horse riding, which helps them to overcome fear, enhances their self-confidence and teaches them to take care of and respect animals. The children learn to cultivate their own garden. Seeding, planting, patiently taking care and finally harvesting, is a very important and healing experience for every child with development disorders. The village life, close to nature, with all opportunities and freedom for games and sport, has in itself a healing effect, both physical and psychological.

Most important however for the healing process of the child is the family life itself. Here he/she finds proper care, safety and, most important, love. Like plants need sunshine for their healthy development, children need a relationship with someone who loves them unconditionally and for no special reason, who will never reject them as a person, who sees their unique personality and possibilities for development and who is there when needed, with patience and an open ear. Our experience is that many wounds, obstacles and hidden pains can slowly become manageable, softened or even cured with this approach.

The Nadomak Sunca team of co-workers includes experts on pedagogy, psychology and therapy. In some cases however, external help, such as psychotherapy or remedial teaching help is needed. In such cases, Nadomak Sunca, sometimes in cooperation with the Centres for Social Welfare, can dispose of a network of therapists in the region. There is also a close cooperation between the house parents of Nadomak Sunca and the staff of the Oprtalj Primary School which includes a special teacher (pedagogue) and a psychologist.

Supervision and Follow-up of the Centres for Social Welfare

Once a child is placed in a Nadomak Sunca family by a social worker of one of the Centres for Social Welfare, the relationship with this social worker, which has in the past often been important to the child, is maintained. Naturally, the intensity of this relationship is not as before and when everything goes well, the contact is reduced to a visit once or twice a year. When problems arise, the contact between the house parents and the social workers intensifies. Because both parties are very motivated to release children out of a negative spiral and to give them a better future, this cooperation is usually very positive and inspiring.

Case Histories

(The names of the children mentioned in the cases have been changed for reasons of privacy.)

Dejan

Dejan came to Nadomak Sunca at the age of nine. His history was as follows: mother suffered from schizophrenia, father officially unknown. They lived in a big city, and suffered badly from the war, which had just started. The mother was not capable of giving proper care to her child, sometimes even completely neglecting him. At certain times they were homeless. For these reasons, Dejan had been taken away from the mother at the age of three and was placed in a state institution (orphanage).

At the age of eight Dejan was placed into foster care with a farmer's family in the countryside. He greatly enjoyed the relatively free life, close to nature. He loved the farm animals, especially the cows. In school, however, severe problems started to develop. Dejan did not learn to read and write as quickly as the other children and was considered to have a rather low IQ (later it turned out that he was suffering from dyslexia). He had to repeat the first class. He was keen to make friends but finding this difficult, started teasing and irritating other children. Finally, Dejan was locked in a negative spiral and his behaviour became more and more aggressive. There was hardly any communication between the school and Dejan's foster parents. In the end, the only solution was to place Dejan in a new surrounding. This was when he came to Nadomak Sunca.

The first impression he made was that of a small grown-up. He handed back to me the pile of clothes we had prepared for him in the cupboard of his new room and insisted on unpacking and arranging his few belongings by himself. Shortly after, he showed me his greatest treasure: a couple of pictures from a stay in Italy at the age of four or five. There he had been staying with a family who offered a vacation to an orphanage child in a war situation.

When we put Dejan in the bath on the first evening, it seemed to be an unknown experience to him, which he clearly enjoyed – luckily enough, because he was in need of many more baths before the crust of dirt on his body was completely removed. A few days later there was a moment that I noticed that he had fallen and hurt himself, but did not want to show his pain. He bit on his teeth and wanted to walk away. I asked if it hurt and if I could see the wound. To my surprise he let me take him on my lap and comfort him.

And suddenly he started to cry and did not stop for 15 minutes. These kind of incidents were repeated quite frequently.

When he first experienced how we celebrated a birthday party of another child in the family, he was absolutely astonished and informed about the possibility of him having such a party and such presents on his birthday as well. Often, when I saw him brooding somewhere in a corner and asked him if everything was OK, he answered me that he was thinking about his birthday (which was still more than six months away) and wondering which presents he would get.

Not long after his arrival, we noticed that Dejan started showing strong unconscious bodily reactions like sweating and bedwetting. At first he did not seem really aware of this. Later he became more and more annoyed, but the symptoms just grew worse He started to stool in his clothes, usually several times a day, but always after he came home from school. We tried different therapies, but nothing seemed to help. As a final attempt, Dejan agreed upon an extensive hospital examination, but no physical defects were diagnosed. About nine months later these reactions stopped quite suddenly again.

At school, he made good progress. Soon it turned out that he was the best in his class in mathematics. His teacher liked him and the class was small, which enabled her to give him extra attention. He also had help of an external therapist, which soon had a positive effect on his dyslexic problems. However, writing never became his favourite means of self-expression. He preferred drawing and painting, for which he showed great talent. He found a few good friends, but also liked to do things on his own. He was not constantly teasing other children any more when he needed attention.

Now nearly five years have passed since Dejan's arrival at Nadomak Sunca. He has grown into a tall adolescent. He is rather calm and usually absorbed in some activity: woodwork, mending his bicycle, working in the garden. He still has phases during which he broods, complains, quarrels and cries, apparently for hardly any reason, like many other children of his age. But on the whole he is a steady, good-hearted fellow, very loyal to his family and friends.

Kristina

Kristina was born in a region which suffered badly from the war. When she was four years old, she, her younger brother, and her mother were hit by a shell. Her brother was killed and Kristina and her mother were badly wounded. After this incident, long years of regular hospitalization followed for Kristina. Her left knee had been smashed and as a result her upper leg did not grow any more. Many painful operations have been needed to artificially lengthen her leg.

When Kristina was eight years old her father died of cancer. Her mother, who never overcame all these traumatic events, was mentally not stable enough to take care of her. Shortly before her ninth birthday, Kristina came to Nadomak Sunca. From the first moment it was clear to the house parents that Kristina was used to being treated as 'something special'. As an only child in a household of grown-ups, as a victim of a terrible event, as a special patient in the hospital – she was always placed in situations in which she was provided with exceptional treatment. Parents, doctors and care workers had all wanted to make it up to her. No wonder our little 'princess' initially had some problems being one of many in the big Nadomak Sunca family!

Only a few months after Kristina's arrival in Oprtalj, she had to undergo another operation to lengthen her leg. She had to spend all summer in the hospital when other children had holidays and enjoyed themselves. When she finally came out, she was hardly recognizable. She looked like a pale shadow of her old self. Because she was in constant need of strong painkillers, her appetite had completely vanished and she weighed less than 30 kilos. For six months to come, she still had to wear a steel instrument around her leg, which was fixed through the bone itself. This caused all kinds of complications like infections, high temperature and sudden bleeding. During this whole period there was not one night Kristina could pass without having nightmares or fierce pains. At the end of this trial, another operation was being scheduled because of a complication with her knee. But through the international Nadomak Sunca network, a second opinion was arranged. A Dutch orthopaedic surgeon suggested alternative therapy, which turned out to be very successful and the surgery could be avoided.

Since these events a few years have passed. Kristina has grown into a healthy and beautiful young adolescent, talented, interested in other people and in life and eager to discover the world. She still has many friends, also outside of Croatia, and all kinds of opportunities are open to her, so the world seems to lie at her feet. But unfortunately, her ordeal is not over yet. By now, Kristina's left leg is already 5 cm shorter than her right one and in about a year's time a final operation will have to take place. Again the Nadomak Sunca network is being activated to find ways to avoid that she has to pass through the same traumatic hospitalization experiences once more. The possibility is being explored of a new and far less painful treatment, possibly in cooperation with the medical team that treated her so far in Croatia, in an advanced orthopaedic clinic in Italy.

Mateo

Mateo's mother became pregnant with him when she was still a minor. The father has, until now, never been identified. The mother's parents put her out on the street because they could not cope with this – to them – painful and humiliating situation. The mother, being still a child herself, did not feel capable of raising Mateo. The first years of his life he spent in a private orphanage run by a church organization. Initially he was regularly visited by his mother. When she decided to marry and have more children, the contact became less frequent. After the birth of her second daughter, the mother and her husband decided to take Mateo into their household.

In the meantime, Mateo had developed into a very lively young child, not able to sit still for more than a few seconds and not able to concentrate on one subject at a time, all kinds of symptoms that led to the term hyperactivity or ADHD. His mother and stepfather were not prepared for the challenges, provoked by children with this kind of behaviour disorder. Mateo was desperately in need of friends and people who would accept him, but, out of fear of being once again rejected, he got into the habit of constantly quarrelling with other children and of provoking everyone within his reach. He drove his mother, who was psychologically still quite unstable, to desperation. His stepfather, who was not around too much, and his mother tried to discipline him with fierce punishments. By the time Mateo was eight years old, things had started to run out of control and a team from the local centre for social welfare had to rescue him from a very threatening situation. He was then placed under the care of a Nadomak Sunca foster family.

His first reaction seemed to be of great relief. He clearly showed that he was happy that he could make a fresh start in this new surrounding and he greatly enjoyed the attention he got. Most of the time he even managed to listen to his new parents and keep some commitments. But still, he had apparently never learned how to play with other children without teasing them or fighting with them. In spite of the fact that the other children of the family were prepared to the situation, they had a difficult time staying calm amongst the shouting, swearing and the constant provocations. In school, no day went by without incidents with other children. In class, Mateo was difficult to handle for the teacher because of his inability to concentrate and he made a sport out of distracting other pupils as well.

Mateo was clearly in need of much attention and of positive experiences. But also of boundaries, because he showed a strong tendency to loose all self-control and his behaviour endangered himself and other children. Taking his friend's bicycle without asking and then crashing it against a stone wall, crossing the main road on roller skates just when a car was approaching at high speed or 'just' throwing stones at other children – are only a few examples of many similar incidents. One of the foster parents needed to be near him all the time, to give the guidance he needed and to avert further catastrophes. Even daily visits to the school were, and still are, necessary to reassure both him and the teachers.

But, luckily most people feel sympathy for Mateo. No wonder – he is small and friendly looking with black hair and shiny blue eyes, usually in a good mood and full of enthusiasm for something, which happens to occupy his mind at that moment. He also has some special gifts. He is very good in reading, which makes up for his total lack of understanding or interest in numbers and calculations. He has talents for acting and music. He recently started to learn to play the guitar and progresses rapidly. He also possesses an exceptionally beautiful voice and proudly sings solos on all possible occasions.

Future Possibilities for the Children

Our wish is that each child that we take into care will eventually find its own path towards independence. That he will follow his inner voice in finding out which unique qualities and aspects of his personality need to be developed. Many of our children suffer from gaps in their emotional and psycho-social development. To be able to catch up with this, they need time. The governmental support for young people in residential and in foster care stops, with few exceptions for gifted students, at the age of 18. Our experience is, however, that many youngsters at this age are not ready yet to stand on their own feet without any form of support. Especially young people who grew up in institutions where food and care had always been 'automatically' provided, do not possess of sufficient independency skills. The danger to become caught, once again, in a negative spiral, is evident.

Nadomak Sunca does not handle age limits as where its responsibility stops. The house parents, in a way, will always continue to support their children. But from a certain age onwards, family life is usually not the most suitable option any more. However, a great lack still exists in Croatia for programmes for this particular group of people of 18 years and onwards, which support them into independence.

Some Ideas and Opinions on Improvement of the Present Situation in Croatia

At this moment, about half of the total amount of children in care in Croatia grows up in institutions. Therefore, we think that a move towards de-institutionalisation is a positive strategy, as long as it is carried out carefully and that international experience and know-how is taken into account. We plead for open adoption, well-organized and more professional foster care and, when necessary, modernized residential care in smaller units. An important motivation for the government to decide for this policy should be that the immense expenses now used to run institutions, could be saved and used for more effective means in the field of social care.

Well-organized and professional foster care should include:

*   thorough preparation of future foster parents, including courses and practical training;
*   participation of the children in important decisions;
*   thorough preparation of the children for their new situation;
*   a professional support system for foster parents;
*   more substantial financial aid from the government for foster families, enabling at least one member of the foster care couple to be a professional parent.

Further we see that it is neither realistic nor effective to cut off all possibilities of governmental aid at the moment a child turns 18. We therefore, once again, urgently underline the need for youngsters leaving foster care or institutions to have follow-up programmes, guiding them into independence. Such programmes are also an important measure in preventing the criminal tendencies of this vulnerable group. Investing in prevention is, from social and economical point of view, much more effective than investing in prisons or other disciplinary institutions.

Renewal in the field of social welfare is very often initiated by non-governmental organizations. Also in Croatia, NGOs have played an important role in social renewal during the post-war period. Many of these NGOs were and still are (partly) financed by donations from abroad. Now the war in ex-Yugoslavia seems to be more and more distant, foreign donors are less motivated to keep on financing projects, which are dealing with social problems within Croatia, no longer directly related to the war situation. This means that the continuation of some important structural and innovative social programmes is endangered. For example: the running costs of Nadomak Sunca are one-third financed by the Croatian government and the remaining two-thirds are still covered by foreign donations. These donations are collected by Foundations in the Netherlands, Germany and Austria and the volunteers who run them have to put much energy in fundraising to meet these needs.

Nadomak Sunca works towards a more intensive dialogue between the Croatian Ministry of Labour and Social Welfare and representatives of all Croatian NGO's for childcare. Together we should work to find a common path and come to agreement on more substantial governmental participation of innovative social programmes. Negotiations in a period of transition are never easy, but we trust in a positive outcome. We believe that everybody working in the field of social childcare, shares with us the ideal of enabling a promising future to children who were born into a situation with no promise at all.

Implications for the Future?

Family Album

What album! Which family?
About which family should I talk?
I don't have my real family. Do you hear: I don't have it!
Nowadays so many children exist who have never known their families from their birth and their youngest days onwards. They have never seen them or they see them rarely.
Who's fault is this?
Well, the parents fault of course. Non-parents who put them into this world and then send them to a children's home.
Children don't want that. Children are not guilty!
Believe me, I know very well what I'm talking about. Unfortunately, I must admit that I'm one of these children too.
At the moment I live in Oprtalj, a small Istrian city. I also was in Rijeka and in Losinj. I was everywhere, just not with my parents.
I remember my grandfather whom I used to visit once or twice a year. He was gentle, friendly and quiet.
When I'm having a difficult time, I feel he helps me – but not out of this world, because he doesn't live any more.
I always ask myself why it had to be my parents who were so selfish and irresponsible. Why did they create me when they didn't want me? People, don't do such things! Children are not guilty. (Borislava, 12 years old)

Reading List

Delfos, M.F. and Visscher, Nelleke (eds) (2001), *(Foster) Children: an Odd Behaviour!?*, Amsterdam: SWP.

Gil, E. (1991), *The Healing Power of Play – Working with Abused Children*, New York: Guilford Press.

James, B. (1990), *Treating Traumatized Children – New Insights and Creative Interventions*, New York: Simon and Schuster.

Chapter 7

Living with Foster Siblings – What Impact has Fostering on the Biological Children of Foster Carers?

Ingrid Höjer and Monica Nordenfors

Introduction

Placing children in foster care is an important and often used measure within the area of child welfare. In Sweden, 14,000 children were looked after in public care as of 1 November 2001. Seventy-five per cent of these children, 10,500, were placed in foster homes (Socialstyrelsen, 2002). Fostering has a great impact on all the members of families who foster. It affects the life of the husband and wife, and it affects the life of their children. Through research on foster care we have gained knowledge about the impact of fostering on the lives of foster carers (Kälvesten, 1974; Vinterhed, 1985; Wåhlander, 1990; Bebbington and Miles, 1990; Havik, 1996; Triseliotis et al., 2000; Höjer, 2001). However, the situation of children of foster carers is more seldom the focus of the work of researchers, and when it is, their situation is often mirrored through the eyes of adults. From research results, one can see that foster carers most often think that their children have benefited from their family being engaged in fostering. In some cases there were discrepancies between statements of adults and young people and children, foster carers were to some extent more positive than their children (Kaplan, 1988; Part, 1993; Poland och Groze, 1993; Twigg, 1994; Pugh, 1996; Talbot, 1997; Familjeplejen i Danmark, 1998; Höjer, 2001).

The study 'Growing Up with Foster Siblings' focuses on the experiences of children of foster carers. This study is one of the research projects in the programme 'Parenting and Childhood in Modern Family Cultures' at the Department of Social Work, Göteborg University. The predominant aim of the study is to find out what a childhood with foster siblings is like, and more specifically, how growing up with foster siblings affects relations in the family. The study is financed by the Swedish foundation 'Allmänna Barnhuset' and by the Swedish Council for Working Life and Social Research.

The aim of this chapter is to introduce the study and some of if its first results, as they were presented at the EUSARF conference in Trondheim in September 2002.

Method

Children and young people have a different perspective of everyday life and relations (compared to the perspective of adults (Alanen, 1992; Qvortrup, 1994), a certain 'child perspective'. Children are active participants in the process of making family connections (Brannen et al., 2000) and in childhood research childhood is seen as a period in its own right. Tiller (1991) emphasizes that a child perspective must emanate from they way children themselves apprehend and interpret the context they live in.

In the initial planning of the study, we were therefore anxious to ensure that the voices of children of foster carers would be heard .The intention was to gain knowledge about their situation through their own participation, and to make the research questions emanate from their experiences, not from our own perceptions as professionals and researchers. We wanted to use research methods where children and young people would have a chance to take an active part, and therefore our choice of methods came to be focus groups, discussion groups and a questionnaire.

Focus Groups

The first step of the study was to gather children and young people who lived with foster siblings in three focus groups. In these focus groups children of foster carers could share their experiences with us, and with each other.

Focus groups were before 1980 mostly used in market research, but in the last two decades have became popular as a method within social science, preferably applied social research. The distinctive features of focus groups are the following: group members meet on one occasion, for a limited time with the aim to acquire specific knowledge of a certain topic (Wibeck, 2000). Focus groups can be used as the only research method, but can also be combined with other methods (Morgan, 1997). Focus groups form a useful method at different stages in a research project, but are especially practicable in order to gain knowledge of an unexplored field (Wibeck, 2000).

We invited children of foster carers from agencies in Gothenburg to participate in the focus groups, and we ended up with 17 participants from

9–22 years, divided by age in three groups: 9–12 years (seven participants) 13–17 years (six participants) and 18–25 years (four participants). We were two group leaders, one who mainly asked questions, and one who mainly observed. Each group session lasted about two hours. All sessions were recorded on tape and each tape was transcribed word for word.

All children and young people who participated in the focus groups were very active and committed, and provided us with a lot of new information. They all appreciated to have this opportunity to talk to peers who shared their experiences, something which several of them said they had wished for.

Discussion Groups

Our idea with the discussion groups was to create an opportunity to enter more deeply into issues and interesting questions that had arisen in the focus groups.

Again, children of foster carers from agencies in Gothenburg were invited. Thirty children announced their interest in participating, but when dates for group sessions were set, only 16 children and young people in the ages between 11 and 23 years had the opportunity to join the groups. We divided the participators by age into three categories: 11–14 (seven participants), 15–17 (five participants) and 18–25 (four participants). We were two group leaders, and met each group three times. Every session lasted for one-and-a-half hours. Group sessions were recorded on tape and later transcribed by us.

Questionnaire

Statements from focus groups and discussion groups formed a basis for a questionnaire with 60 questions directed to children and young people who lived, or had lived, with foster siblings. Participants of discussion groups also helped us to answer the first 'testing versions' of the questionnaire, which we tried to improve after having heard the comments from group members.

One of the problematic factors was how to design questions for respondents who had experience of living with more than one foster sibling. Quite a few of our group members lived, or had lived, together with two or more foster siblings and their had very diverse experiences from each sibling. Therefore, the most desirable design of the questionnaire would have been one where these different experiences could be seen. We tested a type of design where we had several sets of questions for up to four foster siblings, but it turned out to be clumsy and also confusing for respondents. Eventually we rejected all such attempts and instructed respondents to choose the foster sibling who had stayed for the longest period of time in the family, and stick to that chosen sibling while answering the questions. Some respondents told us that this was somewhat awkward for them, because their experiences were so significantly different. We are aware of this difficulty, but we still feel this design to be the best from an analysing aspect.

Questionnaires were sent to foster families who were members of one of the organizations for foster carers in Sweden (Familjehemmens Riksförbund), and also to foster families with children placed by the social boards in Gothenburg and six other municipalities in Western Sweden. All in all, 1,067 questionnaires were sent out.

The questionnaire was also placed on a web site, available through a homepage at the Department of Social Work. Those who had the questionnaire sent to them by post could also choose to use the web site while answering the questionnaire. For a few days the address was out as a link on some popular sites for young people, and during those days we received several answers on the web version of the questionnaire. The following table shows answering frequency for the questionnaires:

Table 7.1   Frequency of filled in questionnaires

Identity	Frequency
Web answers	224
Foster care organization	282
Social boards in Göteborg	115
Other municipalities	58
Unknown identity	5
Total	684

We had to trust foster carers to make the questionnaires available to their children. Some families from the foster care organization did not have biological children at all, or did not have biological children of suitable ages, but we could not know who they were. Such families were asked to send in a note that told us of their inability to participate, which 155 families did. Nevertheless, we cannot know if there were more families than these 155 who could not answer because they did not have children of their own and/ or children of suitable ages. Likewise, we cannot be sure how many of the recipients of postal questionnaires chose to answer via the web version. All these factors make it difficult to account for the percentage of answers, we can only observe that 684 children and young people from all parts of Sweden sent us filled in questionnaires.

Results

The following presentation is an account of the first analysis of the findings from focus groups, discussion groups (in the presentation these groups are not separated, both are denominated 'interview groups') and questionnaires. As the final analysing work is yet far from completed, this presentation is limited to a descriptive level.

General Attitude

Results both from the interview groups and answers of the questionnaire show that a majority of foster carers' own children consider fostering to have had a positive impact on their lives. This positive attitude is in many cases linked to this presumed 'pedagogic effect' of fostering. Fifty-two per cent of those who answered the questionnaire (44 per cent of boys/men and 57 per cent of girls/women) declared that fostering was a good thing because you learned to be considerate towards other people. This positive attitude is to a large extent in concordance with foster carers' general attitude, even if the tendency is not as strong among the children (Höjer, 2001).

Participation in the Decision to Start Fostering

One question of interest is to what extent children of foster carers were involved in the initial discussions that preceded the decision to become a foster family. From answers in the questionnaire, it is evident that a majority (63 per cent) of the respondents were asked about their opinion before their parents decided to start fostering, 22 per cent did not participate in the decision, and 15 per cent were unsure whether they did participate or not.

Some of the children and young people in the interview groups said they were too young to have an opinion when the family became a foster family, and the answers from the questionnaires show that 30 per cent were less than six years of age when the family started to foster for the first time. The following table shows the age of children of foster carers when their parents started to foster.

Table 7.2 **Age of children of foster carers when their parents started to foster**

Age	Percentage N=673
0–5	30
6–10	37
11–15	26
16 or older	7
Total	100

Some of the participants in the group interviews doubted that their parents would have considered their opinion, they thought their parents would have chosen to foster even if they themselves had been negative. Nevertheless, 80 per cent of respondents who answered the questionnaire stated that their parents considered their opinion on whether to start fostering or not.

Relations to Parents

In the group sessions the participators displayed feelings of pride over their parents. They felt that their parents really accomplished something important by their assignment as foster carers. Parents were usually described as caring and competent. A difference could be seen between the way group members talked about their mothers and fathers. Female carers were to a higher extent than male carers described as very competent and capable, with high ambitions to be never failing supervisors of family interactions. Some of the female group participants talked about their mothers as what can be described as 'omnipotent carers', who had an urge to care for everybody in need. These girls were all in their early twenties, and could be said to have a somewhat critical attitude towards their mothers for what they felt to be 'excessive' caring behaviour.

Decreased time and attention Children who are placed in foster care have in many cases experienced neglect and/or abuse. They have a great need for attention and demand a lot of foster carers time. Therefore biological children of foster carers are likely to experience decreased access to parental time and attention when their parents become foster carers (Poland and Groze, 1993; Twigg, 1994; Pugh, 1996; Höjer, 2001).

Decreased parental time was one of the central themes in the group discussions. Children and young people were very much aware of the need for parental attention towards foster siblings, but they felt that they also had a right to attention from their parents. Some of the group participants described situations where they often had to wait, sometimes in vain, for parents to find time to listen to them. One boy (age 16), who has had many foster siblings throughout the years, said that he had to make an appointment with his mother if he wanted her to find time for him.

> I really would have liked her to spend time with me. She has not got the time for all of us … so one has to line up and wait for a call.

In the concluding group session of each age group, the participants were asked to work in pairs, and to formulate sentences of what they would like to tell their parents (and also what they would like to tell their foster siblings and their social workers). In all age groups, when it came to writing to parents, group participants wrote sentences like 'Don't forget your own family!', 'Be sure to do things together with you own children!', 'Don't forget to talk to us, too!'.

In the questionnaire there were several open questions where respondents could formulate their own opinions and ideas. Some respondents found it easy to express themselves in writing and apparently took the chance to make their points, while some were less interested and wrote only short answers or simply did not write anything at all. Therefore it is not possible to draw conclusions from the frequencies of written answers of these open questions. Still, these written answers furnish us with important knowledge of the respondents' experiences. One example of such an open question was when respondents were asked to write down what they felt had made the greatest impact on their lives when the family started to foster. Thirty-six of the respondents answered that the greatest change was that they had *less time with their parents*. One respondent wrote:

> The attention of the parents was drawn to the foster child. We have also got attention but it was not like before. We almost never do anything alone with mum or dad; there is always someone else there.

Some questions in the questionnaire were formulated as statements on which respondents could choose to agree or disagree. One of these statements was about parental time and formulated like this: 'The foster sibling acquires so much time from my mother/father that there is no time left over for me.' Twenty-three (mother) and 16 (father) per cent respectively of respondents stated that they did not get any time with their parents due to their commitment as foster carers. Consequently, a majority of respondents disagreed with this statement, which might depend on the 'strong' formulation of 'no time'. Still it is worth to notice that about one fifth of respondents stated that they have no time with their parents because they are too busy with the foster sibling.

Expectations from parents of support to foster siblings   In group sessions, another central theme was how children and young people felt that their parents expected them to be good and supportive to foster siblings. Some of the group participants told us that it was understood that as they themselves had been lucky enough to have good parents and a good home, they were obliged to tolerate difficult behaviour from foster siblings. Group participants were told to let foster siblings be with them and their friends, even though some of them felt this as a difficult task to put up with.

There were group participants who felt that if they failed to live up to these parental expectations of supportive behaviour, they made their parents disappointed, which was something they really wanted to avoid. In the questionnaire, 37 (mother) and 30 (father) per cent respectively agreed with the statement 'My mother/father becomes disappointed in me if I don't treat my foster siblings nicely'.

Taking responsibility for well-being of parents   From group discussions as well as from questionnaire answers, it was evident that children and young people felt responsible for the well being of their parents. In the group sessions we listened to frequent stories where group participants displayed their worry for their parents. They knew how committed their parents were to their task as foster carers, but they also knew how hard and tiresome this task could be.

This knowledge also made children and young people very considerate towards their parents, a consideration which at times prevented them from informing their parents of their own problems. As Talbot (1997) also found, children of foster carers' are aware of the strains of fostering, and therefore they do not wish to burden their parents by telling them about their own difficulties. The following quotation is an example of feelings both of worry and of responsibility towards parents:

> Soon one does not have a mother any more … my mother does the work of 15 people. She never complains … I don't want to take time from my mother, I don't want to talk to my mother about my problems because I don't want to make her even more tired. (Girl aged 16)

In the answers from the questionnaire, 60 (mother) and 47 (father) per cent respectively agreed with the following statement 'I try to be good and supportive towards my mother/father when she/he is troubled because of my foster sibling'.

Relations to Foster Siblings

Relationships between siblings can be good or bad, easy or complicated in any family. Siblings can relate differently to one another, and sibling relations may display envy and competition as well as care and friendship.

When it comes to the relationship between children of foster carers and foster children, statements are of many different kinds. Some of the young people in the interview groups told us that they related to foster siblings in the same way as they related to biological siblings. In the questionnaire respondents could show their point of view concerning this matter by agreeing or disagreeing to the following statement: 'My foster sibling feels like a biological sibling'. The following table shows the answers of this statement:

Table 7.3   'My foster sibling feels like a biological sibling'

Answers	Percentage N=669
I completely agree	47
I partly agree	37
I neither agree nor disagree	8
I partly disagree	8
I completely disagree	13
Total	100

According to results from the questionnaire, almost 50 per cent of the respondents said they completely agree that foster siblings 'feel like' biological siblings.

In the interview groups, some participants said they enjoyed having a big family. In that respect they found foster siblings to be a great asset – they contributed in a nice way to life in the family, they made it livelier and noisier in a positive way, and they were important as friends and companions.

Answers from the questionnaire concerning relations to foster siblings are displayed in the following table:

Table 7.4　Relations to foster sibling

Character of relation	Percentage N=673
Very good	41
Rather good	34
Neither good nor bad	17
Rather bad	6
Very bad	2
Total	100

Results from the questionnaire show that three fourths of the respondents have a good (very good or rather good) relation to foster siblings, and many of the participants of the interview groups said that they liked their foster siblings and that they appreciated their company.

Factors that Influence Relations

Difference of age　The following table shows the age difference between respondents and their chosen foster sibling.

Table 7.5　Age difference between respondents and chosen foster sibling

Character of relation	Percentage N=636
15–3 years younger	12
2 years younger–2 years older	26
3–5 years older	20
6–10 years older	29
11 years older or more	13
Total	100

When we analysed statements from interview groups, we found that the age difference between group members and their foster siblings had an impact on their relationship. Group members with considerably younger foster siblings seemed to have a better relationship than those who were close in age. Some of the group members, who had foster siblings the same age as themselves, told us about several occasions of competition and rivalry at different levels.

One problematic issue was the competition for friends. Foster siblings wanted to be with the same friends as our group members, which was not always something that they appreciated. One boy (aged 12) described how his foster brother, who was the same age, always followed him and his friends, trying to have as much attention as possible. He found to be immensely annoying. He also told us how his foster brother always took every chance of 'showing off', and tried to outsmart him at any given opportunity.

Several group members from the 'middle groups' (aged 14–17) described something that can be called *identity theft*. They described how foster siblings close in age wanted to *be as them*. One girl told us how her foster sister dyed her hair exactly the same colour as she did, and how this girl would repeat her exact statements when they chatted with friends:

> This is the worst thing, it's worse than when they say 'mum' and 'dad'. I don't mind that as much as her wanting to be like me. (Girl, age 15)

One of the boys (aged 17) told us how his foster brother, who was two years older, had inherited some money. The first thing the foster brother did was to buy an outfit that was identical with his own, so they were dressed as twins – something he did not appreciate at all.

According to answers from questionnaires, there is a significant connection between age difference and relations to foster sibling. The following cross table shows age difference as related to relations with foster siblings.

Figures in Table 7.6 show that those who are younger or older than foster siblings, also have better relationships with them.

Secrets The issue of s*ecrets* was often mentioned in the group conversations. Evidently, children of foster carers have to find ways to handle the *keeping of secrets*:

Several of our group participators declared that foster siblings often told them secrets, which they had to promise not to tell anyone. One girl (aged 16) described how her foster brother (12 years of age) had told her about 'secret things' that happened each time he visited his birth mother. He was really troubled, but she had to promise not to tell anyone, especially not the foster parents. If she told anyone he would 'never tell her anything else ever again'. This girl was very caring in her attitude towards her younger foster brother, and she was puzzled – how should she handle this matter? She felt that she

Table 7.6   Age difference related to relation to foster sibling (p<0.01)

Relation to foster sibling	Age difference				Total
	15–3 years younger n=76	2 years younger– 2 years older n=164	3 years older– 5 years older n=125	6 years older or more n=267	n=632
Very good relation	49	32	33	50	42
Rather good relation	33	38	36	29	33
Neither good nor bad relation	16	18	23	16	18
Rather bad relation	2	8	6	4	5
Very bad relation	0	4	2	1	2
Total	100	100	100	100	100

was the only one he truly confided in – could she betray him? Or should she tell her mother – was that the best thing for her foster brother? This example can be said to be representative of some parts of the group discussions.

In the answers of the questionnaire, 43 per cent of the respondents stated that they had experienced foster siblings telling them secrets, and 20 per cent found this to be something that troubled them.

To know things about foster siblings that you could not tell friends was also quite common, according to group discussions. Several of the group participators had such experiences. One girl (12 years old) told a long story about how her tongue slipped, and she told her friends something about her foster sister that she was not allowed to do. However, as it turned out, it did not matter 'because it was so awful that nobody believed me anyway!'.

In the answers of the questionnaire, 70 per cent answered that they had had experience of knowing things about foster siblings they were forbidden to tell friends, and 15 per cent answered that this worried them.

In the group discussions, some participators told us that their parents sometimes told them things about the foster siblings that they had to keep secret. This was not as tangible an issue as the two latter, but still it was something that at times affected their lives. In the answers from the questionnaire, 61 per cent had experiences of having received information about the foster siblings that they were not allowed to tell them, and 15 per cent found this to be something that troubled them.

Apparently, a majority of the foster carer's own children have had experience of secrets connected to fostering and foster siblings, but this did not seem to trouble all respondents. Still, 15–20 per cent of those who answered the questionnaire stated that keeping different kind of secrets was something that worried them.

Responsibility and Worry Directed towards Foster Siblings

Responsibility Brannen et al. (2000) show how children frequently take responsibility for siblings, and that they also include a moral imperative in this responsibility – taking care of your siblings is something you *should* to. Dunn (1985) found that even small children gave care to siblings and worried about them. Obviously, giving care to siblings and worrying about their well-being is something children normally do. However, living with foster siblings seems to introduce yet another dimension when it comes to responsibility and worry. When we talked to children and young people who participated in the interview groups, it became evident to us that quite a few of them took a lot of responsibility for foster siblings, and that they also worried about these siblings to an extent that to us appeared to be more than what children 'normally' do. Especially the older girls talked a lot of how they worried about their foster siblings.

In the answers from the questionnaire, respondents stated that they take a considerable responsibility for their foster sibling. The following table shows the distribution of answers to the question 'Do you take responsibility for your foster sibling?'.

Table 7.7   Responsibility for foster siblings (p<0.05)

Do you take responsibility for your foster sibling?	Percentage boys N=257	Percentage girls N=411	Total percentage N=668
Very often	18	28	24
Rather often	43	42	42
Rather seldom	17	14	15
Very seldom	12	7	9
Never	10	9	10
Total	100	100	100

Results from the table show that 66 per cent often or rather often take responsibility for their chosen foster sibling. Some gender differences can be seen, girls/women take more responsibility than boys/men (p<0,05). In analysing this answer, the connotation of the word 'responsibility' must be considered. For some respondents 'taking responsibility' may imply to baby-sit a couple of times, and for others it may signify a more overarching commitment that will have a significant impact on their lives. In the questionnaire the 'responsibility question' was followed by an open question where respondents could describe their ways of taking responsibility. One hundred and seventy-eight boys/men and 309 girls/women chose to answer that question. These answers constitute an understanding of what the issue of responsibility meant to the respondents. Table 7.8 shows these answers after they were categorized.

The table shows that 16 per cent of the respondents take the same responsibility for foster siblings as they do for biological siblings. Answers in the other categories show that a substantial part of the responsibility consists of practical help and baby sitting, but also of emotional and physical support and defence.

Table 7.8   Domains of responsibility for foster siblings

Domains of responsibility	Percentage boys N=178	Percentage girls N=309	Total percentage N=487
The same responsibility as I take for biological siblings	12	18	16
Babysitting	13	15	15
Educate, reprove	11	7	8
Defend, protect	9	6	7
Practical help	20	17	18
Emotional support	13	17	16
Plays	8	4	5
General support in difficult situations	4	4	4
I let sibling be with me and my friends	4	3	3
Support-family	0	4	3
My foster sibling is older than me, so I don't take any responsibility	2	2	2
I don't take any responsibility	4	3	3
Total	100	100	100

Worry

> What will happen to her in life? How will such a small creature survive, with such experiences of hurt and pain? Why does a child have to go through such a hell on earth? (Male respondent, 26 years old)

From what our group members told us, we got an understanding of how much they worried about their foster siblings. This concern emanated from different circumstances: For example, group members were worried that foster siblings would have to move back to birth parents against their own will. They were also worried about what happened when foster siblings visited birth parents – maybe they were not treated well, and maybe they had to see things that were bad for them. Sometimes the young people who participated in the groups also worried about the foster siblings own behaviour, that they would fall into drug and/or alcohol abuse, or that they would be used and badly treated by 'unsuitable' friends.

In the questionnaire answers to the question 'Do you worry about your foster siblings' are displayed in Table 7.9.

Table 7.9   Worry about foster siblings (p<0.01)

Do you worry about your foster siblings?	Percentage boys N=255	Percentage girls N=407	Total percentage N=662
Very often	3	11	8
Rather often	18	31	26
Rather seldom	33	31	32
Very seldom	26	17	20
Never	20	10	14
Total	100	100	100

There is a significant difference between girls and boys (p<0.01). Twenty-one per cent of boys and 42 per cent of girls state that they worry very often or rather often. This was also evident in the interview groups, were girls talked more about their worries than boys did.

In the questionnaire there was also an open question where respondents could describe what constituted their worries. Table 7.10 shows those answers after they were categorized.

A lot of respondents worry about the future – what will happen to their foster siblings? They are aware of the vulnerability and the risks in their foster siblings lives, and the impact it might have on their future. More girls than boys are worried that their foster siblings will be unhappy, and more boys than girls worry about foster siblings getting hurt or falling ill. There are also quite a few (12 per cent), who are worried about problems foster siblings might have with birth parents. To sum up the results from this question, it is obvious these answers display a lot of 'worries' that are specifically connected to the characteristics of fostering, something that was also an issue in the interview groups.

Age differences There is also a difference related to age difference between children of foster carers' and their foster siblings, as is shown by Table 7.11.

Figures from both tables show that biological children of foster carers take more responsibility and also worry more for their foster siblings the wider the

Table 7.10   Reasons for worrying about foster siblings

Reasons for worrying	Percentage boys N=120	Percentage girls N=250	Total percentage N=370
Same as for biological siblings	5	5	5
Drug/alcohol abuse, criminality	8	8	6
What the future will be like	20	26	24
'Feeling bad' – problems, anxieties	10	17	15
Getting hurt, fall ill	17	8	11
Get into fights and trouble	7	5	6
Problems at school	2	4	3
No friends, be left out	9	7	8
Have to move from foster home	5	6	6
Problems with birth parents	12	12	12
I don't worry	4	1	1
Problems for biological family members	1	1	1
Total	100	100	100

age gap is upwards in age. Nevertheless, it is worth noticing that also biological children who are younger than their foster siblings still state that they take responsibility for, and also worry about, their foster siblings.

'Loss of innocence' As mentioned before, one of the most positive effect of fostering from the foster carers' point of view was that their own children learnt about caring for other people, and appreciate that they themselves had been fortunate enough to have a good home, and therefore should share with people who were less fortunate. This could be summarized as a *lesson of empathy*, which foster carers in most cases thought they had succeeded in giving to their children (Höjer, 2001).

However, there is also another side to the coin. Children of foster cares might also learn too much about the hardship of children, about abuse and neglect. Pugh (1996) designates this as a 'loss of innocence'. In the interview groups some of the participants told us about 'terrible things', like knife threats and frequent threats of suicide, both connected to the foster sibling while he/she was placed in the foster family, and also to members of the foster siblings' birth family.

Table 7.11   Responsibility for foster siblings connected to age differences between biological children of foster carers (BC) and their foster siblings (FS) (p<0.01)

Do you take responsibility for your foster sibling?	Age difference				
	BC 15–3 years younger than FS N=73	BC 2 years younger–2 years older than FS N=163	BC 3–5 years older than FS N=126	BC more than 5 years older than FS N=266	Total percentage N=628
Very often	12	22	23	31	25
Rather often	22	41	50	46	43
Rather seldom	16	17	12	17	15
Very seldom	18	10	11	4	9
Never	32	10	4	2	8
Total	100	100	100	100	100

Table 7.12   Worry for foster siblings connected to age differences between biological children of foster carers (BC) and their foster siblings (FS) (p<0.01)

Do you worry about your foster sibling?	Age difference				
	BC 15–3 years younger FS N=76	BC 2 years younger–2 years older than FS N=161	BC 3–5 years older than FS N=124	BC more than 5 years older than FS N=262	Total percentage N=623
Very often	5	6	12	8	9
Rather often	18	24	20	31	26
Rather seldom	21	34	32	34	32
Very seldom	36	16	23	17	20
Never	20	19	13	10	14
Total	100	100	100	100	100

Conclusion

When children of foster carers describe their everyday life, fostering has a great impact upon the relationship between parents and children. Children and young people usually show an understanding attitude towards the needs of foster children, and also towards their parents' strong wish to make the fostering task successful. Still, it is evident that their own needs at times are neglected, and that they keep their problems to themselves to a high extent, which in some cases can have destructive effects.

Another salient result both from interview groups and answers of questionnaires is how children of foster carers have strong feelings of responsibility towards their parents and their well being. Brannen et al. (2000) find that children in families are often active care *givers*, not only care *receivers*. Giving care was also what many group participants found to be their 'family mission'. These young people were anxious to be supportive and helpful towards their parents, as well as towards their foster siblings.

When listening to children of foster carers, it becomes obvious that these children and young people are far from passive members of the foster family. They certainly take an active part in the fostering assignment. Living with foster siblings has a great impact on their lives, both good and bad.

Most children and young people seem to cope adequately, and to benefit in many ways from living with foster children. The 'empathy lesson' has been quite successful, these are children and young people with an unusually well developed capacity for caring and for understanding other people – siblings, parents and peers. However, they also have to pay a price for this 'empathy lesson'. They often have to accept less access to parental time and attention, and sometimes also a noisy and chaotic atmosphere at home.

These children and young people need to be acknowledged. They are by no means just passive members of the foster family, they perform an active part in fostering, for which they should have credit and acknowledgement. It is important to give them the attention they rightfully deserve, and to find ways of giving them and their parents' time together, even though fostering is time consuming

References

Alanen, L. (1992), *Modern Childhood*, Jyväskylä Universitet.
Brannen, J. and Heptinstall, E and Bhopal, K. (2000), *Connecting Children*, London: Routledge.

Bebbington, A. and Miles, J. (1990), 'The Supply of Foster Families for Children in Care, *British Journal of Social Work*, Vol. 20 (4), pp. 283–307.

Cautley, P.W. (1980), *New Foster Parents: The First Experience*, New York: Human Services Press.

Dunn, J. (1985), *Sisters and Brothers. The Developing Child*, Cambridge, MA: Harvard University Press.

Familjeplejen i Danmark (1998), *Kaerlighed og naestekaerlighed. Om leveforholdene for plejefamiliers egne börn*, Köpenhamn.

Havik, T. (1996), *Slik fosterforeldrene ser det. Resultat fra en kartleggningsstudie*, Bergen: Barnevernets Utviklingssenter på Vestlandet.

Höjer, I. (2001), *Fosterfamiljens inre liv*, dissertation, Department of Social Work, Göteborg University.

Kaplan, C. P. (1988), 'The Biological Children of Foster Parents in the Foster Family', *Child and Adolescent Social Work Journal*, Vol. 5 (4), New York: Human Sciences Press.

Kälvesten, A.-L. (1974), *40 fosterfamiljer med Skåbarn*, Stockholm: Almqvist och Wiksell Förlag AB.

Morgan, D.L. (1997), *Focus Groups as Qualitative Research*, Thousand Oaks, CA: Sage.

Part, D. (1993), 'Fostering as Seen by the Carer's Children', *Adoption and Fostering*, Vol. 17 (1).

Poland, D. and Groze, V. (1993), 'Effects of Foster Care Placement on Biological Children in the Home', *Child and adolescent Social Work Journal*, No. 10, s. 153–64, New York. Human Sciences Press.

Pugh, G. (1996), 'Seen but not Heard? Addressing the Needs of Children who Foster', *Adoption and fostering*, Vol. 20 (1).

Qvortrup, J. (1994), *Barn halve priset. Nordisk barndom i ett samhällsperspektiv*, Esbjerg: Sydjysk Universitetsforlag.

Socialstyrelsen (1995), *Ovisshetens barn*, SoS-rapport 1995:8, Stockholm: Socialstyrelsen.

Socialstyrelsen (2002), *Barn och unga – insatser år 2001*, Statistik socialtjänst 2002:7, Stockholm: Socialstyrelsen.

Talbot, C. (1997), 'Sons and Daughters of Foster Carers. Children and Young People who Foster', copy of speech for IFCO conference, Vancouver, July.

Triseliotis, J., Moira, B. and Hill, M. (2000), *Delivering Foster Care*, London: British Agencies for Adoption and Fostering (BAAF).

Twigg, R. (1994), 'The Unknown Soldiers of Foster Care: Foster Care as Loss for the Foster Parent's Own Children', *Smith College Studies in Social Work*, Vol. 64 (3), June.

Vinterhed, K. (1985), *De andra föräldrarna*, Stockholm: Skeab.

Wåhlander, E. (1990), *Familjehem – stöd och hjälp*, Stockholm: FOU-rapport no. 133.

Wibeck, V. (2000), *Fokusgrupper*, Lund: Studentlitteratur.

PART III
YOU GET IT OR YOU DO NOT: MAINSTREAMING IN EDUCATION, ETHNIC ORIGIN AND COMPETENCY LEVEL

Chapter 8

Including Youngsters from Residential Care in Mainstream Schools – Is It Possible?

Arne Tveit and Bjørn Arnesen

Introduction

This chapter will focus on children living in residential care and their inclusion in mainstream schools. Supporting the normalization of young people in residential care is a key issue. This urge to live normal lives among the young residents is, according to research results on a broad scale, their main motivation for changing behavior and finding a 'new direction' in life. One of the best opportunities and arenas for social inclusion and normalizing is the municipal, mainstream school system. For many young residents in care this arena has, however, proven to be a painful road to achieve acceptance and inclusion from peers as well as the professional community. We hope to show through this presentation that it is possible to succeed with inclusion when certain conditions are taken into consideration and specific methods are applied.

We have for the last 7–8 years been engaged in practical development and research in the field of residential care and educational placement. Our first project was a national survey conducted in 1995–96, which looked into the educational opportunities and placement of children living in residential care (Ollestad and Tveit, 1996). More recently we have been involved in different projects and evaluation studies in municipalities of Bjugn, Melhus and Trondheim in the central region of Norway (Arnesen and Tveit, 1998, 1999; Bonesrønning et al., 1999; Arnesen et al., 2000).

Youngsters placed in residential care often express as an important goal for the future to be like their peers. If they are to achieve this goal, connection to mainstream school is a main task. It is important for these youngsters to show their peers that they have succeeded in being equal, and the mainstream school also gives them ample possibilities to make friends and be a part of the normal peer social life. For those who are out of the mainstream school system the impact to other peers is that something is wrong, and they thereby confirm that they are outside the community of peers. The result is lack of information and possibilities of making commitments with other peers. The school history for youngsters placed in residential care is mostly a story of exclusion, bullying, social and academic shortcoming, runaway behaviour and so on (Arnesen et al., 2000; Hermodsson, 2000). Nevertheless, the main goal for young people staying in residential care is to be like their peers. Connection to mainstream school is both the fulfilment of a goal and a dream for most residents.

One of the main tasks for residential care institutions, as it is for schools, is to do whatever is necessary to motivate the young people to learn in a broad sense. International and Norwegian studies point out that only a smaller part of residents in residential care cope with the demands and obstructions that exist in being a part of the school community. A Norwegian study of a residential care unit (Clifford and Arnesen, 1997), emphasize that staff were important in the transition to care in the institution, although they were not so important as the other young people there. Most of the informants had little contact with other young people before admission, or felt excluded both at school and in other contexts. One of the main reasons was that the transition to an environment where one met other young people with comparable experiences, and where they experienced a measure of understanding and acceptance, was overwhelming. The sense of belonging to a group, especially a group of equal peers, was described as a major and significant experience by more than half of the informants. The fact that so many of these young people are disaffected and distrust the teachers and other helpers is important to acknowledge. This aspect has to be taken into consideration in regards to the experiences from the projects in Trondheim and mainly Bjugn, which we will present later in this paper. The main challenge for the youngster who has experienced so much rejection is often closely connected to the amount of adaptation and support given when he or she for the first time is received in a new school setting. Many schools are unprepared, understaffed and lack the necessary competence and routines. The schools need to establish a system of preparedness, or some sort of 'first-aid' unit, to make this transition work as well as possible. There has to be a great deal of effort put into cooperation between residential care units and the local school and in supporting the youngster in a way so he or she can handle social rules, peer relations and activities, and finally in making the necessary adjustments to the municipal school system. The challenge is first of all to motivate and support the young people to manage the more challenging mainstream school with its variation of peers and henceforth the need of equivalent social skills.

Inclusion for All – Except Children with Challenging Behaviour?

Integration and inclusion has been the official policy in Norway for more than twenty years. Public figures show that over 99 per cent of all children between 7–15 years of age attend their local municipal school. This does not seem to be the case for children living in residential care. Our research (Ollestad and Tveit, 1996) shows that 34.4 per cent of the children up to age 15 living in public residential care received their compulsory education in segregated settings outside mainstream schools. Our sample of institutions consisted both of institutions with short-and long-term attendance, but the number of segregated pupils did not differ significantly between the two. Furthermore we found that of the approximately two-thirds of our sample who attended the local school, almost 60 per cent received part or all their education in separated settings within the mainstream school. It is natural to question if our research data is outdated, since it goes back to the mid-1990s. Unfortunately there is little new data to verify our findings. More resent research directed towards the exclusion of children and adolescents with behavioural and emotional problems tend to support our conclusions. All in all our and newer surveys reveal a tendency towards extensive segregated education for children who challenge the school system through their behaviour.

The Educational Law of Norway allows special education in special units both within and outside the mainstream school. For some children with special problems and needs such placement is regarded as necessary. The placement must, however, be based on a specialist assessment by the local 'Pedagogisk-Psykologisk Tjeneste' (Psychological-Educational Services), and in each case the local school board/or principal must make an *enkelt vedtak* (statement of provision of special resources). The parents have the right to make a complaint about this *enkelt vedtak*.

For the last 50 years the grounds for making the decision to place a young person outside the mainstream should always be considered only if it benefits the need of the individual child. However, through a change in the Educational Law in 2000 the local education authorities (e.g. the local headmaster) can exclude a child from school and have it moved to a neighbour school or some special unit on the grounds that he or she is a menace to fellow pupils or teachers. We don't have data that indicates what this new policy has led to. There is reason to believe that the target group at hand will experience increased exclusion. Our data from 1996 before the law was changed reveals that for as many as 50 per cent of the children in the survey who received their education in separate settings, a specialist assessment was lacking. This result indicates that for a great number of children in residential care their placement in special units or settings may be based on grounds other than their special educational needs. This in itself represents a serious violation of these students' legal rights.

On the whole the issue of placement is a complex one. Available international research data (Kauffman and Lloyd, 1995, p. 15) show 'that place alone is not the critical ingredient in helping students attain important social and academic goals'. Even more than other children, the ones living in residential care need acceptance, understanding and care. They want to be regarded as normal children and youngsters, especially amongst their peers. On this basis the educational placement of students living in residential care raises some important challenges. These children are uprooted from their neighbourhood, families and friends and have to adjust to a completely new, often very different setting, with new adult and peer relations in the institution as well as in school. They are removed from their home environment, often in a crisis situation and are very vulnerable. They may be in a state of mind somewhere between shock from the separation from their home environment and hope for the future. For many of these children placement in a mainstream school setting from day one proves to be a disaster. Our survey shows that the schools as well as the institutions have great difficulties in establishing the right educational provisions to meet the individual needs of the students. One of the reasons for this is the fact that the placement is often made without preparation. Necessary information is lacking and teachers report that they feel more or less like they are blindfolded in their attempt to meet the individual student in the most appropriate way.

In Norway some municipal authorities are seriously looking into different ways of coping with these problems. A main strategy seems to be an introduction of a temporary small and supportive educational unit either within or outside the local school, which has as its main objective providing a safe and prepared introduction to the mainstream school. The greatest danger in choosing this temporary solution is, of course, that it ends up as a permanent segregated educational placement. As we will illustrate in the next section experience shows that the local school authorities seem more likely to succeed in the transition from the segregated setting into the mainstream when certain measures are taken and obstacles overcome.

The Phase Model – a Three-level Strategy

The project we have studied most closely the last five years is taking place in the municipality of Bjugn in the region of Fosen in Sør-Trøndelag County. The population of the commune is approximately 4,700 people and there are four schools that all educate children in the age 6–15 years. Within the boundaries of the commune there are situated two residential care units, one public and one private, with a total number of 12–18 residents mainly in the age of 12–18 years. These institutions represent a unique challenge to the local schools and support units. The institutions started early in the 1990s and the local competence and experience in addressing the problems these children represent in the educational field was at that time rather slim.

Our part in the project has been a diverse one, partly as evaluators and partly as counsellors. We have been able to follow it very closely and have documented several interesting results (Arnesen and Tveit, 1998, 1999; Arnesen et al., 2000). The main object of this paper is to present the core of the project and some new experiences concerning the transition into mainstream school that have not been published previously.

In developing an adaptive approach to the education of young people living in residential care this and other projects have developed what is named as a phase-model. It has three different levels: the receiving level, the stabilization level and the transition level.

In another project at a school situated in Trondheim staff have developed (Bonesrøning et al., 1999) a system where they offer all these three levels within the framework of the local school and the ordinary classroom setting. This is probably the ideal way of securing a good inclusion. In the Bjugn-project, however, due to the high amount of students from the institutions and other local conditions, they have chosen to establish a separate unit to take care of the first two levels in this approach and to contribute to the realisation of the third level, the transition into the local mainstream school.

Since the project started in 1996 the main focus had been on building up competence in the support unit and improving the quality of the receiving and stabilization process. Less attention had been given to the difficult task of working towards and within the mainstream school to attain full inclusion. There were of course some students who had been successfully included but far too often one of two things happened. The student was either kept too long in the separate unit before entering into the transition process, or the mainstream schools refused to take serious responsibility and the special unit worker would follow the residential care student all the way as a permanent extra resource/teacher. The student might therefore be physically integrated, but would not necessarily feel included.

Focus on the Transition Level

From the very start of the project the fear of making this separate unit, called 'Nylandet', a permanent placement for the target group was highlighted. During the school year 2001–02 special measures were finally undertaken to counteract such a development.

We at MKA were asked to assist and give counselling to the separate unit in this respect. The task was called 'Nylandet in the local school' and it addressed the challenge of how the staff (teachers and social workers) from the separate unit could work successfully towards and within the local school to support the transition process in collaboration with the mainstream teachers. The main target that was focused by the staff from the separate unit was the complex area of how to gradually transform responsibility over to the mainstream classroom teacher and reduce their own importance and relationship with the student and hence prepare their withdrawal.

Through dedicated work towards this aim the staff developed a number of criteria to indicate the de-escalation of their own presence in the mainstream school in the process of a successful inclusion of the student:

1   the student must be prepared and motivated both socially and academically;
2   the mainstream teachers must be prepared and dedicated to the task and an adaptive educational programme must be implemented;
3   the classmates must be informed and motivated;
4   the residential care institution must be informed and prepared for the change and a closer collaboration with the mainstream teachers must take place;
5   the possibility to temporarily reverse the process and escalate must be kept open;
6. the process must be continuously evaluated.

The experiences from applying this set of criteria are limited but positive. During the school year of 2001–02 seven of 12 secondary level students (13–15 year olds) attended the local schools most or all of the time. The other five were still mainly in the support unit. Some of them came into the residential care institution later in the school year and needed more time to be able to handle the transition into the mainstream school. For the seven residential students who attended the mainstream schools applying the criteria above seemed to increase the level of success. When the support staff managed to withdraw from the class room parallel to a stronger engagement by the classroom teacher, when the classroom teacher had the necessary help to put up an adaptive programme both academically and socially and when the level of accept towards the 'residentials' amongst peers and staff had improved, the students seemed to manage to stay on and become a part of the local school.

Two Main Obstacles

The staff from the support unit do, however report of some important obstacles that must be overcome to ensure more lasting results. One of these has to do with the lack of recognition from the mainstream teachers in regarding the staff from 'Nylandet' as a genuine support group. Traditionally schools have had to depend a great deal on their own, without much outside help. There is no culture for mixing different vocational groups and diverse competence in school. The teachers have had the arena much to themselves. Social workers therefore have a hard time being recognized as equal partners in Norwegian schools, although there are now some positive signs of change in this attitude (Klefbeck and Ogden, 1995; Tveit and Ollestad, 1996; Lichtwark and Clifford, 1996; Arnesen and Tveit, 1998,1999; Arnesen et al., 2000).

A second obstacle is the lack of cooperation and opportunities for shared reflection between the professionals from the mainstream school and the separate unit. Time is blamed as the main reason for this condition. Our experience is that lack of time is far from the only reason. The mainstream teachers report that they have little experience from colleague support and reflection amongst themselves. School in Norway has very little tradition for professional colleague guidance. This is far more the case within the social and health care systems.

The school authorities in Bjugn were aware of this problem and therefore supported the introduction of a guidance program in all the schools. This program originates from Great Britain (Ward, 1996, 1998) and has been adapted from a British and milieu oriented context to a Norwegian and school-oriented context (Arnesen, 2000; Tveit, 2001). Ward named his framework 'opportunity-led work' in our Norwegian version we named it 'decision-oriented work'. The method is based on the professional's consciousness towards making decisions in their encounter with young people. In short, this method focuses on the great number of opportunities you meet in your everyday job and how to get into the best position to help the young people, creating opportunities and thus achieving long-term results. So the crux of the matter is the skill of the individual social welfare worker and educator to see and make use of the opportunities at hand. Our experience from working with this method on a broad scale within a number of schools is that it enhances the amount of resources present in the professional community within the different systems and it increases people's faith in own ability and practice (Tveit, 2001).

This was also a side effect in Bjugn but we have too little data to conclude the impact of introducing this method as to level of effect on contributing to better collaboration and professional acceptance between the mainstream teachers and the staff from the separate unit. To implement such a method it has to be followed up by the schools' leadership giving it priority amongst the daily routines. There has to be set off an appropriate amount of time and the guidance sections have to be structured and prepared.

These two main obstacles have to get the attention from everyone it concerns or they will hamper the necessary process of attaining successful inclusion for young residents under care into the mainstream school. Collaboration and understanding between teachers, support staff and residential staff is a crucial issue.

All in all the results from Bjugn and Trondheim should draw more attention to the possibilities than the obstacles. The professionals in both the school and the care system would facilitate the inclusion process if they adapted some of these positive experiences, such as focusing on the importance of highlighting the transition period and a follow trough system similar to the phase model described in this chapter.

Summary

This chapter presents experiences that especially highlight the transition period for a young resident arriving at a new mainstream school.

To support the normalization of young people living in residential care is a key issue. The municipal mainstream school represents a main arena for normalization and inclusion. Traditionally the school system has fallen short in providing adequate competence and sufficient support in fulfilling this task especially in regards to the special needs required for young people from residential care.

The phase model with a three level strategy presented in this paper focuses on the need for a mode of adaptation and a high level of acceptance. Six explicit criteria have been developed to facilitate this transition process

Two main obstacles are underlined by the support staff: 1) The widespread lack of recognition of other vocations than teachers, such as social workers, within the school system; and 2) The low consciousness amongst teachers for the need of mutual reflection and colleague guidance.

Collaboration between teachers, support staff and residential care workers is crucial and in the daily work at school the different professionals must find methods of enhancing reflection and guidance from colleagues.

References

Arnesen, B. (2000), *Hvordan styrke kompetanse gjennom læring av egen praksis?*, Embla 5/2000, s. 36–43.

Arnesen, B. and Tveit, A. (1998), 'Evalueringsrapport', *Tilpasset grunnskoleundervisning for institusjonsbarn i Bjugn kommune*, Rogneby Kompetansesenter.

Arnesen, B. and Tveit, A. (1999), 'Evalueringsrapport', *Tilpasset grunnskole-undervisning for institusjonsungdom i Bjugn kommune*, Trondheim: Midt-Norsk Komptansesenter for Atferd.

Arnesen, B., Jahnsen, H., Nergaard, S., Ollestad, A. and Tveit, A. (2000), *'De umulige' – er det mulig? Grunnskole – og ungdom bosatt i barneverninstitusjoner*, En bok om problematferd og inkludering, Lillegården kompetansesnters skriftserie 2/2000.

Bonesrønning et al. (1999), *Sverresborgprosjektet: Et prosjekt med fokus på å utvikle et skoletilbud for ungdom som bor i ungdomshjem*, Trondheim: Sverresborg skole.

Clifford, G. and Arnesen, B. (1997), *Drømmen om selvstendighet. Ungdom vurderer opphold ved en utredningsinstitusjon drevet av det fylkeskommunale barnevernet*, Arbeidsrapport 3/97, Barnevernets utviklingssenter i Midt-Norge.

Ollestad, A. and Tveit, A. (1996), *Barnevernsbarna – en segregert gruppe i skolen! En undersøkelse om grunnskoletilbudet til barn og unge bosatt i fylkeskommunale barneverninstitusjoner*, Rogneby Kompetansesenter.

Tveit, A. (2001), *Fokus på beslutningsprosessen – presentasjon av en veiledningsmetode*, Norsk Skoleblad 29/2001, s. 24–6.

Tveit, A. and Ollestad, A. (1996), 'Teachers and Residential Care Workers: They Meet and Talk, but do they Cooperate?' (translation of an article published in a Norwegian journal for social- and childcare workers, *Embla* 1/96).

Ward, A. (1996), 'Opportunity-led Work', *Social Work Education*, No. 14, pp. 89–105.

Ward, A. and McMahan, L. (1998), *Intuition is not Enough*, London: Routledge.

Chapter 9

Anti-discriminatory and Anti-oppressive Practice: Working with Ethnic Minority Children in Foster and Residential Care

Toyin Okitikpi

The focus of this chapter is anti-discriminatory and anti-oppressive practice and working with children from ethnic minority backgrounds who are in care. Generally I am interested in the experiences of these children in the care system and in considering the issues that they face. More specifically I am interested in looking at the children's:

- psychological wellbeing; as well as
- their emotional, cultural and educational development.

It is the contention of this chapter that to be able to work effectively with minority children in care there is a need to understand not only the problems they present, but also to recognise the impact of other issues on their lives. For example, the negative views held about minorities in society do affect the children's perception of themselves, their connection to their environment and their sense of belonging. Ultimately this chapter is interested in discussing different ideas that may be useful when working with children from minority backgrounds irrespective of their ethnicity or cultural background.

Introduction

As in other areas there is often a mismatch between how academics and opinion formers define a particular concept and the meaning attached to the same concept by practitioners and lay observers. As Thompson (1998) observed:

> Many writers use the term 'anti-discriminatory practice' in a broad sense to refer to forms of practice that challenge discrimination and oppression, while

others take a lead from Philipson (1992) in drawing a distinction between anti-discriminatory practice and anti-oppressive practice, reserving the former for a narrow, legalistic approach to inequality. (Thompson, 1998, p. 77)

For many people anti-discriminatory and anti-oppressive practices are indistinguishable as they mean the same thing. In other words, both are taken to mean a way of acting and being which does not discriminate unfairly or oppress others, giving everyone a fair chance and being aware of it. Put plainly, it is about having a sense of fairness, treating people equally and treating people as one would expect to be treated oneself. In my view there is clarity in this description of anti-discriminatory and anti-oppressive practice because it is devoid of the contortions that academics, opinion formers and commentators get themselves into in their effort to provide a coherent and precise explanation of the concepts.

At some level attempting to define anti-discriminatory and anti-oppressive practice is fraught with difficulties because one would have to begin by asking problematic questions. It requires, in some cases, ontological shifts and concepts that are characterised by contradictions and paradoxes but at the same time the concept has tangible expressions in its manifestation. In other words anti-discriminatory and anti-oppressive practices can be manifested in people's attitudes and reactions and these in turn can be expressed in the behaviours that are displayed.

However despite the difficulties inherent in trying to define the concepts, I would suggest that at its simplest anti-discriminatory and anti-oppressive practice fosters an approach that challenges preconceptions about a (racially, culturally, gender, sexuality and ethnically) binary world. It is an approach that understands the wider societal discourse of injustices and discrimination and the power imbalances in society. Anti-discriminatory and anti-oppressive practice also recognises the importance of the client worker relationship and the profound effect that dyadic relationship can have on the experiences of minority children in care. Like their majority counterparts, children from ethnic minority backgrounds are taken into care for a variety of reasons; however, their experiences differ from other children because of the additional factors with which they have to contend. For these children the experiences of being a minority in society and the physicality of being away from home may fuel the their sense of isolation, disorientation, dislocation and powerlessness. It is the contention of this article that anti-discriminatory and anti-oppressive practice encourages a reflective and reflexive approach because it both encourages awareness and compels practitioners to challenge the inequalities that exist and to examine not just their practices but also their attitudes and beliefs about others.

In this chapter the term ethnic minority is not used as a euphemism to mean Asian children or children of African Caribbean and African background. Rather it is used to mean children who are of different ethnicity/cultural background compared to the majority population of the country where they live. In my view to use the term ethnic minority exclusively when only referring to Asian children or children of African Caribbean and African background is to ignore the social realities of many children in different European countries.

The Politics of Identification

Throughout Europe there are growing numbers of children whose parents are from a different ethnic and cultural background to the majority population. It is these children that are often classified as children from ethnic minority backgrounds. In essence the term ethnic minority is but a shorthand classification for denoting that the children's origin is of a different ethnic background compared to the indigenous majority population. However the need for such classification is based on an historical legacy that believed in the inherent differences, racially, ethnically and culturally, within the human family. For convenience sake and to justify, in many cases, the treatment of a large number of people, the human race was divided, and in some cases subdivided into a hierarchical structure with Europeans enjoying a favoured position (Jahoda, 1999; Kohn, 1996). However, as has already been made clear since the 1950s, these classifications of the human family into differentiated groups and the subsequent belief in the superiority of one group over another is an arbitrary social construction that has no scientific validity (Tizard and Phoenix, 1993; Okitikpi, 1999). Yet despite the disqualification of such differentiation the *idea* of a hierarchical human race still persists and, in some respect, it shapes the way people view others who are different from themselves. Indeed the importance of this legacy cannot be ignored or underplayed because, generally, it forms the basis upon which people from different countries and different ethnic and cultural groups relate to each other in society.

Understanding the Present

In essence, to understand the impact of the historical legacy on the physical, emotional and psychological well being of the individual is to understand the personal experiences and social realities of ethnic minorities in any society. Ethnic minority children are placed in care, either with foster families or in residential accommodations for many different reasons. Like their majority counter-parts, it could be argued that ethnic minority children also share the same dreams and aspirations about what they would like to happen to them while in care. For example, in many instances, rather than being in residential care they may prefer to be part of a family. Like others they would also like to be loved and supported. In essence they are looking for stability, safety and the sense of security that being in a family implies. If they were in foster care they would still be looking for the same but with more certainty and unconditional acceptance. Of course for many children residential care is not just a fall back position or a second option but in fact the best option. At its best residential care can provide a safe, caring environment that has the child as the focus of all attention. Since the child's presence is their raison d'être, residential units can ensure the child's needs are met and that the child is helped to make sense of his/her life within a safe and protective environment. However, the point of departure between ethnic minority children and children from the indigenous population are the children's uncertainty about their sense of belonging and the views that are held about them and the assumptions that are made about ethnic minorities by 'others' in society. Habermas (1994) suggested that for any social phenomena to have a meaning one has to take account of history and in my view this is an interesting starting point. In addition both Habermas (1994) and Eagleton (1991) further suggest, in their different ways, that the oppression of any particular social or cultural group can only be comprehended in relation to the social totality. In essence Habermas and Eagleton are asserting the centrality of both history and context as a means of understanding the present. In this context, the 'background noises' such as social exclusion and disengagement, political disenfranchisement and racism and the way ethnic minorities are perceived by the majority population cannot be ignored or divorced from any analysis of the experiences of ethnic minority children's lives in care. In other words, the starting point for developing a deeper level of understanding about the lives of children from ethnic minority backgrounds in foster care or residential care, is by taking account of not just their need for stability, although this is important, but by also taking account of the 'background noise' and its effect and impact on the lives of the children.

It's a Question of Integration

In many respects anti-discriminatory practice is not only about providing non-discriminatory services and provisions – it is also, paradoxically, primarily about integration and the means by which minority people, irrespective of their background, can be accepted on equal terms in the society. Integration is about a sense of belonging, unconditional acceptance as a member of society, with the same freedom of movement and access to the same services and provisions that are available to the majority population. However, the term integration and all that it implies is problematic for a number of reasons. At the heart of the term are concerns about what it is to be from a minority background in society and what status is or should be afforded to such groups. Aside from the politics of 'difference' and race there are also other complications that impinge on whether integration is the most appropriate means by which to judge how minorities have settled into the country. But before exploring these complications it worth setting out in brief the fault line of the discussion about the kinds of society that best accommodates minority groups (Okitikpi, 2002). Although the ideas set out below originally emerged from a PhD thesis, (Okitikpi, 2002) that explored the experiences of black and white couples in intimate interracial relationships, nevertheless the basic ideas are also applicable in this case. In essence the fault lines are between:

- *acculturation*, which holds that in an open society it is inevitable there would be a process by which a new racial and cultural identity would be forged by the incoming group. The assumption being that the incoming group would hold on to some of their cultural identity and at the same time they would 'borrow', adapt and adopt other traits, both from the indigenous population but also from other minority groups with whom they share social space;
- *assimilation*, which is about the absorption and incorporation of the minority population into the social and cultural values of the majority population. In this instance the minority are accepted on the condition that they forego their culture, norms and values. This is seen as a fair exchange for living in the host country;
- *integration*, which is seen as a 'melting pot' society characterised by the merging and eventual erosion of racial, cultural and genetic difference. Here there would not be any distinction between different cultural/ethnic groups. It is about combining and adding together different groups to form a 'different' whole. This suggests or gives the impression that the

majority population would not usurp the minority population but instead it would integrate the different social and cultural values in an expansive rather than in a reductive way;

- *multiculturalism*, where advocates of this view accept that a totally integrated racial and cultural society is unlikely to materialise, but they assert that there can be a society that is pluralistic and respectful of the different cultural groups within society. Under the slogan 'equal but different' the emphasis is on a pluralistic society where there is an acceptance and tolerance of racial, cultural and ethnic differences. In essence this approach is not too dissimilar to what Fulcher (2002) describes as 'cultural safety', where the emphasis is on respecting, understanding, appreciating and accepting the range of cultural differences that exists between groups;

- *separatism*, where the advocates of this view assert that the history of minority and majority is characterised by oppression, racism, inequality and discrimination. For minority and majority groups to progress there would need to be a clear separation between them. The idea is that people from the different minority and majority groups would be self-contained in their cultural havens with little or no contact between the groups. The expectation would be that people try and maintain the purity and cultural authenticity of their respective group.

In my view, the relationship between ethnic minority groups and the majority population in most European countries has an element of all of these different positions, though there are of course people from the different groups that encourage a particular position. However I would argue that ultimately the aim of anti-discriminatory and anti-oppressive practice is to provide an environment in which competing groups feel themselves as stakeholders and active members of society with the same rights and obligations as others. Importantly it is about creating an environment where people are able to understand that their advancement or lack of advancement in society is not necessarily because of the presence of others.

From a slightly different angle but with similar intentions Soydan (1998), developed a cultural sensitive social work typology that attempted to make sense of different models of social work practice with ethnic minority clients. The three models identified by Soydan were categorical diversity, transactional diversity and universal diversity (for detailed explanation of the three models see Vincenti in this volume). Although Soydan's typography refers to both social policy and social work, I shall concentrate on the social work aspect.

Briefly, categorical diversity is akin to a universalistic service provision that takes little notice of cultural differences. Rather, the aim is to provide a colour-blind service that focuses on the need of the individual irrespective of their ethnicity. Transactional diversity is not dissimilar to the multicultural approach described earlier, as Vincenti highlighted:

> Cultural groups develop an understanding of their culture when meeting, or encountering other groups. The focus is upon the development and maintenance of the boundaries surrounding a cultural group – thus any process of intervention and treatment must be initiated from the groups own definition of their problem. (Vincenti, 2002, p. 6)

Finally, universal diversity takes account of differences in all its varied forms including; economic position, physical and mental capabilities, age, gender, and religion (Vincenti, 2002). Soydan, like others (Dominelli et al., 2001; Aluffi-Pentini and Lorenz, 1996; Thompson, 2002), is attempting to grapple with the complexities of multi-cultural, multi-ethnic and pluralistic societies and to try and provide both an explanation and an analysis of their configuration and at the same time put forward ideas that would arrest social fragmentation, sense of alienation and social exclusion within and between different members and groupings in society.

Children at the Centre

Working with ethnic minority children is characterised by a complex set of dynamics that are problematic, paradoxical and at times incoherent and inconsistent. As Thompson (2002, p. 1) also observed: 'Social work with children, young people and their families is demanding and challenging work.' There are a number of publications that highlight the experiences of black children in the care system (Barn, 1993; Dominelli, 2002), and others attempt to provide templates on working with black and ethnic minority children in care (Small, 1986; Banks, 1995). While such publications should be welcomed they sometimes present a simplistic and, in my view, uncomplicated discussion about being a minority in a strongly monocultural, mono-ethnic environment. They often present a clear-cut description of the lives of minority children and the problems they encounter. In addition they appear to suggest that the needs of the children are fundamentally different from the needs of the indigenous white children. In my view, while there are indeed differences between ethnic minority children and the majority children, I would also argue that minority children do not live in a vacuum and they too go through similar emotional, psychological and social processes as described by Erikson (1968), Freud (1901) and Bronfenbrenner (1979). Children from minority ethnic backgrounds too are trying to make sense of their world in the midst of a socio-structural context that appears to be both hostile and unconcerned about their needs. Like their majority peers they are also trying to find solutions to such basic questions as 'Who am I?', 'From where do I come?', 'Where do I belong?' and 'What is going to happen to me?'.

In my view these are fundamental questions that all humans are moved to ask irrespective of their gender, racial or ethnic background. In other words these are basic questions that are not exclusive to or just the preserve of the majority children. Ethnic minority children are also caught up in the search for *self*, a sense of identity and stability and fulfilment in an environment that sometimes appears unpredictable and incoherent.

Particularity in Generality

There are as many differences and similarities *within* ethnic minority children as there are *between* ethnic minority children and the majority children. In other words although ethnic minority children may be considered as a group, because of their experiences, it is equally important to recognise that *all* children irrespective of their ethnicity or cultural background share certain peculiarities. For example, the position of children in relation to the adult world, children's levels of dependency, their developmental needs and the social factors that impact on their development are all shared issues. However, as well as recognising the areas children share in common it is also important to particularise each child's experiences. It is often the case that by describing a child as coming from an ethnic minority background one is using the term to signal the need for sensitivity, understanding and a certain degree of self-consciousness. While it is important to acknowledge the child's ethnicity and their cultural background because a great deal would or, indeed, should flow from such identification, it is however not enough to rely on such a limited 'tag'. Such a limited description deprives the child of their cultural fluidity, their familial idiosyncrasies as well as the potential for the development of an emerging self-identity. It is by taking account of all these competing factors, with the paradoxes, fluidity and the uncertainties involved that one could begin to fully understand the needs of children of ethnic minority backgrounds.

Working with Minority Children

In working with children from minority backgrounds I have tried to suggest that there are a number of strands that need to be taken into consideration before any effective work can be embarked upon with them. As highlighted earlier, the children exist within a social context that has a strong opinion about the position of minority groups in society and as a result the children have not only had to come to terms with being in care they have to also live in a society that finds their presence difficult to accept unconditionally. In order to work effectively with minority children I believe there is a need to understand the importance of developing effective *communication*, higher levels of *educational* expectations, encouraging the children's involvement in *extra curricular activities*, connecting the children to their *cultural communities* and an appropriate level of their involvement and *participation* in the planning of their care. To elaborate on each point mentioned:

- *Developing effective communication*. It is widely agreed that communication is an important element in any relationship. Communication is not just about giving and receiving information it is also about ensuring that, in this case, the children's voices and their world is at the centre of all considerations. In other words, communicating with children involves listening to them and helping them to develop the necessary skills that would enable them to get their views, feelings and ideas across. However this has to be approach in a realistic and meaningful way. Over the past few years it has become fashionable in social work and social welfare circles to talk about empowerment, user participation and other 'user friendly' terms. Workers are encouraged to listen to the children, often uncritically, and children are asked to make decisions about aspects of their life that no child should be given the burden to carry. There is often a mistaken belief, in my view, that children should be looked upon as mini adults who, given the all the necessary information and choices would be able to make decisions that would have a profound effect on their lives. It is sometimes forgotten that it is their circumstances that have placed the children in such positions and that if they weren't involved with the welfare system they would have caring parents who would 'involve' them, *sometimes*, in the decision-making processes of the household, but they would not be given the sole responsibility of deciding every aspect of their lives. Many children, in my view, would be happy for adults to make the important decisions that affect their lives, and they would be happy with an 'appropriate' level of consultation. It is important to acknowledge that children's participation in the decision making process should not mean an abdication of adult responsibilities and the acceptance of all that the child demands. Adults have a difficult yet a pivotal role to play in children's lives. The issue, which is worth further consideration, is about trust and the extent to which the child could trust the adults making the decision on their behalf and whether they truly have the children's interest at heart. So, what is being advocated is that communication in this instance is about developing a meaningful relationship with the child that transcends mere verbal exchanges and the passing of information. It requires and indeed demands genuineness, the development of a trusting relationship and at the core is a total concern about the child's wellbeing.

• *Looking to the future: higher level of educational expectation.* It has been the case, certainly in the UK, that children in the public care system fair less well, educationally, in comparison to the rest of the children in the population. More disturbingly children in care are more likely to be homeless, unemployed, in prison and in mental institutions. Education is not only highly valued in most societies, it is also viewed as both a liberator (Okitikpi, 1999) and a means by which people can develop the necessary social capital. Education is the means by which people are able to improve, not just their financial situation, but also their social, psychological and environment conditions. Because education is so importance it is incumbent on those charged with the responsibility of caring for the children to ensure that they too are able to compete in the world of work. It has sometimes been suggested that children in care have a great deal more to worry about than educational achievements and the level of qualifications they are able to obtain. There is an assertion that the children may have experienced emotional and psychological traumas and that the focus should be on helping them to heal the pain. In other instances it has been argued that the children's identity and their cultural backgrounds should outweigh educational considerations. In my view I would suggest that `these assertions are somewhat shortsighted. While it is the case some of the children may indeed need help and support and maybe even specialised therapy, this should not be at the expense of their future prospects. If they have emotional and psychological peace and they have been enabled to develop a well-rounded sense of self all these would count for very little if they are unable to read and write and they leave school with no qualifications. Lack of education and qualifications means the children, in late adolescence and adulthood, would continue to depend, in some form, on the state for their continuing existence.

- *Encouraging the children's involvement in social activities.* There is always the danger of assuming children in care do not have access to a range of extra curricular activities as their peers. However, institutions, particularly residential units, thrive on uniformity and a group focused approach, whilst to some extent an extra curricular activity is about individual aptitude, interests and capabilities. It demands understanding the particular interest or interests of the child and enabling them to either to develop it or pursue it to its ultimate end.
- *Importance of cultural connections.* In Britain, the National Occupational Standards for Child Care at Post-qualifying Level highlighted the need for children to remain not just within their family environment but also within their community network. It further suggests that children and young people should have their identity reaffirmed through the promotion of their religious, cultural, racial and linguistic background. While these are of course very important, in my view, the need to connect the children to their 'cultural community' dominates the way the children are perceived. In other words the children's ethnicity becomes the only point of connection to the children and other aspects of the child's development are ignored. In this instance culture, race, identity and the child's ethnicity is presented and discussed as a fixed and unyielding phenomenon. In reality the child does need to be connected to their cultural community but account also needs to be taken of their social class, their familial background, their aspirations and a recognition and allowance for the child to borrow, change and subvert any aspects of the 'cultural background' they may wish. Too often, in my view, connecting to ones cultural background implies a rigid and total acceptance of what in essence is an already diluted culture that is then presented at the authentic culture. As Kreps and Kunimoto (1994) observed:

> Every individual is composed of a unique combination of different cultural orientations and influences, and every person belongs to many different cultural groups. It is important that we recognise the influences of many cultures on our lives. Based on our heritage and life experiences we each develop our own idiosyncratic identity. (Kreps and Kunimoto, 1994, p. 3)

Conclusion

As I have tried to convey in this chapter, anti-discriminatory practice is not an easy option. It is a difficult, complex and dynamic approach that challenges organisations and practitioners. The expectation is not just about providing a tolerant and understanding environment, though this is very important, it is also about taking account of the views, feelings and experiences of ethnic minority children in care and encouraging an integrative, tolerant and equal opportunity social environment. In addition, issues of justice, fairness, and Human Rights, particularly article 22 of the Rights of the Child, cannot be ignored or sidelined in discussions about anti-discriminatory, anti-oppressive practice.

Although not a child in care, the killing of Benjamin Hermansen, a 15 yearold boy of mixed parentage (Norwegian and Ghanaian extraction), by three white young Norwegians highlights the simmering and growing tension that exists between host country and those they perceive as 'others'. Benjamin's death illustrates the need for an urgent debate about how best to forge a society in which the minority population is experienced as valued and enriching rather than a threat to the culture and identity of the majority population.

References

Aluffi-Pentini, A. and Lorenz, W. (1996), *Anti-Racist Work with Young People: European Experiences and Approaches*, Lyme Regis: Russell House.

Banks, N. (1995), 'Children of Black Mixed Parentage and their Placement Needs', *Fostering and Adoption*, Vol. 19 (2), pp. 19–24, London: BAAF.

Barn, R. (1993), *Black Children in the Public Care System*, London: Batsford.

Bronfenbrenner, U. (1979), *The Ecology of Human Development: Experiment by Nature and Design*, Cambridge, MA: Harvard University Press.

Cheetham, J. and Small, J. (eds) (1986), *Social Work with Black Children and their Families*, London: Batsford.

Dominelli, L. (2002), *Anti-oppressive Social Work Practice*, Basingstoke: Palgrave Macmillan.

Dominelli, L., Lorenz, W. and Soyden, H. (2001), *Beyond Racial Divides: Ethnicities in Social Work Practice*, Aldershot: Ashgate.

Eagleton, T. (1991), *Ideology*, London: Verso.

Erikson, E. (1968), *Identity: Youth and Crisis*, New York: W.W. Norton.

Freud, S. (1901), 'The Psychology of Everyday Life', in J. Strachey (ed) (1953), *The Standard Edition of the Complete Psychological Works of Sigmund Frued*, vol. 6, London: Hogarth Press.

Fulcher, L.C. (2002), 'Cultural Safety in the Delivery of Out of Home Care', paper presented at the 7th EUSARF Congress, Norway.

Habermas, J. (1994). 'The Tasks of a Critical Theory', in *Social Theory, Social Polity*, Cambridge: Blackwell.

Jahoda, G. (1999), *Images of Savages. Ancient Roots of Modern Prejudice in Western Culture*, London: Routledge.

Kohn, M. (1996), *Race Gallery: The Return of Racial Science*, London: Vintage.

Kreps, G.L. and Kunimoto, E.N. (1994), *Effective Communication in Multicultural Health Care Settings*, London: Sage

Okitikpi, T. (1999a), 'Identification of Mixed Race Children', *Issues in Social Work Education*, Vol. 19 (1), pp. 93–106, Sheffield: ATSWE.

Okitikpi, T. (1999b), 'Educational Needs of Black Children in the Care System', in R. Barn (ed.), *Working with Black Children and Adolescents in Need*, London: BAAF.

Okitikpi, T. (2002), 'Managing Intimate Interracial Relationship', PhD thesis.

Small, J. (1986), 'Transracial Placement: Conflict and Contradiction', in S, Ahmed, J. Chetham and J. Small (eds), *Social Work with Black Children and their Families*, London: Batsford.

Soydan, H. (1995), 'A Cross-cultural Comparison of How Social Workers in Sweden and England Assess a Migrant Family', *Scandinavian Journal of Social Welfare*, Vol. 4 (2), (April) Munksgaard Kobenhavn.

Tizard, B. and Phoenix, A. (1993), *Black, White or Mixed Race*, London: Sage.

Thompson, N. (2002), *Building the Future. Social Work with Children, Young People and their Families*, Dorset: RHP.

Thompson, N. (1998), *Promoting Equality. Challenging Discrimination and Oppression in the Human Services*, London: Macmillan.

Vincenti, G. (2002), 'Social Work Models and Methods when Interacting with Ethnic Minority Children Place within Residential Care, with reference to a Danish Context', paper presented at the 7th EUSARF Congress, Norway.

Chapter 10

Children's Needs for Self-expressive Play (with the 'Forgotten Group' as a Special Case), Presented as an Important Issue for Residential Care

Brian Ashley

Introduction

Earlier papers by the author have argued the need for better provision for children's self-expressive play. Regardless of continued advocacy from many sources, policy makers place very low priority on this need. The present chapter attempts to collate the long-standing evidence. The author has also previously highlighted the special needs of the developmental stage of pre- and early adolescence, which he has designated the 'Forgotten Group' because his comparative studies have shown this stage to be generally neglected in such provision throughout the world. This chapter presents this case for important consideration also within the field of residential care. The chapter also assumes that the role of the adult in children's play is to respond to the initiatives of the child and suggests the following essential principles which adults need to understand in order to provide appropriate support to children's play in the home and the community and institutions.

Principle 1: that all children and youth need space and time to develop self-directed play independently of the control of adults – even parents/parent substitutes or teachers.

Principle 2: that play in the way it is defined in Principle 1 must be differentiated from play as it is otherwise generally understood and used in the educational world.

Principle 3: that the role for adults such as parents, teachers and community workers in children's free play could be to create the external conditions around children and youth which are necessary to give them this opportunity for self-directed expression in play and leisure and for self-directed learning.

Principle 4: that, due to institutional and social trends, the pre-adolescent stage of the 'Forgotten Group' presents special needs which are largely neglected in such provision.

The author believes that these principles may present a significant and special problem for residential care. The underlying question is whether policy makers consider sufficiently the special need to apply these principles within residential care. The implication is that this question should be given special emphasis in the design, management and the programmes of residential care and in the selection and training of residential care workers.

The Child's Need for Space and Time for Free Play

A Clarifying Definition of 'Free Play'

Over ten years ago at the IPA International Congress in Tokyo the author chaired a session of over 100 expertsfrom all over the world on children's play. Their discussion was directed to find the best definition of play to give the most scope for the full development of the child. They decided that it should be 'activity freely chosen by the child itself to meet needs which arise from within the child itself and directed towards goals chosen by the child itself'.

Children need space to pursue their own goals as well as engaging in activities which are created for or imposed upon the child from outside itself. Play within spaces or programmes devised by adults or institutions, does not necessarily satisfy the inner real needs of children. Play used to meet goals decided from outside the child, for instance in childcare or education or sport, even if with the best interests of the child in mind, was considered by these experts as a more limited interpretation which, if overemphasized, can risk the full or widest potential of play for the child.

Adult Planners and Decison-makers Need to Understand the Child's Perception

Adults planning for or making decisions about children's space, need to understand this essential requirement for children to have some space and time where they can initiate and control the usage themselves. Adults require to learn to understand and cherish the true hidden meaning of the activity for the 'player' or 'user', rather than to concentrate upon the superficial understanding they derive from observing the activity itself. The precise nature of children's play or free use of space is rarely understood. It is often assumed by the adult observer to be the external appearance of that activity, whereas to the child 'player' the activity may be something much different and have an essential nature only appreciated internally by the 'player'.

Fantasy is an Important Developmental Process in the Child's Management of 'Reality'

Maybe the play activity has no 'meaning' in the adult sense, but is an ephemeral phase or tool of an inner developmental process for the child which will never be 'realized' in the outside world. The hidden internal processes are first concretized into the reality as understood by the child and only gradually, if at all, into that reality as seen by the adult. If adults react and intervene too quickly from their view of reality they can inhibit the social developmental process of self-management of reality by the child It is this development of self-management of reality which prepares a child for social change and develops the capacity to cope with a continually changing reality. Children need to learn to cope with the reality in a society which is changing too rapidly for most adults to assimilate. This is the most disqualifying aspect of the role of the adult as interventionist in children's play. In many cases the reality of the child is likely to be nearer the future real situation they have to learn to cope with, than the known experience and less adaptable time-fixed reality of the adult. Even the process of studying the activity (and certainly the describing and recording of it, as in research which tries to 'understand') most likely distorts the goal for the child. This concentration by adults upon the activity itself could be detrimental to the attainment of the inner meaning for the 'player'.

Theory and Research Emphasize the Need of Children to Control their own Space

Child development theories have long maintained that child-initiated and child-controlled use of both physical space and space in time is not only beneficial but, indeed essential, for the mental and social development of the child . Increasing population growth in some parts of the world and increasing urbanization in the whole of the world, is steadily diminishing the availability to the child of natural or unplanned free spaces. This results in restricting the space available for children to space which is planned by adults. At its best, this provides them with limited opportunities to use spaces which are designated for them for purposes or activities decided upon or controlled by adults. At its worst it limits them to finding space for themselves in a society planned by adults largely for their own adult perceived needs.

Children's Need to Express Themselves Requires Trust from Adults

Freedom of the child 'player' to express and develop needs and interests which emerge from within the child itself, requires adult trust in the capacity of children to make decisions. It requires trust in minimalizing the need of the adult to intervene or control the process. Adults generally, even those who work professionally with children in child-care and education, have great difficulty in accepting that children have the capacity to make responsible decisions for themselves although some research evidence would suggest otherwise.[1] Children's need for self-expression is restricted by the intervention, direction and control of adults. Adults, through superimposing their view of the needs of children and their adult interpretation of children's use of space, distort the provision for and use of space by children and deny them the usage which children themselves need and want.[2]

Summarizing this General Case

Children require but, in modern urban society, do not get, adequate physical space and space in time to express their own intrinsic needs.[3] Unfortunately it is adults, who have the responsibility to ensure that children have that opportunity but who often are the greatest obstacle to children's achievement of that opportunity.[4] Parents if they used their great opportunities in time and contact, especially in the child's earliest years, could counteract this tendency. Unfortunately they often lack the confidence to challenge the power and influence of the professional view that the important developmental process is that which takes place within educational institutions. In face of such weighty opinion parents feel themselves deskilled and they become brainwashed to support the professional views and to subscribe to the same aims and methods.[5] It may be necessary for residential care to assess the implications of comparing this description of the attitudes and responses of parents with those of residential workers in the caring role of substitute parents.

The Case for a Support System for the Modern Family

The Disappearance of Informal Support Systems in the Modern Community

Socio-ethnological researchers have, for a long time, emphasized the importance of the social context in understanding the different social needs arising within different and changing cultures and the requirement for professional agents to respond with a cultural awareness. The deskilling of parents is part of the influence of social change. The increasing spread of large-scale urbanization is removing the institution of the traditional extended family where there was no strict boundary between a family unit and the surrounding social system which continued to be a support and relationship resource. Children had close relationships with children from other families within the wider social system. Children were encouraged to develop within a child culture in which they learned from each other with a minimum of adult interference or supervision. This traditional family is being rapidly replaced by the so-called nuclear family which is established often far from family and friends. This small unit is separated from the wider social system. and becomes inward-orientated. It is difficult for wider social networks to develop and the modern unit lacks the informal support and advice available in the traditional system. Current research suggests that, as a result, most parents in society today require support in developing their parenthood on a firm basis. This need is not confined to parents with problems or in difficulty. The support which is required is to meet the uncertainties and questions of normal everyday life. This kind of support is not readily available in the complex and swiftly changing society of today. The absence of such support can lead quite easily to the development of problems which are costly to society. The provision of such a simple support system, readily available to all and easily accessible from the home, could prevent such problems occurring and therefore save society those future costs.

The Importance of Brain Stimulation in the Earliest Years of Childhood

Further research, which maps electronically the neurological development of the brain from or even before birth, clearly demonstrates the importance of stimulative social activities between mother/mother substitute and child to create in the brain the neurological network necessary to receive learning and to facilitate new learning. If this network is not stimulated from the earliest age then the child is less able to receive and respond to future learning experiences.

The development of this brain network is not a simple physiological process but is dependent on continued appropriate stimulus within these close inter-personal relationships in infancy. The important basis for such relationships between mother/substitute and child is free self-expressive play where child and mother reciprocate. If appropriate stimulation is delayed, then the undeveloped network hinders learning capacity long into later years and it is increasingly difficult to repair the deficiency. This explains why children, who, for reasons of family, cultural or environmental deficiency, do not respond at the expected level to institutional learning, can rarely be helped by institutions to reach the normal level of response. Even compensatory programmes using special additional resources within institutional learning have not succeeded in repairing the deficiency. It is particularly difficult for institutions to offer the individual stimulus within the close inter-personal relationships necessary for such reparation. Programmes have increasingly had to be orientated outside the institutions and to emphasize family support programmes from the earliest age.[6] This indicates the need for the residential care institution in the role of parent-substitute also to give special attention to this need for individualized and close inter-personal support to children. The residential institution with relatively high staff/child ratios and with much time for close personal adult/child contact could consciously create supportive programmes designed to facilitate and stimulater self-expressive learning. Through such conscious awareness of the limitations of other institutions in remedying earlier deficiencies and lack of stimulation, the residential institution could make a significant contribution in redressing the balance for children who have suffered these lacks.

The Significance for Early Learning of Mother/Child Relations and Experience in the Home

Recent educational and early years learning research, has established the amount and importance of the early learning accomplished within the normal family and home. Measurement of the capacity of the child to understand the basic precepts which are necessary for developing institutional learning shows that most of these are already learned at an early age within the home and family and that the normal child brings this capacity with it when beginning institutional learning. Comparing the extent of this capacity with the comparatively short period of time taken to achieve it, leads experts to the conclusion that this process of home learning is the most effective learning process offered by modern society at any age or stage of development. The judgement of researchers is that the effectiveness of this home learning is due to the fact that it is largely child-initiated within a personal relationship and context familiar to the child and which the child can influence. It also differentiates itself from institutional learning in that it is based upon questions which emerge from the child, arising out of the reciprocal play-learning process, rather than, as in institutional learning, questions being prompted by the adult within adult-initiated activities. Sometimes the presentation of this argument for supported home learning is seen as an attack on institutional care and education and an attempt to preserve the mother in a dependent home-centred situation. Far from being so, it can be presented as an essential preparatory and complementary process to increase the preparedness of the child for the institutional process and therefore making it more likely that the child will achieve its full potential in that process. It also increases the awareness of the mother/substitute of the importance of her role in her relation with the child in the home and, therefore builds up parental self-confidence and self-esteem.The lack of these two qualities in the parental/substitute role has been shown to underlie most problems of early care in the family and of child abuse. Creating this awareness and developing these qualities should therefore be an important goal of the preparation and training of all staff in residential care.

The Need for Continually Available Non-specialist Support

This evidence of the importance of the role of an active and aware parent/ substitute role in the home early learning process provides the argument for an adequate family support system to be developed to work with the parent and child from birth. Many young parents lack the awareness, capacity and confidence to develop the home learning process. Support to develop this capacity at this stage is likely to be more effective and less costly than to wait for the problems to emerge within the educational institutions and then try to take remedial action. Of course it will be argued that many countries already have an excellent system of prenatal care and of advice and support for parents of newborn children. The tendency, however, is for such advice and support to concentrate upon health and physical care and for it to reduce in extent gradually during the child's first year and later to be more orientated to problems which emerge rather than upon on-going readily available support. The early learning research points to a need for support which is less specialized than these existing support health services. It requires a support service which helps all families with the important home early learning function. This support needs to be available near the home and easily accessible to all families. It needs to accept parents as they are and not attempt to direct or control them. It must be responsive to family initiated questions It, therefore, requires to be able to offer the same kind of professional help and knowledge to the parents/substitutes as the help which high quality home early learning experiences offer to children. Parents need to be helped to experience and discover within a process similar to that which they need to offer their children. Because the help or training is being offered to parents and not children, it requires an expertise in facilitating adults as equals in the process of learning how to help their children's development. The training process has to use understanding of group dynamics in helping adults to learn to help each other. All training for residential care staff and all consultative help to such staff in their work roles, should be based on this same process and expertise.

The Application to Residential Care

The implications of this importance of parent and family support and engagement in the early development and informal education of the child, has, in the case of children in residential care, to be equally assumed by the residential institution itself and added to the responsibility for primary care The question arises as to whether residential care does not also suffer from some of the deficiencies ascribed above to health and physical care services in over-concentrating upon physical well-being. This additional home learning task within self-expressive play relationships, for many staff within residential care, may reveal similar needs to those of young parents coming to parent-support centres. The author's research with such parents shows that they attend as much for their own needs of social contact with other adults as for the needs of their children to play with other children. Strong evidence of this need of the adults to meet and support each other in learning their home supportive role is shown by the fact that an increasing proportion of those who attend parent support centres are parents with very young, even newly born children. These parents are obviously not coming for direct help to their children but rather for their own needs as parents. Many support centres have started special 'baby cafes' for this need group. In such meeting places advantage can be taken of the young parents' eagerness to learn about their new babies. They are the obvious group to be provided with knowledge about the advantage of 'early learning' for their children and supported to develop their own capacity to help their children. They can be helped to facilitate the self-expressive play of their children and to observe and learn from that expression, so that they can provide wider opportunities for the child to explore further. Their increased self-esteem and confidence in this parental role can then enable them to provide the essential basis and support for the future self-confidence and independence of their children. By learning the importance of self- expressive play and its results in infancy, they can prepare themselves for ensuring that their child continues to get the opportunity in space and time for such self-expression in its future life. Even when the child enters and becomes engaged in the institutional process which tends to neglect such opportunities. Parents who have been helped to be aware of the importance of these self-expressive opportunities can, in the future, present a challenge to institutions to change their practice towards more self-expressive learning for children. Training and staff development of residential staff, should anticipate similar needs in such staff as these discerned in development of parental support.

The Case for Planning, Design and Provision of Space for Self-expressive Play to be Age-differentiated

Designs are Orientated to Children's Needs as Understood by Adults

It is unfortunate that designers of space for children seem to be most successful when designing for a structured process or goal which they can understand as adults. Thus they are very successful in designing space and equipment for indoor educational activities in childcare institutions and schools – especially for younger children who follow, without question, the latent direction of the adult responsible for the design. A similar aim by adult designers to provide structures or spaces for a manifest activity or for needs as understood by adults, has tended to dominate the design of outdoor space and equipment for children.

In most modern societies it is the youngest age-group of children which receives the most attention in the provision of designated public outdoor play space, through the provision of yard play spaces. These small spaces are usually given high priority in community planning and are assumed to meet the needs of children. Yet research has long indicated that the limitation of space and the lack of variety of experience provided by their design and equipment means that they appeal only to the youngest age-group with limited capacity for movement and who have, as yet, little experience of the use of space.

Structure Reduces Free Expression

Structure and equipment aimed at stimulating particular play activity recognisable as such by the adult designer, tends to restrict the user possibilities to those which prompted the design. Lindholm's research in Sweden showed that children find this self-fulfilling and circular process boring and restrictive. Occasionally they overcome the boredom temporarily by distorting the use of the structure or design towards their own needs and to uses which have been unplanned and unforeseen by the designer. It is this ingenuity and need to manipulate the environment, which the designer should provide for. This need to manipulate their environment has been demonstrated by other researchers who have suggested that children to do not play 'in' or 'on' spaces but more 'with' spaces. Titman in her English studies suggested that children need to 'relate to' a space and this is easier for them to do with natural facilities than with artificial structures. Designers and planners even though they often understand children's needs for creation, invention and challenge have not discovered how to provide for them without structuring their choices. The requirements of adult society for such community spaces to accord with their need for tidiness, order and structure are also a constraint upon design (see note 3). But nearly 50 years ago the pioneers of Emdrup adventure playground in Copenhagen and Lollard Street Adventure Playground in London did not allow themselves to be inhibited by such constraints.[7] The challenge to professionals in our modern goal-oriented society and planning process is to discover how to design and protect space for a child-directed expressive process which does not have, in adult terms, a recognisable 'meaning' or manifest goal. Unfortunately, in studying or making provision for children's use of space, all adults tend to take ready-made models or measures from adult experience or 'meaning' into and impose them upon the child's world. Again there is opportunity for the residential institution with the special advantages of time to give attention to these needs of children to design, create and use freely, their own spaces.

Adults Working with Children's Play Need Special Training

The evidence is that adults generally, even those who work professionally with children, have great difficulty in accepting that children have the capacity to make responsible decisions for themselves, although some research evidence would suggest otherwise, particularly as children move up in age and development stages (see note 1). This suggests that a more age-differentiated approach is required for the planning for use of space by children. Simply to provide a space and designate it for use by children generically, as if they were a homogeneous need-group, is not sufficient. Different space and provision is required for different developmental stages. There is also a need for provision of adults whose main role, rather than directing the activity, is to preserve those spaces for children's own use, as defined earlier. These adults need to be differently trained to adapt to the role of facilitator and supporter of children's own interests rather than that of teacher or leader or animator working towards adult imposed goals. Such a policy would result in giving all children, even up into the adolescent ages, chances to develop and express their own age- or development-related interests within spaces provided for them.

Childcare and Educational Institutions tend to Restrict Self-expression

As the small child grows and develops capacity for and need of more movement and self-directed experience, it reaches the age of entry to the child care institution and its use of both space and time becomes increasingly adult directed and controlled. Play, though given attention in the programme, is seen as a tool towards the goals of the institution, rather than meeting the inner needs of the child. Freedom for free self-expresssion is gradually more limited within the institution and increasingly directed towards time outside the institution – either in the home or in the local environment. But now, for the growing child, these self-expressive needs are more difficult to meet in the home because they encroach upon the needs of others. In residential care, which for some children replaces the home, it may be that this encroachment upon the needs of others is even more likely and, therefore, the need for private space and time even more significant.

These institutional restrictions on self-expression increase as the child enters and moves through school. At the same time the tension between the adult-directed process and the needs for self-expression increases, especially as the child is moving into that developmental stage of pre-adolescence when there is an increasing need to develop independence from adults in general. It is these special needs of this developmental stage to which this chapter draws attention. The terms 'stage' or 'group' are used because the special needs arise from the physical, psychological, and social tasks which children have to solve for themselves, immediately prior to, or during the early stages of adolescence. Experience and research shows that with each generation these tasks have moved gradually down the age scale and that the developmental tasks are not related to homogeneous age groups but that children move into, through and out of the stage at different ages and at different rates. They, therefore, present an almost insoluble problem for institutions like schools or for other services which are organized on a homogeneous age-related basis. This tension is repeated in the family where there is often conflict between the increasing self-expressive needs of the child and the needs of others in the home. Outside the home the child's growing need for independence and greater capacity for movement widens the child's possible area of use of the local environment but rarely gives them access to any more planned provision of space. This lack of suitable space for them and their interests in the local area poses a problem of supervision for parents who often must institute a restriction upon the movement of the children which is exactly contrary to their strongly emerging needs for independence.

Most governments concentrate scarce resources upon the homogeneous processes within age-related institutions. They give decreasing attention to any leisure-time provision outside the institutions for the older children (see note 3). There is need to have increasing concern about the lack of support for this group at this time.

Modern Social Trends Create Need for Special Attention to the Stage of the 'Forgotten Group'

Modern Children are Isolated from the Community

Certain trends in modern society leave this group ill-prepared for the independence which they seek. The small nuclear family does not provide the links with and introduction to, the wider community which were possible in the traditional neighbourhood. Children are socialized in intensive close relationships within the small egocentric family unit and, due to lack of free and open contact of the unit with others in the community, the children are isolated from the wider social system. Any contacts they do have with adults are selective and arranged and not part of a continuing everyday social context. They get no experience of seeing how different social and economic roles function or of how different generations relate to each other in the community. They have no opportunity of learning how to handle wider relationships or of developing increasing social competence and independence within the community. In cities today this trend is compounded by adult fears of the danger to children in the complex of strangers in the wider community. It is clear that there is a risk that residential care institutions, because of their nature, may insulate children from the community even more than the ordinary family home.

Institutional Socialization Increases this Isolation

Increasingly socialization of children takes place within institutions. These institutions can be seen to continue the process of adult supervision and direction and of isolating the child from the wider social system. These institutions provide a uniform pedagogic programme which takes little account of local community or culture Social experience is largely confined to a caring process controlled and supervised by a special group of adults, usually women, who manage the environment to emphasize the relationships of children within homogeneous groups of other children. Conflict and differences are suppressed in order to maintain harmony (see note 2). Children are even more isolated than in the family from the wider social system and real life learning experiences.

This process of isolation and separation from learning within the community and the consequent lack of preparation for independence of adult control and supervision continues within the school. Here the process becomes more institutional and more controlling. Institutions for younger children being care-orientated are, at least, child-centred. Schools, having an educational or instrumental goal orientated outside of the child itself, become increasingly programme-centred. Because the units or classes are larger the process becomes more structured and adult-directed. Pressure to concentrate upon programme and goal lead to an increased emphasis upon learning and experience within the institution and to a continued isolation from the community.

Tension Increases between Adults and the 'Forgotten Group'

It is precisely at the stage of the 'Forgotten Group' that the tension between the process within the school and the developmental needs of the pupils becomes unavoidable. Until this stage children have been largely concerned with the concrete and practical manifestations of learning. When only interested in the 'what' of learning, the superior experience of the adult makes direction and obedience to adult rules tolerable or even to be welcomed. But now in this developmental stage children also develop the capacity for abstract thought and become interested in the 'why'. Children at this stage need to test and prove for themselves and make their own decisions. Adult experience and direction and rules are part of the world to be questioned. Children who have reached this stage of beginning to prove and test have difficulty in accepting, without question, adult control and intervention in their decisions. Adult directed and goal-oriented institutions, like schools, show depressing lack of evidence that they realize and accept the need of children for self-expressive space. Even if they do see the need it is almost impossible to cope with such individual needs within the structured system. The programme cannot be individually questioned. There is no time or space in the institution for individual reactions or problems arising from social or emotional difficulties or experiences. The children are, therefore, left to resolve such needs outside the institution in their own time. But many families find that the home cannot provide for them either, especially as the questioning of adult authority and intervention applies equally to parents. Even the most sympathetic parents are often seen as intervening adults who lack understanding.

Research Shows that Risk Factors Emerge and Increase at the Stage of the 'Forgotten Group'

The problem caused by increasing need for independence is heightened by the fact that, at no time in their socialization to this point, have these young people been prepared for independence and making their own decisions within the community. They have, as has been shown, been isolated from that community. Evidence all over the world shows that it is in this developmental stage that the first signs of behavioural problems begin to manifest themselves. Yet study of provided space in different parts of the world (see note 3) reveals that it is precisely at this stage that there is the most significant lack of suitable provision. Outside the home there is still no planned provision of space for this transitional stage between controlled and supervised childhood and the relative freedom and autonomy of older youth. The free-ranging of these children seeking opportunities to test and prove their social development without adult control, places strain on neighbourhoods planned by adults for the needs of themselves and their families.

Lacking Opportunity for Independence the 'Forgotten Group' orientate Themselves to Social Relations within their Group

Experience shows that in this developmental stage and faced with this dilemma the 'Forgotten Group' turn to each other in their developmental need for support in their experiential learning. Boys seek themselves to groups of other boys of similar background and experience. Girls tend to develop 'best friend' relationships. Research shows that the 'Forgotten Group' pursue activities in order to cement the group or friend relationships. They are more interested in their social existence with their friends in the group than in the activity itself. Children who are slower in developing or have difficulty in making contacts can lack these supportive relationships from their own age group. They may withdraw and become isolates or develop other maladjustments such as seeking status by trying to dominate or bullying children in a lower developmental stage. The increase in 'bullying' or 'mobbing' may be one aspect of the lack of socially meaningful or supportive relationships. The kinds of activity chosen by the 'Forgotten Group' depend on the main factors of educational background and opportunity and resources. Those of good educational ability who are succeeding in school tend to find socially acceptable group pursuits, often of an intellectual nature, whilst those who are not succeeding in school often find socially unacceptable or even delinquent pursuits. In both these main groups there are those who are in a social and economic situation which permit them to find suitable space, for instance, in private homes, for the group to meet and there are those whose social and economic situation forces them out into the community where lack of their own space brings them into conflict with the authorities. Staff in residential homes need to be especially aware of the advantages and disadvantages of group memberships in this developmental stage. The very processes which staff may see as advantageous in managing children by dealing with them in homogeneous groups, may contain the risks of very detrimental effects on the personal and individual development of some children.

The 'Forgotten Group' are Exposed to High Social Risk

It is clear that the 'Forgotten Group' is in a high risk situation. The 'Forgotten Group' has the most available unsupervised free time for the consumption of media. All mass media research shows that the most harmful effects of the questionable aspects of the 'normal' media – such as violence – are when children view without the opportunity to 'test out' or discuss reactions with a mediating adult. The social and developmental tasks of the group, in particular their need to come to terms with their sexuality, make these aspects of the adult world, as illustrated in the media, particularly interesting. Pornography and other 'forbidden' viewing has an exciting element of risk especially as a group or friendship experience. Indulging in such 'forbidden' experiences can be an introduction to even more dangerous experimentation such as misuse or anti-authority behaviour.

Those members of the 'Forgotten Group' from lower social and economic groups will be more prone to attract attention and to be penalized as anti-social or delinquent due to the fact that they are forced to seek public places for their activity. But there is no reason to think that similar behaviour is not found amongst those who have the circumstances to hide their behaviour from direct public notice. Unfortunately it is the case that most decision-makers who control the provision of public space, usually have the private resources to provide private space for their own children and, therefore, do not understand the need in public provision to provide private space for children without such private resources (see note 4).

Provision of Space and Time Worldwide Inadequately Recognizes this Need for Independence and Self-expression

But it is at this developmental stage that public provision for space for free expression becomes most vital. The tension between the needs of children for self-expression and the limitations upon the availability of appropriate space can no longer be concealed and in the case of many children can no longer be coped with. Experience shows that staffed open playgrounds and open centres, within a neighbourhood catchment area, which is large enough to allow for the greater freedom of movement outside the home, but not so large as to threaten the young people with anonymity, are the best form of provision for this developmental stage. Such open and unstructured spaces have the special advantage that they are not age specific and can take in children in this stage of development together with children from the earlier stage who have more difficulty than the rest in coping with the limitations upon freedom. The open and unstructured nature of such provision gives children the opportunity to experiment and seek their own solutions – even to fail and try again. The lack of structured activities suits the group dependency of the 'Forgotten Group' because they are not orientated to activities which select out participants in terms of individual skill or ability but allow uses based on social relationships or group participation. Experience shows that boys like building their own group meeting places and developing group rituals and programmes based upon these meeting points. Girls like opportunities to create their own special 'areas' where they can experiment with colour and design and wish to have 'their own' animals to take care of and relate to.[7]

The Provision of Space for Unstructured Uses by Children is not easy for Adult Society to Tolerate

These spaces, if they are provided, challenge the need of the adult society for order and control. Therefore, as has already been suggested, there is an absolute necessity for an associated provision of adult workers who see their role as to preserve the independence and lack of structure of the spaces and who allow the children to develop their own uses. But more importantly these workers are needed to be readily 'available' for children when needed.[8] Research indicates that children at this stage, while seeking to break away from the constraints of family and institutions, still show the need for access to understanding and supportive adults who are prepared to facilitate their opportunities without determining their choice.

Working with children in this stage of striving for independence in these unstructured situations and being available to provide support to children when they need it and on their terms, makes special demands on the adults who need special training to help them to facilitate and cope with the self-expression of the children. This special training would also seem to be a self-evident requirement in the preparation of staff in residential institutions where children in this stage of development are cared for. The nature of their earlier history and experience is most likely to mean that these children have a particular need for understanding support in coping with these questions.

The 'Forgotten Group' Seeking Independence Pose a Threat to Adults Needs to Control

One possible reason there is no provision for the 'Forgotten Group' may be because of this challenge to adult society to make a form of provision which it does not understand and does not like. Adult society fears children who are experimenting in challenging behaviour. Adults find it difficult to accept the behaviour rather than directing and controlling it. Theory requires that, to encourage and support children's free play, people should be able to work with them less as teachers or leaders or animators in activities which adults regard as important, and more as facilitators who support the emergence of children's self expression. But research shows that people who are attracted to play work and other work with children are themselves people who like to be involved in activity and who tend to focus on the activity in itself as important. They often measure their own competence and improvement in their own performance in terms of ability in the activity. Additionally it has been shown that it is often the view of children as immature, malleable and in need of support, which attracts people to work with them. Those who feel most successful in the work with children, including parents, are those who find it easiest to develop the skills which children themselves aspire to or admire. All of these reasons make it difficult for adults to relinquish the role of exemplar or model or initiator and to adopt a non-interventionist role in the process. Their very success in the manifest activities makes it even more difficult for them to accept that their own prowess may be obscuring even greater potential in the children.[8]

Adult Advocacy for Play Provision Fails due to Misunderstanding of the Real Need

Adult intervention betrays and denies the need of children for self-expression in a variety of ways. The first is the failure of advocates for children's free use of space to describe, in a form which adult policy and decision-makers can accept and approve, the developmental qualities which can be achieved by children through the opportunity for free play or use of space. Child research has shown that the capacity for imagination, to explore, discover and to invent, to develop independence, initiative and responsibility and to manage and adapt to change, can all be discovered and developed in free play. These are qualities which decision-makers in politics, industry and commerce repeatedly say that the adult world requires, especially in the future. Why then has it not been possible to persuade adult society to provide for a self-expressive use of space which could develop them?

The failure is partly due to adults, in their role of advocates for space for children, themselves concentrating upon advocating for a structured programme or for the outward activity, rather than trying to uncover and demonstrate the underlying intrinsic benefits for children. Therefore the space opportunities which are at present provided as a result of their advocacy, are often still not the kind which permit the self-expression which develops the qualities just described. Workers with children themselves, have, as adults, difficulty in accepting the capacities of children to decide for themselves and therefore, in giving them real opportunities for self-expression. There may be good reasons, including a concern for safety, why the adult is reluctant to relinquish control over the activity. But even here research has shown that adults are often unnecessarily protective and that understanding preparation and training of children however small, can permit them to engage in many so-called dangerous activities (see note 5). Such research suggests that adults often use such protective reasons to excuse their own need to intervene in and control children's play. There are also other more questionable reasons, such as the adult's own need to be recognized as important. Or the acquiescence by the adult of the system's requirement to have conformity and to control behaviour, in order to avoid problems. These tendencies are also supported by the attitudes of adults as parents who, though concerned for their children, are often more ready to accept the definition by adult society, especially that of decision-makers and experts in work with children, as to what is best for them, rather than to listen to and encourage the children's own expression of need (see note 5).

Suitable Neighbourhood Spaces are Already Available if their Purpose was Redefined

A New View of a Well-established Community Resource

Decision-makers often excuse lack of provision of free space for the 'Forgotten Group' on lack of resources (see note 3). But in every neighbourhood there already exist public spaces which could be used in this way without any significant extra provision of space by the community – namely playgrounds in schools or institutions. Until recently, these spaces have been controlled and dominated by the institutions to which they are attached. School playgrounds have been seen as unrelated to the main purpose of education and only an ancillary facility for the spare time use of children. They have been given a low priority within the planning and allocation of resources. All over the world their design and appearance tells a great deal about the attitudes of adult society to spaces where only children spend their time. Yet research on children's use of such spaces supports the thesis of this chapter. Forsberg's research on Swedish school playgrounds showed that children, even in such inadequate planned spaces, pursue their own interests and develop qualities which adult society would regard as admirable. Investigations have shown that where such spaces are improved in design and facilities, especially if the children are consulted and can influence the provision, the attitudes of children to the whole school are also improved. Gradually this awareness is being spread by new movements[9] and is having some effect upon the improvement and development of the school playground.

The Playgrounds of Schools and Institutions could be Community Spaces

Some experts, including the author of this chapter, have suggested that the space at present described as the school playground could be redefined. Instead it could become an independent neighbourhood space for children administered for their needs and supervised by workers who facilitate the uses decided upon and controlled by children. This space could also still be used by the school for the free interests of children in their own time but, because the design of the space could be planned in consultation with children and administered for them, it would not be dominated and restricted by the school's other purposes as at present. Children's natural interests in exploration, experiment and discovery and the need to express these and other interests would almost certainly mean that the space designed in this way could, amongst other aims, support the educational interests of the school. But these educational interests in this domain of children would not be allowed to be superordinate to the self-expressive needs of children. These spaces would be design-related to the ages of the children normally attending the institution or school with which they were associated. Because school provision is usually planned to relate to suitable age-related catchment neighbourhoods these spaces would, therefore, fulfil the need to have age-related free space for children in each local community. A fundamental difference from the present system would be that these independent neighbourhood spaces would not be controlled by the school or restricted by school opening times and timetables but, with supportive workers in attendance, could be freely open to access for local children at all times. An added but crucial advantage of this answer to the provision of space would be that the needs of children with handicap to also play and to have use of free space could be met in these same spaces. In the restricted availability of space to children, these particular children are more disadvantaged than most. Of the spaces provided for children, very few, at present, are designed to facilitate use by children with handicap. It has been demonstrated[10] that children with handicap can play with other children if the space is designed to enable their participation. Increasingly it is the policy to integrate children with handicap within the normal school. So if the school playground became a neighbourhood play space designed for the needs of children associated with a particular neighbourhood school it could also be designed to facilitate the play of children with handicap attending that school. One of the findings of the author in developing play facilities, adjusted to the needs of those with handicap, was the importance to plan for the supportive adults, like parents and assistants, who accompany the children with handicap if they are to have a chance to play. These accompanying adults need to find the play space comfortable and pleasant for them, for example with sheltered sitting places with a grill and simple catering facilities, so that they stay and give the children ample time to use the play space. Otherwise the uncomfortable adult restricts the child's time, however enjoyable. This was an important finding which should be applied to all neighbourhood play spaces. All these questions need to be answered in how space is provided, used and controlled in residential care.

Playgrounds of Schools and Institutions could be Administered as Neighbourhood Spaces for Local Participation in Democracy and Community Development

If these neighbourhood play spaces are pleasant for adults to visit then they may create the opportunity, which is lacking in nearly every modern neighbourhood, for natural relationships to develop between adults and children, in a context of free choice.This blend of relationships could be facilitated if parents and other local adults were encouraged to support the independent play workers in the administration of the play space. Projects of this kind can be used to redevelop community relationships and supportive networks which are sorely needed in modern housing areas.

Even child users could join in this administrative board. This process of participation in the administration of their own neighbourhood domain and in the process of consultation about design and usage, would be an important way to promote community participation by the adults as well as providing a real way of educating children especially those in the higher age group towards democracy and acceptance of responsibility. In this way the needs of children as they grow through the development stages would be met and they would gradually be able to understand and take more responsibility for their actions. This would provide a more realistic way than the artificially constructed methods within schools for them to assume responsibility. Research with older adolescents has shown that, even though they have values and attitudes which adult society would find admirable, there is still a great reluctance to give them real responsibility. The only point in the research enquiries where adolescents were at issue with adult values was over the question of direction and control. They wished to be trusted to make their own decisions for themselves. The management of their own neighbourhood's play space would be one opportunity for them to do so.[11]

Concluding Summary

The chapter has stressed that all provision for children's free play should be age differentiated and orientated to the specific needs of age and developmental stage. The failure to recognize such differentiation and specificity is the prime reason for the lack of adequate provision for children's real needs of self-expressive play. This is particularly important at the developmental stage of the 'Forgotten Group'. Although the chapter has used the generic term 'children' it is important to emphasize that an aspect of the developing independence of the 'Forgotten Group' is that they think of themselves less as 'children' and would aspire to be regarded as 'young people'. Similarly the generic term 'play' has been used throughout the chapter, but, for similar reasons, it could be expected that the 'Forgotten Group' would prefer their free time interests to be described by a separate term, presumably after consultation with them leading to their agreement.

The author, having studied and worked with the developmental stage of the 'Forgotten Group' in many different situations in different parts of the world and whilst very familiar with various forms of residential care is aware that he has not fully investigated, as an involved participant, the special implications and applications of his argument to residential care. It is hoped that the general argument in the chapter will be sufficient to raise the special issues. The author would like to see these issues being worked out within residential care. His experience suggests the value of a consultant, independent of the particular situation, is particularly necessary in invoking new policies and new methods to deal with the special issues raised within the chapter. Firstly, it would be imperative that the implications for staffing and training of staff were carefully worked through at the highest policy making level before any attempt, experimental or otherwise, were to be instigated. At each step the understanding and support of those at the highest decision-making level, starting at the political, would be imperative. Too often staff at fieldwork level are left to stumble upon solutions emerging from their professional and practical needs. But these solutions, to succeed, need a helpful or understanding environment. The changes and adjustments in attitudes are so crucial that the help of an independent adviser is invaluable, in preventing forward steps at any level before the necessary preconditions are ensured. The adviser can ensure that the time is taken and the preparations made to cope with the tensions which will arise when the new policies are implemented at each level. Above all the consultant can work to preserve the helpful environment long enough for the changes in the processes to be firmly established and given time to become effective. The author has worked in this way as adviser in the implementation of new methods of dealing with the issues raised in the chapter. This experience leads to a conviction that the main reason for lack of adequate provision to deal with these needs of children is the intolerance of the system to the demands which the new methods make upon its understanding. It is here the consultant gives the greatest service by helping to explain the tension to the system and to contain the strains upon the system long enough to allow the practitioners at field level to cope with the changes and demands which the new policy places upon them. Having suggested the need for change in this chapter the author is willing to take the responsibility to help in the process of implementing the new policies and processes necessary.

Notes

*　In the following notes and references IPA = International Association for the Child's Right to Play – originally the International Playgrounds Association – with members now in over 47 countries and which holds international congresses in different parts of the world every three years.

1　Professor Frank Self of Hartford College, Connecticut described in a paper to the International Symposium on Children's Safety in Edinburgh 1989 his own research into and development of the use of normal tools and kitchen utensils by pre-school children for their own activities. He maintained that careful education of the children into the usage and careful preparation of the tools to enable their manipulation by even young children could remove the so-called dangers from such usage. His experience was that children managed all implements and self-managed the activities with no difficulties and no accidents.

　　Also the practice within adventure play (see note 7) demonstrates how children can be supported by trained workers to handle risky situations, tools and materials with safety.

2　For instance, the author, whilst in Scotland developing public play programmes recruiting children from different socioeconomic areas, noted that inexperienced workers saw the attitudes to equipment of children from poorer backgrounds, who had not had the opportunity to learn to handle and take care of personal property, as purely intentionally destructive or delinquent. Or, in projects in Sweden, the play of boys from some immigrant backgrounds practising for the outwardly physically expressive and active male role of their culture, were seen by childcare workers , especially women from the majority culture, to be excessively noisy and exhibiting harmfully aggressive, problem behaviour. In these and similar cases adults saw such behaviour as needing to be restricted and controlled.

3   The descriptive references in different parts of the chapter to international developments and policies is based on the author's own experience from international study visits and reading and in correspondence and discussion with experts from different parts of the world.

4   In his capacity as a member of the International Council of IPA the author sought support from international aid agencies for play projects among homeless city children in Bombay initiated by the Indian branch of IPA. It was made clear by those making decisions on development grants that play had great difficulty in being accepted as a sufficiently prior claim on aid funds.

5   These views are part of the conclusions from working with parents in different projects in Europe and also in Japan but, in particular, from a four-year development project in Sweden. The project was to research into the forms and methods of 'open pre-schools' which are used in Sweden to support parents who are at home with their young children. The research included a questionnaire survey of all parents using 24 open pre-schools in five different local authority areas. The research was published in Sweden as part of the report of the government supported project.

6   As examples: the changes in the orientation of the Head Start policy in the USA. from purely institutional support towards family support; the highly respected Bernard Van Leer Foundation which had for many years supported developmental education projects for all age groups of children and young people all over the world, including assistance to institutional forms of care, reassessed its funding policy and now for over five years has redirected all its funding efforts to early learning community projects providing direct support to mothers/mother substitutes and their children; in Scotland the author worked voluntarily for some years as a training consultant to the Royal Scottish Society for the Prevention of Cruelty to Children. This organization has over 100 years experience of working with investigation of and case work with families with child abuse problems. In 1995 this organization changed its name to Children 1st to indicate a change of emphasis from investigation of problem cases towards a preventative role in the support of families and children under stress.

7   The famous Emdrup Adventure Playground in Denmark, the first of its kind, was developed during the Second World War to give children chances for free expressive play. Children were encouraged to play with fire and use all kinds of tools and all kinds of scrap materials to invent their own facilities. They built and rebuilt huts to create their own 'shanty town'. In deference to possible adult criticism it was surrounded by earth banks to deaden sound and provide cover. It has continued as a playground until the present time and is an accepted children's domain.

The English play pioneer Lady Allen of Hurtwood, a landscape architect and pioneer in children's leisure provision, wished to create free expressive play spaces in the centre of London immediately after the Second World War. Frustrated in her attempts to obtain official planning approval she turned to bombsites awaiting redevelopment. There (for example, at Lollard Street) she encouraged free adventure play. Her policy included always employing professional leaders as facilitators of the children's play and of the democratic participation of the children in the programme.

These pioneering examples have inspired the adventure playground movement which has spread worldwide. Unfortunately official community planning has difficulty in taking the risk of adult disapproval. As a result the development of this type of provision is sparse and usually confined to areas, like Lollard Street, awaiting development and where community planning is less interested. This has led to adventure playgrounds being associated with areas of social blight – whereas they could be important social meeting places for all children.

8   The evidence for these views is based particularly upon a series of research inquiries carried out by the author among students training to be teachers, youth workers and social workers in Scotland. Results have been published in a variety of articles, the first of which was 'A Sociological Analysis of Students' Reasons for becoming Teachers', *Sociological Review*, Vol. 19, August 1971.

9   Examples of movements which are campaigning for improvement of school playgrounds are, in England, 'Learning through Landscapes' and in Sweden 'Skolans Uterum'. There are others throughout the world.

10   The author directed an IPA Sweden project to establish a demonstration 'playground for all' designed for children with handicap to play with other children. The project confirmed the importance of the full-time playworker, not only in supporting and encouraging the efforts of children, but also in being a constant 'presence' for the adults, parents and care assistants, who also often needed support and advice. Her availability created a 'social climate of acceptance' which enabled the playground to be an attractive meeting-place for both children and adults. The experience was used and extended by Stockholm Leisure Department in building another such playground for all 'Bergsgruvan' ('The Mountain Cave'), 1992.

11   The author as Director of the School of Community Studies, Moray House College of Education, Edinburgh, Scotland had over 20 years of experience of developing courses of training for teachers, social workers, youth workers, and community educators. An important component of these courses was a generic course in principles and practice shared in common by the students from different courses and which was based on the experiential group dynamic and community development training methods advocated in this chapter. The school also developed a neighbourhood worker course based on the same principles for adults, including parents, who lived in disadvantaged communities in which the school was involved through community development and community research. Included in those who participated in this locality based training were play workers from community play schemes.

The author now, as a freelance consultant, applies this experience to help community development and family support projects to achieve the objectives this chapter describes.

References

Almström, B. and Ashley, B. (1994), 'Report of a Research Symposium on Play', English summary, Sweden: Skolans Uterum.

Ashley, B. (1965), 'A Playground for All', report of a demonstration project', Sweden: IPA.

Ashley, B. (1985), 'Arbeta i närsamhället' ('Working in the community'), Stockholm: Liber Förlag.

Ashley, B. (1988), 'Den öppna förskolan som ett socialt centrum för barnfamiljer i närområdet' ('The Open Pre-school as a Social Centre for Families with Children in the Neighbourhood'), Stockholm: Norstedts.

Ashley, B. (1990a), 'Den Glömda Gruppen' ('The "Forgotten Group"), Stockholm: Förskolans Förlag.

Ashley, B. (1990b), 'Öppna Förskolan – en lönsam investering' ('The Open Pre-school – A Profitable Investment'), Stockholm Primärvårdsservice.

Ashley, B., Cohen, H. and Slatter, R. (1969), *Introduction to the Sociology of Education*, London: Macmillan.

Bales, R. (1995), *Interaction Process Analysis*, Cambridge, MA: Addison-Wesley.

Elias, N. (1978), *The Civilising Process – A History of Manners*, Oxford: Basil Blackwell.

Eppel, E and Eppel, M. (1969), *A Survey of Adolescent Attitudes*, Oxford: Oxford University Press.

Forsberg, M. (1987), *Skolgårdens Lekspråk* (*The Play Language of the School Playground*), Lund: Signum (summary in English).

Garborino, J. and Bronfennbrenner, U. (1976), in T. Lickona (ed.), *Moral Development and Behaviour: Theory, Research and Social Issues*, New York: Holt, Rinehart and Winston.

Gow, L. and McPherson, A. (eds) (1980), *Tell Them From Me: Scottish School Leavers Write About School and Life Afterwards*, Aberdeen: University of Aberdeen Press.

Keasey, C.B. and Turiel, E. (1997), 'Report of Nebraska Board of Education', Symposium on Motivation.

Kohlberg, L. (1969), *Readings in Child Psychology*, Del Mar: CBM Books.

IPA (1981a), Report of the 8th International Congress, Rotterdam, text of keynote address 1 by Professor Uri Bronfenbrenner.

IPA (1981b), Report of the 8th International Congress. Rotterdam, text of keynote address 2 by Brian Ashley.

IPA (1987a), Report of the 10th International Congress, Stockholm, text of keynote address by Professor Brian Sutton-Smith.

IPA (1987b), Report of the 10th International Congress, Stockholm, Plenary Discussion: 'Violence', report by chairman Brian Ashley.

IPA (1987c), Report of Theme Session 2 by chairman Nina Cosco.

IPA (1987d), Report of Theme Session 3 by chairman Brian Ashley.

IIPA (1990), Report of the 11th International Congress, Tokyo.

IPA (1993a), Report of the 12th International Congress, Melbourne.

IPA (1993b), 'Training of Play Workers as Facilitators', paper by Brian Ashley.

Lindholm, G. (1993), 'Research Report on Analysis of Children's Behaviour on "Green" Playgrounds Compared with Structured Playgrounds', Agricultural University, Alnarp, Sweden.

Mead, G.H. (1934), *Mind, Self and Society*, Chicago: University of Chicago Press.

Norén-Björn, E. (1977), *Lek, lekplatser, lek redskap – En utvecklingspsykologisk studie av barnslek* (*Play, Playgrounds and Play Equiment – A Developmental Psychology Study of Children's Outdoor Play*), Stockholm: Liber Förlag.

Ross, M.G. (1968), *Community Organization*, New York: Harper and Row.

Sutton-Smith, B. (1981), *A History of Children's Play: New Zealand 1840–1950*, Philadelphia: University of Pennsylvania Press.

Titman, W. (1994), *Special Places; Special People. The Hidden Curriculum of School Grounds*, Surrey: WWF UK/Learning through Landscapes.

Young, M. and Willmott, P. (1957), *Family and Kinship in East London*, London: Routledge and Kegan Paul.

PART IV
RESEARCH, A USEFUL TOOL IN RESIDENTIAL AND FOSTER CARE

Chapter 11

Discovering What Makes a 'Well-enough' Functioning Residential Group Care Setting for Children and Youth: Constructing a Theoretical Framework and Responding to Critiques of Grounded Theory Method

James P. Anglin

Background

A review of the British and North American literature on residential care for children and youth over the past 35 years reveals the impressive resilience of this form of service. Despite many rather scathing critiques (Rae Grant, 1971; Rubin, 1972; Steinhauer, 1991; Vail, 1966), revelations of institutional abuse (Bloom, 1992; Collins and Colorado, 1988; Levy and Kahan, 1991), and attempts to eliminate residential programmes altogether (Cliffe and Berridge, 1992; Coates, Miller and Ohlin, 1978), residential care continues to play a significant role in virtually all child and family service systems. Further, while the number of children in residential programmes has decreased significantly since the 1970s, it appears that most jurisdictions have accepted the inevitability of preserving at least a minimal number of residential care programmes in perpetuity. It would seem that, in relation to the social service system as a whole, residential care is something like tip of the iceberg that protrudes out of the water; if you try to remove it, the iceberg moves upward to maintain its overall balance.

In recent decades, a number of political forces and ideological movements have placed considerable pressure on residential care programmes. These have included deinstitutionalization, recessionary economic conditions, increased demand for accountability and quality assurance, the mandating of permanency planning, and the assertion of children's rights, among others.

In recent years, there has been a strong movement in favour of 'homebuilder' and 'family preservation' programmes in North America and internationally. These programmes seek to provide brief interventions into the lives of client families in order to defuse a problem, or resolve a crisis, without having to remove children from their own homes. In the minds of some, traditional residential care has come to be seen as passé, misguided, overly intrusive, ineffective and exorbitantly expensive. In fact, it has become a commonplace belief that residential care for young people is to be avoided at almost all costs. Brown and Hill (1999) say in reference to a 'wrap-around' service that the goals of the programme include 'preventing admission to residential care' (p. 38). Further, the Minister for Children and Families in British Columbia made the following statement in a letter to the editor of a newspaper after the closure of a five-bed group home.

> As a ministry, we strongly believe that children do best with their families and where that is not possible, in a family-type setting – not an institution. Fernwood House clearly played a role in serving children with severe behavioural problems at a time when we had fewer options and less information about how to help these children. *What we now know is that group settings are not the best option for any child*, particularly those with severe behavioural problems, where there is a need for intensive individualized care. [emphasis added] (Boone, 1999)

Such current challenges and strong assertions of beliefs and values have created a need to take a careful, in-depth look at the nature of residential care as a modality of child and youth care work, to provide some current information on how it functions, and to contribute knowledge grounded in current practice to the ongoing debate. Whittaker (2000), in his article 'The Future of Residential Group Care' in *Child Welfare*, the journal of the Child Welfare League of America, states the need this way:

> A full and rigorous examination of the theoretical and empirical underpinnings of residential group care with respect to their implications for current service policy, practice and future research is long overdue and ought to receive the highest priority on the new century's emergent agenda. (p. 60)

This study involving staffed group facilities was undertaken in a spirit of curiosity and with an appreciation of the importance of exploring the nature of residential life and work. It seeks to make a modest but useful contribution to placing residential group care back on the current child welfare agenda.

The Staffed Group Home Study

With funding support from the Ministry for Children and Families in British Columbia, ten group care programmes for young people were visited over a 14 month period. The homes were selected from those within the 'child and family services' sector of the Ministry and the sample did not include programmes from the 'community living' sector (for youth with mental and physical challenges), the 'corrections' sector (for youth in custody under the Young Offenders Act), or the 'mental health' sector (for youth under direct psychiatric care and supervision). The only exception was a 14-bed wilderness programme that operated within a corrections model.

The purpose of this study was to construct a theoretical framework that would offer an understanding of staffed group homes for young people that, in turn, could serve as a basis for improved practice, policy development, education and training, research, and evaluation. Staffed group homes were chosen as the focus of this study given their prevalence in the province and the confusion evident throughout the service system about their desirability and appropriate use. Eight of the ten programmes studied were staffed group homes; four had four beds each, three had five beds each, and one had eight beds. Four of the homes were in large urban areas, two were in small urban areas, one was rural and one was semi-rural. Of these eight homes, one was an emergency shelter, two were receiving homes, and five were longer-term homes (i.e. six months to two years).

In order to provide some comparative information on the boundaries of the group home model, one home combining a married couple and staff (i.e. a mixed foster family and group home model) and one 14-bed wilderness programme (i.e. a group model bordering on an institutional model) were included in the sample. Of the ten homes, six were non-unionized and four were unionized, while four were proprietorships and six were society-based and governed by boards of directors. While the study was in its early stages, one of the homes to be included in the study was terminated, however two former manager/supervisors were interviewed following brief visits to the home while it was still in operation.

Most of the settings were considered by local contracting managers and other professionals in contact with the homes to be 'well functioning', although one was self-admittedly going through a difficult period of transition. Over the course of the study and analysis, the term 'well-enough' functioning (paralleling Winnicott's (1986) concept of a 'good-enough' mother) seemed to better recognize the reality and ongoing struggle characteristic of such settings.

A brief discussion of the relationship of theory and practice in child and youth care will set the stage for a presentation of the study method and the findings of this theory-building undertaking.

The Relationship of Theory and Practice

The influential social psychologist Kurt Lewin has been credited with the maxim: 'There is nothing so practical as a good theory' (Hunt, 1987, p. 4). This assumption provides a basic rationale for this study of group homes. However, this maxim seems to fly in the face of the 'common wisdom' in the child and youth care field. Many practitioners in the human services, including child and youth care workers, react almost viscerally in a negative way whenever theory (or anything that even sounds like theory) is presented or discussed. Those who react in such a way appear to hold a belief that the nature of child and youth care work is first and last hands-on, immediate, concrete, and practical. In contrast, theory is often thought to be by its very nature too abstract, irrelevant, generalized and therefore eminently unhelpful for such practical work with individuals in unique situations. Therefore, to maintain not only that theory can be relevant and useful, but that there is nothing *more* practical than a good theory may call for some explanation.

Lewin's provocative statement that 'there is nothing so practical as a good theory' recognizes and articulates the fact that our psychosocial reality as human beings has an inherent sense of order and purpose to it. Our everyday social world is constructed by purposive action based in the meanings that objects, processes and other persons have for us. The order within human interaction and human life is founded in the systematic organization and interrelation of such human realities as beliefs, values, ethics, thoughts, intentions, purposes, feelings, actions, behaviours and responses. Identifying and clarifying how these complex entities are systematically inter-connected in human experience is a task for theory building. Having an articulated theoretical framework (i.e. a systematic way of thinking) about these elements and dynamics of human action that is coherent, informative and grounded in actual experience is to possess a powerful tool that can have very practical uses and implications for responding to concrete situations, and to the individual and collective actions of others.

A second basic assumption underpinning the approach adopted for this study is the converse of the first, namely: 'There is nothing so theoretical as good practice' (Hunt, 1987, p. 30). What this assumption implies is that in order to develop a substantive theory, one must have access to instances of good practice. Thus, as was mentioned in the previous section, an effort was made to select primarily 'well-functioning' group homes. In the initial selection of homes, what constituted 'well-functioning' was left to the judgment of several experienced workers with long-time involvement in the homes being considered for inclusion. A similar assessment by three such expert informants was considered sufficient to involve a home in the study.

Where the complex work of residential care is being done well, important lessons can be learned about the key elements and processes of the work and the inter-relationships between them. Put another way, this approach holds that work that is consistently being done well is being done in accordance with good theoretical principles, *whether or not the practitioners are aware of them or can articulate them*. This phenomenon is explored in considerable detail by Polanyi (1958, pp. 49–65) in his explication of 'tacit knowing'. One everyday example illustrating this point and cited by Polanyi is that 'the principle by which the cyclist keeps his balance is not generally known' (Polanyi, 1958, p. 49). He goes on to outline the quite complex physical principles at play when someone achieves the balance necessary to ride a bike, but of which very few bike riders are even aware, except in a tacit manner.

Much of the good practice exhibited by child and youth care workers is the result of such tacit knowing. It is well known that skilled crafts people and athletes often cannot articulate precisely how they do what they do. It sometimes takes a less skilled but highly observant and experienced teacher or coach to be able to articulate with some precision the elements and dynamics of an expert activity or performance. 'Knowing *how*' and 'knowing *that*' are two different forms of knowledge (Benner, 1984, p. 2). This study is concerned with examining the 'know how' and tentative articulations of good practitioners, as well as the experiences and perceptions of young people and their parents, as a foundation (or the ground) for developing a theoretical framework in order to more fully understand and be able to account for the nature of residential life and residential child and youth care practice.

The Study Research Method

The method selected as most appropriate to the task of developing a theoretical understanding of group home life and work was the grounded theory method as articulated in a variety of texts by the co-founders of the method, Barney Glaser and Anselm Strauss (Glaser, 1978, 1992; Glaser and Strauss, 1967;

Strauss, 1987; Strauss and Corbin, 1990). Towards the end of this chapter, a perspective on some of the major critiques of grounded theory method will be presented in the context of the approach taken in this research study.

The development of grounded theory was influenced by the emerging tradition of 'symbolic interactionism' (Blumer, 1969; Strauss and Corbin, 1990, p. 24). The emphasis on personal meanings, social interactions and interpretative process characteristic of a symbolic interactionist perspective is evident in the formulation of grounded theory (Glaser, 1992, p. 16).

The basic aim of grounded theory is to generate theory from social data derived inductively from research in social settings (Strauss and Corbin, 1990, p. 23). Critical to the accomplishment of this purpose is a systematic gathering of data through the active participation of the researcher in the phenomenon of interest. The process of immersion in the data is sometimes referred to by sociologists as 'indwelling', and most aptly so in relation to a study of group homes. Such data gathering techniques as participant observation, semi-structured interviews, informal conversations and document analysis are typical of a grounded theory inquiry (Chenitz and Swanson, 1986).

Central to the grounded theory method is the search for a main theme, often referred to in the research literature as a 'core category' or 'core variable', in relation to which most other aspects of the phenomenon of interest can be understood and explained. As Glaser states, 'the goal of grounded theory is to generate a theory that accounts for a pattern of behavior which is relevant and problematic for those involved' (1978, p. 93). Thus the researcher is searching the data on a continual and comparative basis in order to discover a core theme that will serve to connect and place in perspective virtually all of the elements of the phenomenon being studied.

The Core Theme

The theme that was found to permeate the data across all of the group homes studied and which encompassed the other major categories was *congruence in service of the children's best interests*. A group home may demonstrate congruence or incongruence to varying degrees across its elements, processes and overall operation, and it may do so with a variety of *congruence orientations*. For example, there may be an orientation toward operational efficiency, to the preferences of the staff, or to reducing the budget. In actuality, there are always competing interests and intentions within an organization as complex as a group home, and *full congruence* throughout an organization can best be understood as an ideal state never actually achieved in reality.

In this study, each home was found to be engaged in what could be termed a *struggle for congruence*, and what was discovered to be at the centre of most of the struggles was the intention to serve 'the children's best interests'. Related and virtually synonymous terms such as 'child-centred' and 'child-oriented' were also used by research participants to express this notion, but *the children's best interests* wording seemed most precise and evocative of the ideal being sought in practice. At the same time, while most of the homes in this study gave at least some evidence of holding this goal as an ideal, some of the homes clearly were not being guided in their work by such a focus. Further, no home was fully consistent in making all decisions on this basis (nor could one expect them to be), given both the competing interests that form the reality of group home operation and the natural variability of staff in their understandings and abilities to achieve congruence in their actions.

The concept of *children's best interests* has become a widely accepted notion in international instruments such as the United Nations Convention of the Rights of the Child (United Nations, 1989) as well as in the child welfare and child protection literatures in North America and the United Kingdom (Alston, 1994; Goldstein, Freud and Solnit, 1973, 1979). It is interesting to note that even the first book on residential child and youth care published in North America by August Aichhorn (1935) includes the notion of acting 'in the child's interest' (p. 194) as a touchstone for child and youth care practice. Therefore, it should not be too surprising that this longstanding and currently dominant concept was echoed in the words of some of the supervisors and managers of homes and agencies within the research sample.

Other major competing interests observed within the homes, and present in all homes to varying degrees and in various manifestations, included cost containment, worker preferences, and maintaining control. However, in this sample of largely well-functioning homes, it was evident that the core challenge was to achieve *congruence in service of the children's best interests*. The specific processes and interactions found to be most significant in creating such congruence will now be outlined.

Basic Psychosocial Processes

The ongoing comparative analysis of the data generated in this study revealed three dominant and pervasive psychosocial processes related to the central problematic of the *struggle for congruence in service of the children's best interests*. While each process is subsidiary to the main theme, each could also be viewed as a core category in its own right in relation to a sub-problem within group home life and work.

1   The most general, or pervasive, psychosocial process identified pertains to the overall development and ongoing operation of a group home, namely *creating an extrafamilial living environment*. The notion of an extrafamilial living environment or 'extrafamilial home' captures a fundamental tension inherent in this form of setting and helps to clarify the group home's unique nature in juxtaposition to foster care and institutional care on the continuum of residential services. As its name implies, a group home strives to offer a home-like environment not attainable within an institutional setting while removing the intimacy and intensity of a family environment. Much of the ongoing confusion and disagreement concerning the need for group homes can be attributed to a lack of appreciation of the importance of the 'extrafamilial home' dimension. In this study, group home managers and staff themselves frequently did not grasp the significance of this defining aspect of group home life. (See Anglin, 1973, for a detailed comparison of the characteristics of group homes and foster homes.)

2   At the level of the carework staff, the primary challenge was found to be *responding to pain and pain-based behaviour*. While the residential child and youth care literature frequently mentions the 'troubled and troubling' nature of the youth in care (for example Hobbs, 1982), and acknowledges their traumatic backgrounds, there is a tendency to 'gloss over' the deep-seated and often long-standing pain carried by these youth. The term 'pain-based behaviour' has been coined to remind us that so-called 'acting-out' behaviour and internalizing processes such as 'depression' are very frequently the result of a triggering of this internalized pain. Perhaps more than any other dimension of the carework task, the ongoing challenge of dealing with such primary pain without unnecessarily inflicting secondary pain experiences on the residents through punitive or controlling reactions can be seen to be the central problematic for the carework staff. One of the observed characteristics of a well-functioning home is a sensitivity on the part of the workers to the need to respond effectively and sensitively to both the youth residents' behaviour, and their own personal anxieties. At the same time, few managers, supervisors and staff demonstrate an understanding of the underlying pain in the residents and within themselves. When it is brought to their attention, there is often a remembrance of the experience of pain, both the resident's and their own, and a realization that they have let this experience slide beneath their

ongoing awareness. This intensive psychosocial process, and its frequent repression, makes acting in the best interests of the residents very difficult, and represents perhaps the greatest potential barrier to achieving a high level of congruence within the home in service of the children's best interests.

3   At the level of the residents, a third basic psychosocial process was identified, namely *developing a sense of normality*. This psychosocial process not only captures the central task, or goal, to be accomplished by the residents, it also serves to define a key element of what constitutes the resident *children's best interests*. There is an apparent paradox at the heart of this process that can be confusing and worrisome to critics of group home care. How can an 'abnormal' (or 'artificial') living environment such as a staffed group home foster the development of normality? Won't the residents simply become institutionalized in such an extrafamilial context? It became evident in this study that what a well-functioning group home can offer residents is *a sense of* normality, thus providing a bridging experience in terms of the residents' readiness to engage successfully in more normative environments. For example, while residents do not 'belong' in a group home, they can develop *a sense of belonging* that they can later transfer to more normative settings, such as their own family or a foster home.

Each of these three psychosocial processes is closely interrelated with the others, and in reality they exist coterminously as three interwoven threads or interrelated facets of the overall struggle for congruence within a home. To illustrate this point, a significant factor in a resident's experience of developing a sense of normality will be the manner in which staff respond to his or her pain and pain-based behaviour in the course of creating and shaping the extrafamilial living environment. Further, these pervasive psychosocial processes are made up of many moment-by-moment interactions between individuals, and some of the most pervasive and pivotal of these interactional dynamics will be outlined next. These interactional dynamics provide an important means for understanding and assessing the degree of congruence throughout a group home organization and its functioning.

Interactional Dynamics

On the basis of a comparative analysis of the interpersonal interactions occurring within the homes as noted during the on-site visits and discussed in interviews, eleven dynamics emerged as most pervasive and influential. This category of *interactional dynamics* identifies the most significant modes of relation between persons within and connected to the group home. These interactional dynamics can be understood as the key relational ingredients of group home life and work and as elements of the larger psychosocial processes already identified. Briefly stated, the dynamics include the following:

1   listening and responding with respect;
2   communicating a framework for understanding;
3   building rapport and relationship;
4   establishing structure, routine and expectations;
5   inspiring commitment;
6   offering emotional and developmental support;
7   challenging thinking and action;
8   sharing power and decision-making;
9   respecting personal space and time;
10 discovering and uncovering potential; and
11 providing resources.

Each of these interactional dynamics can come together with various others in a single moment or episode, much in the same way as various ingredients combine in the preparation of different culinary preparations. The creation of a *residents' best interests* environment can be seen to be largely a matter of combining these interactional ingredients in a highly congruent manner, while sensitively addressing the three major and intertwined psychosocial processes of *creating the extrafamilial living environment, responding to pain and pain-based behaviour,* and *developing a sense of normality.*

Finally, one additional category was also found to be important in completing the framework for understanding group home functioning; namely the *levels of group home operation.*

Levels of Group Home Operation

Organizations such as group homes are not simply assemblages of people, paper, procedures and premises. As the term 'organization' suggests, these elements must be brought together in an organized fashion. As with most such settings, group homes consist of a hierarchy of operating levels, or domains, each with its defined set of roles and responsibilities. In this study, five such levels were clearly evident as reflected in participants' ongoing thinking and action within the homes:

1   extra-agency level (contracting, funding, liaison, etc.);
2   management level (administration, budgeting, resource allocation, personnel management, etc.);
3   supervision level (overseeing care workers, team development, programming, resident care, etc.);
4   carework and teamwork level (working individually and collectively with youth and family members, completing reports, linking with community agencies, etc.); and
5   youth resident and family level (daily living, visiting, etc.).

The word 'levels' rather than 'domains' reflects more explicitly the hierarchical nature of these operational dimensions. The notion of a *flow of congruence* from the higher levels to the lower levels was identified and explored as an important aspect of the core category of *congruence in service of the children's best interests*, and how it comes to be realized (or not) in actual practice. Figure 11.1 graphically illustrates in a synoptic form the theoretical elements of the framework and suggests, with its rectangular cube and sub-cubes encompassed within an oval design, the complexity of their key linkages and inter-relations.

As outlined elsewhere (Anglin, 2003), the findings of this study can be seen to complement and extend previous research on residential group care for children and youth. However, it is suggested here that in addition to the particular outcomes of the study, the use of the grounded theory method is worthy of further analysis for possible use in other child and youth care studies. A review of the literature did not reveal any other published studies of residential care for children and youth utilizing the grounded theory method. Therefore, a brief overview of some of the significant critiques of this method will be presented in the context of the approaches used in this study.

Critiques of Grounded Theory

The grounded theory method was considered best suited for this study given the method's defining purpose of generating theory and its demonstrated utility in other practice-based disciplines (Glaser, 1993, 1994). While a grounded theory approach is focused on generating theory, and is frequently recommended for

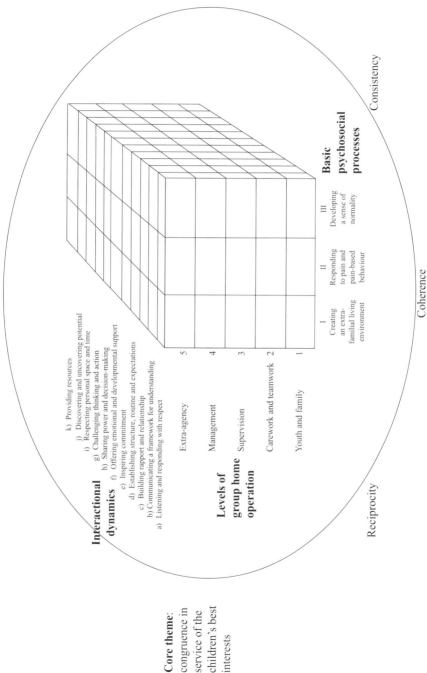

Figure 11.1   Framework matrix for understanding group home life and work

areas without extensive existing research and where the nature of interpersonal and social processes are being explored (Strauss and Corbin, 1990, p. 19), it is also recognized that it is but one method amongst many (Glaser, 1998, p. 45). Any single method will necessarily provide only a partial and limited view of the phenomena it seeks to understand. One major criticism of grounded theory is its alleged inability to adequately address social structures and systemic-level constructs, such as 'authority and power, organizations, organizational careers, status passage, and so forth' (Layder, 1993, p. 20). One of the reasons given for this suggested limitation is the almost exclusive focus on empirical observation and the emergence of theory directly from data collection and analysis, and the rejection of pre-existing theoretical constructs and theories (Layder, 1993, p. 27).

Anticipating and countering Layder's views on social structures and constructs in their examination of symbolic interactionism and grounded theory, Lindesmith, Strauss and Denzin (1975, p. 5) assert:

> Since humans create societies, such abstract concepts as social system, role network, and status demands or values were seen as 'existing' only insofar as humans actively took such objects into account. The meaning of objects arises out of the behavior directed towards those objects. Humans, then, self-consciously produce social worlds, or universes of discourse and meaning.

Further, after noting that some sociological perspectives other than symbolic interactionism and grounded theory 'emphasize one or another exterior structural variable in an attempt to explain the patterned regularities that are observable in all societies and social groups' (Lindesmith et al., 1975), these authors comment:

> An interactionist view stresses neither the interior or exterior influences to the exclusion of the other, but considers both as parts of a single dynamic process … We assume that human behavior provides the primary data with which social psychology deals, and that the explanation of any particular form of behavior requires that its relations to other types be traced and demonstrated. Thus a given kind of behavior is explained in terms of its interrelationships with other kinds of behavior and not in terms of 'forces', 'drives', or anything else which lies outside the behavioral field or which is inferred from behavior. (pp. 8–9)

This ongoing debate has been variously characterized as opposing 'macro and micro' perspectives, or 'structure versus agency', with the structuralists charging the interactionists with being 'astructural' while the interactionists accuse the structuralists of neglecting human agency (MacDonald, 2001, pp. 118–19). For the purposes of this study, perhaps it is sufficient to observe that in keeping with the grounding of theory in data, such aspects as social structures, systems, roles and status will emerge in a grounded theory inquiry only if they are seen to be significant for or by the agents themselves. In this way, the grounded theory approach is seen to encompass elements of structure at least from the perspective of the agents themselves.

Several other issues have also been addressed in critiques of grounded theory. A key issue concerns the assertion by the founders of the method that the researcher should 'enter the research setting with as few predetermined ideas as possible – especially logically deduced, a priori hypotheses' (Glaser, 1978, p. 3). Critics have challenged this admonition on the grounds that it is an unrealistic and impossible state to achieve (e.g. Burgess, 1984, p. 181). Layder (1998) comments 'that we never enter research with a mind clear of theoretical ideas and assumptions' (p. 51), and 'that observation is always saturated with theoretical ideas' (p. 113). Further, Layder (1998) characterizes the Glaser and Strauss (1967) approach as being 'wasteful' and 'dogmatic' (p. 36) in that other forms of theorizing are rejected or simply ignored. While Layder sees benefit in grounded theory's contribution to keeping theory from being 'abstract and removed from the everyday lives of people' (Layder, 1998, p. 18), he proposes 'the simultaneous privileging of theory and data in the emergence of new theory' rather than the approach advocated in grounded theory 'which privileges data against prior theory' (Layder, 1998, p. 169). Layder (1998) proposes the term 'anchored' as opposed to 'grounded' in that the term grounded 'seems to imply an exclusively empiricist position' (p. 113) rather than the more balanced approach to utilizing both theory and data that he advocates.

All observation is indeed imbued with theory, but from a grounded theory perspective, there appears to be virtue in attempting to keep an 'open mind' without pretensions of an 'empty head' by minimizing the bringing forward of, and reliance on, existing theories prior to engaging the phenomena of interest. And while 'complete openness' (Glaser, 1998, p. 44) may not be possible, the researcher's stance needs to be 'receptive to the emergent' (Glaser, 1998, p. 45), and not unduly blinkered by preconceptions. In fact, Glaser even suggests that 'if an existing theory seems quite grounded in data, one can possibly begin with it' (1998, p. 45). However, the initial 'use of existing theory concepts should not also pre-empt the emergence of concepts' (p. 46), as the overarching principle of grounded theory is to let the data speak for themselves. One needs to be open to dropping any preconceptions that are not supported by the data themselves.

Another issue raised by Layder (1998) relates to how one knows when the data gathering is complete for a given study in the absence of some guidance from systemic constructs or prior theoretical formulations. Glaser responds that 'theoretical saturation of a category occurs when in coding and analysing both no new properties emerge and the same properties continually emerge as one goes through the full extent of the data' (Glaser, 1978, p. 53). Thus, in Glaser's view, saturation (knowing when no new data is required) must be determined within the confines of the study data themselves, and all external or pre-conceived formulations are in fact antithetical to this emergent process. However, as Smith (1989, p. 76) observes, 'it is never possible for the researcher to know, with total confidence, that "enough" data have been gathered'. Substantial confidence rather than total confidence may be a reasonable goal, especially given that any study is but one contribution to an evolving body of research and theory, and therefore is subject to further development over time.

A further important issue identified by Brown (1973) relates to the difficulty of inferring causality from observation of incidents and correlations of factors. Brown (1973) points out that 'when we make theoretical statements of the kind that certain things go together or that one thing leads to another, there will usually be plausible rival interpretations about what is going on' (p. 3). It is one of the challenges of using grounded theory to find ways to turn the emerging hypotheses back on to the existing data themselves to seek out discrepancies as well as recurrent patterns, and to gather new data as necessary from situations where the emerging hypotheses can be subjected to further scrutiny and challenge through which at least some of the competing interpretations may be rendered implausible, if not completely ruled out. And paralleling the comment about saturation mentioned above, it is never possible for the grounded theory researcher to know, with 'total confidence', that 'x' causes 'y'. In Brown's words, such 'a decision must involve some element of judgement; is what is sensed in the individual case compatible with the story created from the kaleidoscopic patterns of the analysis?' (Brown, 1973, p. 9). As noted subsequently in Brown's analysis, the systematic checks and the step-by-step tracing of changes required in this process is, in general, 'time consuming and sadly neglected' (1973, p. 11).

A good grounded theory study will take the time necessary to critically test these connections until there are strong and reasonable grounds for suggesting causes and effects. Smith (1989, pp. 82–7) proposes triangulation, a concept explored by Denzin (1978), as at least a partial solution to the challenges of theory development from a primarily inductive process of inquiry. According to Denzin (1978), triangulation may include four tiers, namely the use of multiple methods, multiple slices of data, multiple investigators and multiple theories (p. 294). And as Smith (1989) observes, this is not a means to 'objective truth', but is a means of 'adding depth and variety to the analysis' (p. 85). This study of group homes utilized several data gathering techniques (i.e. participant observation, interviews and document analysis) as well as multiple time, event and site 'slices of data' that attempted to explore the case for possible cause and effect relations where such were suggested by the initial analyses.

In summary, this research inquiry emphasized the interactional rather than the structural elements of group home life and work, however structural aspects did emerge where they had meaning and significance to the participants. And while it is evident that all observation is directed to some degree by prior theoretical assumptions and preconceptions, a concerted effort was made to retain an open and inquiring stance in the face of the emergent data themselves. Further, systematic attempts were also made throughout the study to seek out incidents and situations that offered opportunities for potentially discrepant findings as well as potentially confirmatory and 'saturating' ones in relation to the emerging hypotheses. Finally, the gathering of data utilized several different techniques as well as carefully selected 'slices of data' that served to assist in the exploration of possible cause and effect relations.

Summary and Implications

This research study of staffed group home life and work with children and youth was undertaken in order to construct a framework for understanding and practice. The method utilized was grounded theory, and some of the major critiques of this method have been addressed within the context of this study. It is hoped that the resulting framework matrix (Figure 11.1) and its identified elements and dynamics will assist individuals, agencies, and government departments committed to providing good residential group home care to the young people who need it.

If a service such as group home care is to be utilized, then we need to know how, when and for whom it can best be used, and value it as *a positive choice* in these circumstances. A service that is not valued, or that is considered always to be an unsatisfactory or second-rate option will inevitably deteriorate, and will ultimately reflect these self-fulfilling expectations. Our young people are asking for and deserve the best group care settings that we can provide.

References

Aichhorn, A. (1935), *Wayward Youth*, New York: Viking.

Alston, P. (ed.) (1994), *The Best Interests of the Child: Reconciling Culture and Human Rights*, Oxford: Clarendon.

Anglin, J.P. (1991), 'Residential Care for Children and Youth in Canada', in M. Gottesman (ed,), *Residential Child Care: An International Reader*, London: Whiting and Birch, pp. 48–62.

Anglin, J.P. (1992), 'Children's Rights and the Magic Beanstalk', *Journal of Emotional and Behavioral Problems*, Vol. 1 (3), pp. 36–9.

Anglin, J P. (1994), 'Canada: New Trends, New Perspectives, Radical Changes', in M. Gottesman (ed,), *Residential Child Care: An International Reader*, London: Whiting and Birch, pp. 24–30.

Anglin, J.P. (2003), *Pain, Normality and the Struggle for Congruence: Reinterpreting Residential Care for Children and Youth*, New York: Haworth Press.

Benner, P. (1984), *From Novice to Expert: Excellence and Power in Clinical Nursing Practice*, Menlo Park, CA: Addison-Wesley.

Bloom, R.B. (1992), 'When Staff Members Sexually Abuse Children in Residential Care', *Child Welfare*, Vol. 71 (2), pp. 131–45.

Blumer, H. (1969), *Symbolic Interactionism: Perspective and Method*, Berkeley: University of California Press.

Boone, L. (1999), 'More Options' (letter to the editor, editorial page). *Times-Colonist*, 7 October, Victoria, British Columbia.

Brown, G.W. (1973), 'Some Thoughts on Grounded Theory', *Sociology*, No. 7, pp. 1–16.

Brown, R.A. and Hill, B.A. (1996), 'Opportunity for Change: Exploring an Alternative to Residential Treatment', *Child Welfare*, Vol. 75 (1), pp. 35–57.

Burgess, R.G. (1984), *In the Field: An Introduction to Field Research*, London: Unwin Hyman.

Chenitz, W.C. and Swanson, J.M. (1986), *From Practice to Grounded Theory: Qualitative Research in Nursing*, Menlo Park: Addison-Wesley.

Cliffe, D. and Berridge, D. (1992), *Closing Children's Homes*, London: National Children's Bureau.

Coates, R.B., Miller, A.D. and Ohlin, L. (1978), *Diversity in a Youth Correctional System: Handling Delinquents in Massachusetts*, Cambridge, MA: Ballinger.

Collins, D. and Colorado, P. (1988), 'Native Culture and Child Care Services', in G. Charles and P. Gabor (eds), *Issues in Child and Youth Care Practice in Alberta*, Lethbridge, Alberta: Lethbridge Community College, pp. 83–94.

Denzin, N.K. (ed.) (1978), *Sociological Methods: A Sourcebook*, 2nd edn, London: McGraw Hill.

Glaser, B. (1978), *Theoretical Sensitivity*, Mill Valley, CA: Sociology Press.

Glaser, B. (1992), *Basics of Grounded Theory Analysis*, Mill Valley, CA: Sociology Press.

Glaser, B. (ed.), (1993), *Examples of Grounded Theory: A Reader*, Mill Valley, CA: Sociology Press.

Glaser, B. (ed.), (1994), *More Grounded Theory Methodology: A Reader*, Mill Valley, CA: Sociology Press.

Glaser, B. (1998), *Doing Grounded Theory: Issues and Discussions*, Mill Valley, CA: Sociology Press.

Glaser, B.G. and Straus, A.L. (1967), *The Discovery of Grounded Theory*, Chicago,IL: Aldine.

Goldstein, J., Freud, A. and Solnit, A.J. (1973), *Beyond the Best Interests of the Child*, New York: Free Press.

Goldstein, J., Freud, A. and Solnit, A.J. (1979), *Beyond the Best Interests of the Child*, New York: Free Press.

Hobbs, N. (1982), *The Troubled and Troubling Child*, San Francisco, CA: Jossey-Bass.

Hunt, D.E. (1987), *Beginning with Ourselves: In Practice, Theory and Human Affairs*, Cambridge, MA: Brookline Books.

Layder, D. (1993), *New Strategies in Social Research*, Oxford: Polity Press.

Layder, D. (1998), *Sociological Practice: Linking Theory and Social Research*, London: Sage.

Levy, A. and Kahan, B. (1991), *The Pindown Experience and the Protection of Children: The Report of the Staffordshire Child Care Inquiry*, Banbury, England: Cheney and Sons.

Lindesmith, A.R., Strauss, A.L. and Denzin, N.K. (eds) (1975), *Readings in Social Psychology*, Hinsdale, IL: Dryden Press.

MacDonald, M. (2001), 'Finding a Critical Perspective in Grounded Theory', in R.S. Shreiber and P.N. Stern (eds), *Using Grounded Theory in Nursing*, New York: Springer, pp. 113–57.

Polanyi, M. (1958), *Personal Knowledge: Towards a Post-critical Philosophy*, London: Kegan Paul.

Rae-Grant, Q. and Moffat, P.J. (1971), *Children in Canada: Residential Care*, Toronto: Leonard Crainford.

Rubin, S. (1972), 'Children as Victims of Institutionalisation', *Child Welfare*, Vol. 51 (1), pp. 6–18.

Smith, R.S. (1989), 'Diversion in Practice', unpublished Master's thesis, University of Leicester, Leicester, England.

Steinhauer, P.D. (1991), *The Least Detrimental Alternative: A Systematic Guide to Case Planning and Decision Making for Children in Care*, Toronto: University of Toronto Press.

Strauss, A.L. (1987), *Qualitative Analysis for Social Scientists*, New York: Cambridge University Press.

Strauss, A.L. and Corbin, J. (1990), *Basics of Qualitative Research: Grounded Theory Procedures and Techniques*, Newbury Park: Sage.

United Nations (1989), *Convention on the Rights of the Child*, New York: UNICEF.

Vail, D.J. (1966), *Dehumanization and the Institutional Career*, Springfield, IL: Charles C. Thomas.

Whittaker, J.K. (2000), 'The Future of Residential Group Care', *Child Welfare*, Vol. 79 (1), pp. 59–74.

Winnicott, D.W. (1986), *Home is Where we Start From: Essays by a Psychoanalyst*, London: W.W. Norton.

Chapter 12

An Evaluation of Abused Children's Behaviour following Intervention: A Follow-up Study in Greece

Helen Agathonos-Georgopoulou, Kevin D. Browne and Jasmin Sarafidou

Introduction

Child abuse is a serious global problem with grave consequences to the child victim but also to society. Researchers and clinicians have identified serious effects to the child's development, behaviour, intellectual functioning and social competence. The estimates of incidence levels in combination with the findings related to the detrimental outcomes to children, the demands on the service system and the costs involved, have contributed to the consideration of the phenomenon of child maltreatment, of all types, as a public health problem (WHO, 1999). The definition established by WHO is the following:

> Child abuse or maltreatment constitutes all forms of physical and/or emotional ill-treatment, sexual abuse, neglect or negligent treatment or commercial or other exploitation, resulting in actual or potential harm to the child's health, survival, development or dignity in the context of a relationship of responsibility, trust or power.

Violence against Children as a Meeting Point

Today, violence against children acts as the meeting point of two substantial movements which correspond to internationally accepted conventions and initiatives of international organizations. One is the movement promoting children's change of position in society, from objects of protection to subjects of rights (UN CRC, 1989). The other is linked with WHO's strategies 'Health 21:21 goals for the twenty-first century' via goal 3 'A good start in life' and goal 7 'Reduction of injuries from violence and accidents, including violence in the family', the Strategies on Child Protection and the currently running campaign on family violence as a public health issue (2002). All countries are called to: a) define the problem by collecting data related to morbidity, mortality and the factors contributing to both; b) understand the problem on the basis of the identification of risk factors and research outcomes; c) identify and evaluate alternative types of interventions; and d) implement interventions and promote new knowledge. To accomplish all these strategies, it is important to promote research at all levels, based on objectivity and respect of each country's identity and cultural uniqueness.

Follow-up studies of maltreated children manifest considerable methodological difficulties. One is linked with issues of definition and the source from which the sample has been drawn. The absence of an internationally accepted definition so far, has affected the criteria for the inclusion of children in the study, resulting in as numerous sets of criteria as the studies themselves. Nowadays, the almost international acceptance of the UN Convention on the Rights of the Child, setting basic standards for children's quality of life, in conjunction with the recent WHO definition of child maltreatment as a public health problem, can act as sound bases for the development of common methodological approach in research. Other methodological concerns in follow-up studies relate to the use of a control group, the size of sample, the mean time in years between referral and follow-up and the different instruments used to measure outcome (Lynch and Roberts, 1982; Oates, 1985). The need still remains for studies to take a longitudinal perspective on the developmental effects of child maltreatment, considering all possible mediating variables (Augoustinos, 1987; Gibbons et al., 1995).

The effects of child abuse on the child's behaviour, although differing according to the child's age, relate to aggression as a common denominator. Preschool children have been found to show aggression towards peers while in the home they are characterized by both aggressive and aversive behaviours such as hitting, yelling and destructiveness when interacting with parents and siblings (Lahey et al., 1984). During adolescence, abuse outcomes are linked with antisocial or violent behaviour. The findings of a classic longitudinal study of 232 males from violent and non-violent low-income families have suggested that 22 per cent of the abused, 23 per cent of the neglected and 50 per cent of the rejected boys had been later convicted for serious juvenile crimes such as theft, auto theft, burglary or assault, compared to 11 per cent of boys from matched comparison families (McCord, 1979). As most information is being derived from samples of delinquent populations, conclusions must be cautiously drawn until further prospective studies are made. In the general literature on child development, a lot of attention has been devoted to finding explanations for the origin of child behaviour problems. Such explanations would be helpful in planning and in implementing the most appropriate types of intervention and prevention.

Recent Literature Review

A lot of attention is being focused in the relationship between child behaviour and family functioning. A most recent literature review (Van As and Janssens, 2002) on this subject, focused on four aspects of family functioning and their relationship to children's behaviour problems: parenting styles, intergenerational relationships, family structure and family interaction patterns. The authors conclude that child behaviour problems are related to a lack of parental support, an imbalanced parent-child relationship, a lack of cohesion and structure in the family, and a poor quality of communication between parents and children.

Each one of these aspects of family functioning and all of them as an entity, are linked with child abuse and neglect. Another association between child abuse psychopathology and family functioning is the crisis in the relationship between the parents, which precedes and/or follows separation and divorce, during which children may be 'used' by parents. The child, in his unconscious urge and need to unite the parents and preserve the family, may become 'difficult', by being unable to control these urges. Transitions in the family's developmental route and the new demands they impose on the members may also generate conflict leading, mainly, to the physical abuse of the child. Problems in communication within the family may also relate to children's behaviour problems, leading to parental aggressive behaviour and physical abuse.

The above findings led us to the follow-up study of an initial clinical population of physically abused and neglected children which were referred to a multidisciplinary team at the Institute of Child Health during a ten year period, for assessment and treatment.

The Study

Clinical Population

The initial clinical population consisted of 197 children and their families, ages from one week to 17 years, living in the Greater Athens area. Most cases were referred by the Aghia Sophia Children's Hospital in which the team was located and, therefore, there was a higher degree of awareness of the problem of child abuse and neglect amidst medical and nursing staff. Other cases were referred by welfare agencies, schools, legal agencies and some private doctors.

The follow-up study comprised 89 children and their families (45 per cent of the original sample), who were assessed 2–12 years later (mean: 7 years). The age of children on follow-up was from 5 to 24 years (mean: 11.4 years). Most of the families found were subjects of intervention, of various types, by the team and by other collaborating services. Sample attrition was due to the families' frequent change of domicile, a characteristic of abusing families, and/or family break up and of unknown relocation. Families were reached by letters explaining the scope of the study and then were visited at home by the research psychologist. Pediatric assessment was done by the team's pediatrician upon the child's and the family's visit to the Institute of Child Health.

The aims of the follow-up study were: a) to describe the personal characteristics of children 2–12 years later, such as health, growth, schooling, sexual behaviour, living arrangements, relationships with significant others; b) to identify children's characteristics from referral to follow-up, such as re-abuse, accidental injuries, use of medical services, social life, possible placements out of home; c) to compare a number of family variables linked with abuse, assessed both at referral and on follow-up for negative or positive changes overtime; d) to evaluate parents' criminal and violent behaviour from referral to follow-up, the help sought and parental views for the disclosure of abuse; e) to assess children's behaviour and to compare the child's behaviour within two groups and situations, abused children who stayed at home during intervention vs those removed from home, and abused children who were re-abused vs those not re-abused (as to parents' self-reports); f) to test for associations between positive and negative changes in abusing families and the abused child's behaviour; g) to examine whether any of the characteristics upon referral which are used to determine abuse can also predict behaviour problems later. This presentation will focus on the follow-up data related to the assessment of children's behaviour and the related comparisons.

The instrument used to assess children's behaviour was the Rutter Behaviour Scale A2 (1967), completed by parents, as it met with the study's requirements as an outcome measure. Although this scale is addressed to children in the general population and not specifically to abused children, its wide use has included children in different settings and situations, including children in care.

The Rutter Behaviour Scale was completed by parents or caretakers of 70 children ages 7 to 16 years, living at home or in residential care. The mean Rutter Total Score (RTOT) was found to be 14.4 (SD 2.3). The subscales scores were as follows: a) emotional 2.4 (SD 2.3); b) conduct 2.4 (SD 2.4); and c) health 3.0 (SD 3.5). For the purposes of this study, only the total scores (RTOT) were used in the analyses.

In the first analysis, children's behaviour (Rutter RTOT) was compared with respect to three grouping factors: a) child at home (n=39) versus child removed (n=60) during the intervention; b) re-abuse (n=52) versus no re-abuse (n=28) by mother; c) re-abuse (n=39) versus no re-abuse (n=50) by father. Results revealed that children who were removed from home during intervention had a RTOT of 17.4 (SD 10.2) in comparison with those that stayed at home, who presented with a RTOT of 11.2 (SD 7.7). This difference was statistically significant (p< .005), with those children who were removed showing more behaviour problems. Children who were re-abused by their mothers had a significantly higher RTOT of 17.0 (SD 10.2) compared to those who were not re-abused who had a RTOT of 10 (SD 6.9). This difference was significant (p<.006). Similarly, children re-abused by their father had a higher RTOT of 17.7 (SD 8.9) compared to those not re-abused who had a RTOT of 12.12 (SD 7.1). This difference was statistically significant (p< .016) with the re-abused children showing more behaviour problems. The changes in families (positive and negative), from referral to follow-up, were assessed with the use of the McNemar test, on all comparable variables.

Statistically Significant Changes

Statistically significant positive and negative changes were observed on follow-up on a number of family variables (Table 12.1).

On follow-up, 32.4 per cent of abusing families had moved from 1 to 2 rooms to three to six room accommodation, while only 2.8 per cent had moved to a smaller house. Among all families, 37.1 per cent had fewer changes three years before follow-up while for only 10 per cent the situation was the opposite. Social isolation was another area of positive change; 38.9 per cent of families who were seriously socially isolated at referral, were on follow-up living in conditions described as with 'none or fair' social isolation, while the reverse change occurred in just 5.6 per cent of families. Mothers' satisfaction from their own life improved; 38.2 per cent of mothers not satisfied at referral, were found satisfied on follow-up while only 5.5 per cent changed negatively. Almost half of the parents (56.5 per cent of fathers and 45.9 per cent of mothers), who on

Table 12.1   Positive changes in abusing families on follow-up

	Variables of positive changes P
Increased number of rooms	.001**
Fewer house changes during last three years	.002*
Less social isolation	.001**
Improved maternal satisfaction from own life	.001**
Father with less rigid attitudes on child's obedience	.001**
Mother with less rigid attitudes on child's obedience	.001**
Social worker's evaluation of less stress in the family	.001**
Social worker's evaluation of less stress with other relatives	.001**
Fewer life events for mother, last year	.043*
Fewer life events for mother, last month	.002**

follow-up believed that children should respect and obey their parents, changed on follow-up to a less rigid attitude towards child rearing. The social worker's evaluation of family stress revealed also positive changes; 47.1 per cent of the families evaluated initially as living under stress were found to live under 'not considerable stress', while only 4.4 per cent changed negatively. Similarly, 38.4 per cent evaluated as experiencing stress with relatives at referral, had 'not considerable stress' on follow-up, while only 2.7 per cent changed in the opposite direction. In the area of life events, families improved, as well; 29.5 per cent of mothers who had experienced a total score of 4 or more life events at referral, as assessed by the Paykel Scale (Paykel et al., 1971), reported 1–3 life events in the year preceding follow-up, while in 11.5 per cent of the cases more life events were observed. Similarly, 36.3 per cent of mothers who reported 4 or more life events within the last month prior to referral, reported 1 to 3 life events in the month before the follow-up, while 11.3 per cent changed in the opposite direction. Negative changes of families from referral to follow-up were fewer and were associated with family disruption and the difficulties that mothers were facing (Table 12.2).

From the parents who lived together at referral, 38 per cent did not live together on follow-up, while only 1.3 per cent that was not living together at referral joined each other on follow-up. In relation to mothers' worries, 31.5 per cent of mothers who did not worry about living conditions at referral, did so on follow-up, while in 11.1 per cent of cases the opposite held true; 25.9 per cent of mothers who did not worry about work upon referral, did worry on follow-up, while 5.6 per cent changed in the opposite direction; 33.3 per cent of mothers who did not worry about personal matters upon referral, did

Table 12.2   Negative changes in abusing families on follow-up

	Variables of negative changes P
Natural parents not living together	.001**
Mother worries more about living conditions	.034*
Mother worries more about work	.012*
Mother worries more about personal matters	.001**
Child does not live with both natural parents	.001**

so on follow-up, while only 3.7 per cent worried more when they were seen again. Lastly, 42.7 per cent of children who lived with both natural parents upon referral, did not live with them on follow-up, while none of the children who did not live with both their parents at referral, joined their parents on follow-up. No changes (positive or negative), were observed in families from referral to follow-up in relation to all other compared factors.

Children's behaviour on follow up was associated with the presence of certain risk characteristics for physical abuse upon referral. These 15 characteristics comprise a screening instrument, which was devised earlier on the original population of 197 abused children and a control group , to be used for the prediction of child maltreatment, within the domain of secondary prevention (Agathonos-Georgopoulou and Browne, 1997).

Among all 15 factors considered as predictors for abuse within the Greek cultural milieu, only three were found to be associated with disturbed behaviour on follow up, as evaluated by Rutter's Total Scores. Children who were evaluated to have problems with bad personal hygiene (as 'dirty') at referral, depicting neglect of parental, namely maternal care, were found with a RTOT of 15.4 (SD 10.1) in comparison to those found with adequate personal hygiene (as 'clean'), who showed a RTOT of 9.2 (SD 6.8). Children with a greater number of life events within the last year prior to referral had significantly higher RTOT (RTOT 15.8,SD 10.4) than those that did not (RTOT 8.5, SD 5.5). Lastly, children who had 'other illnesses' (other than a full list of expected illnesses during childhood) prior to referral, had a significantly higher RTOT (RTOT 18.6, SD 7.7), in comparison with those that had a better health record, showing a mean RTOT score of 12.8 (SD 9.7). A further statistical analysis of children's RTOT scores and the significant predictors revealed that the most significant factor was 'Parents with adverse life experiences'. All the remaining variables seemed to be related with this factor.

The analysis of positive and negative changes in families from referral to follow-up resulted to an index of family change. This analysis revealed that children's RTOT is linked with families' changes. The more the negative changes of the families from referral to follow-up time, the higher the RTOT, therefore the children's behaviour problems. Positive changes in the families resulted in children exhibiting fewer behaviour problems.

Discussion

The results of the follow-up study are to a considerable extent in accordance with those of other similar studies on physically abused and neglected children. In this study, the children's behaviour as depicted by the Total Score (RTOT) in the Rutter Behaviour Scale A (2) for Parents, was used as an objective outcome measure. The mean RTOT found in the study (RTOT 14.4, SD 9.5), is considerably higher than the scores found in other research among non-abused children in the general population. The study confirms the effects of maltreatment on children's behaviour. In Greece, Koulakoglou (1993), in a general population sample of one thousand children 7–12 years in Greater Athens Area, found a mean RTOT of 7.9. Vorria (1994), in a study of an institutional sample of 9–11 year old children found a mean RTOT of 12.6, while the RTOT of the non-institutional control group was 6.0. Other findings of the use of the Rutter Scale A2 for Parents disclose differences in RTOT scores according to origins of samples. Hodges and Tizard (1989), in their study of an ex-institutional sample of 16 year-olds found a mean RTOT of 7.6. The high RTOT observed in this study denotes considerable psychiatric disorder. In Rutter et al.'s classic study (1970), 54.5 per cent of those children finally diagnosed as showing psychiatric disorder scored 13.0 or more compared with 6.0 in the general population. The same study found that 15.1 per cent of boys and 8.1 per cent of girls in the general population obtained scores of 13 or more compared to 70.8 per cent of the boys and 66.6 per cent of the girls in a clinical population. Similarly, in France, Fombonne (1989), in a clinical sample of children addressed to a child psychiatric outpatient department for children 6–11 years, found a mean RTOT of 16.5. In the same study, a sex differentiation was observed as boys presented with a mean RTOT of 17.2 in comparison to girls who were found with a mean RTOT of 15.5.

Children Having Been Removed from Home

In this study, children's RTOT was found to be related to children having been removed from home. Children who were removed presented with more behaviour problems (RTOT 17.4, SD 10.2) compared to those who stayed at home during intervention (RTOT 11.1, SD 7.6). The behaviour of children who stayed at home was more problematic to that found by Koulakoglou (1993), and Hodges and Tizard (1989), but closer to Vorria's institutional sample's score (1994). Nevertheless, it is difficult to say whether children developed behaviour problems as a result of having been removed or whether a child's behaviour problems contributed to its removal from home. It may be suggested that the abusive experience had a negative effect on the children's behaviour and that by removing them from home this made matters worse than better. The same question applies in the case of the findings of re-abused children by either mother or father who scored higher that those not re-abused. Were children re-abused because parents could not cope with their behaviour problems or was it that their re-abuse contributed to the development of behaviour problems among children? In the domain of child maltreatment theory and research, this question is a pseudo-dilemma, as both are intrinsically linked.

The comparison of children's behaviour (RTOT), with each of the risk factors predictive of physical child maltreatment revealed statistical significance as per three factors: a) children's bad state of hygiene upon referral, 'dirty' children presenting with more behaviour problems; b) parents with a greater number of life events within the last year prior to referral, with more life events correlating with more behaviour problems; and c) the presence of 'other illnesses' prior to referral, a bad health record, related with more behaviour problems on follow-up. It could be argued that children with a bad health record were neglected by their parents, mainly their mothers, who described them as presenting with behaviour problems (Oates, 1985). A bad health record before referral may acquire two meanings; either that a child may have been perceived as 'sick' by its parents –often the mother- on the basis of a distorted relationship, or that a truly vulnerable child may later develop behaviour problems.

Staying at Home with Support or Short-term Care and Re-unification?

The main issues that emerge from follow-up studies are, firstly, that of implications of the research results for practice and general social policy measures within the specific country and/or cultural milieu; secondly, the wider implications in the domain of further research needed in order to answer questions. In this study, the high levels of behaviour problems scores found among the children removed from the family suggests two things. Firstly, that a lot of these children would have been much better at home if support was offered to their family. Secondly, in case of entering care, it should have been short-term with therapeutic orientation, aiming at re-unification. The evolution of long term residential care to short term therapeutic care should be a priority target of social policy in Greece. At present, although the number of children admitted to residential care is diminishing, few alternatives are offered to meet newly emerging needs. Following European trends in child protection, very few children enter care because of poverty, which is being replaced by reasons related to family malfunctioning and the effects on children, child maltreatment of all types, neglect and abandonment and children with behaviour and conduct problems who are relinquished by the parents as they are unable to cope with them. The problem is that institutional care has remained rather static in terms of programs and staff training, unable to meet children's needs. In the midst of this situation of child protection, there are some good programs operated mainly by non-governmental organizations that function as small family-type units with 15 to 20 children. Foster care, although with a history of more that 70 years of operation in Greece, has functioned with a limited spectrum until a few years ago when it was regenerated. A fairly recent law supports foster care as a scheme for both adults with physical handicaps and mental health problems and for children needing to be cared away from their birth families.

This follow-up study revealed high levels of behaviour problems scores among children with a history of abuse, much higher than the general population, while resembling those of clinical samples. Findings suggest that the treatment needs of the child should not be overlooked while concentrating on the multiple problems of the family. The implementation of the United Nations Convention on the Rights of the Child in child protection, requires a reconsideration of the child from object of protection to subject of rights. This automatically entitles the child to all possible measures for treatment and rehabilitation as it is the child who should be the primary 'client' of the system.

The implications of the study findings for further research at international level suggest that priority should be given to a number of issues. More research is needed on the various 'developmental careers' of abused and neglected children, namely, on the relation of early exposure to maltreatment with conduct disorders and on criminality in later life. The investigation of pathways from childhood to adulthood requires an analysis of a quite complex set of linkages over time (Rutter, 1989a). Research suggests that antisocial personality disorder in adulthood is almost always preceded by conduct disorder in childhood, suggesting that continuity looking backwards is very strong (Rutter, 1989).

Another area for further research is the issue of 'cost' as a result of a child's removal (Stratton et al., 1988). More knowledge is needed not only about the 'cost' to the child but also to the family as whole, to the parents as individuals and to the siblings. Central to the evaluation of 'costs' is the concept of 'loss' and how it is transcribed to everyone involved. Furthermore, it would be interesting to see how this 'loss' is transcribed to the professionals involved and to the agency dynamics. Especially in the case of residential care for abused and neglected children, these dynamics among all partners involved, the parents, the child itself, staff and the state or the agency in a parental surrogate role, need a thorough consideration as research priority. Lastly, research emphasis should be given to both risk and protective factors together with interactions between them (Rutter, 1983). As Rutter points out (1989a), individuals may be 'immuned' to types of psychological adversities that may enable them to function better, later on in life. Follow-up studies of abused children, based on sound methodology, have a lot to contribute towards answering these questions while raising new.

References

Agathonos-Georgopoulou, H. and Browne K.D. (1997), 'The Prediction of Child Maltreatment in Greek Families', *Child Abuse and Neglect*, Vol. 21 (8), pp. 721–35.

Augoustinos, M. (1987), 'Developmental Effects of Child Abuse: Recent Findings', *Child Abuse and Neglect*, No. 11, pp. 15–27.

Convention on the Rights of the Child, United Nations (1989).

Fombonne E. (1989), 'The Child Behaviour Checklist and the Rutter Parental Questionnaire: A Comparison between Two Screening Instruments', *Psychological Medicine*, No. 19, pp. 777–85.

Gibbons, J., Gallagher, B., Bell, C. and Gordon, D. (1995), *Development after Physical Abuse in Early Childhood*, London: HMSO.

Hodges J. and Tizard, B. (1989), 'I.Q. and Behavioural Adjustment of Exinstitutional Adolescents', *Journal of Child Psychology and Psychiatry*, Vol. 30 (1), 77-79.

Koulakoglou, C. (1993), 'The Development of the Fairy Tale Projective Test in the Personality Assessment of Children', unpublished PhD thesis, University of Exeter.

Krug, E., Dahlberg, L.L., Mercy, J.A., Zwi, A.B. and Lozano, R. (eds) (2002), *World Report on Violence and Health*, Geneva: WHO.

Lahey, B.B., Conger, R.D., Atkeson, B.M. and Treiber, F.A. (1984), 'Parenting Behavior and Emotional Status of Physically Abusive Mothers', *Journal of Consulting and Clinical Psychology*, No. 52d, pp. 1062–71.

Lynch, M.A. and Roberts, J. (1982), *Consequences of Child Abuse*, London: Academic Press.

McCord, J. (1979), 'Some Child Rearing Antecedents of Criminal Behaviour in Adult Men', *Journal of Personality and Social Psychology*, No. 37, pp. 1477–86.

Oates, K. (1985), *Child Abuse and Neglect: What Happens Eventually?*, Sydney: Butterworths.

Paykel, E.S., Prusoff, B.A. and Ulenhuth, E.H. (1971), 'Scaling of Life Events', *Archives of General Psychiatry*, No. 25, pp. 340–47.

Report of the Consultation on Child Abuse Prevention (1999), WHO, Geneva, 29–31 March, Document WHO/HSC/PVI/99.1.

Rutter, M. (1967), 'A Children's Behaviour Questionnaire for Completion by Teachers: Preliminary Findings', *Journal of Child Psychology and Psychiatry*, No. 8, pp. 1–11.

Rutter, M. (1983), 'Statistical and Personal Interactions: Facets and Perspectives', in D. Magnusson and V. Allen (eds), *Human Development: an International Perspective*, New York: Academic Press.

Rutter, M. (1989a), 'Pathways from Childhood to Adult Life, and Psychiatry', *Journal of Child Psychology and Psychiatry*, Vol. 30 (1), pp. 23–51.

Rutter, M. (1989b), 'Intergenerational Continuities and Discontinuities in Serious Parenting Difficulties', in D. Cichetti and V. Carlson (eds), *Child Maltreatment*, Cambridge: Cambridge University Press.

Rutter, M., Tizard, J. and Whitmore, K. (1970), *Education, Health and Behaviour*, London: Longmans.

Stratton, P., Davies, C. and Browne, D. (1988), 'The Psychological Context of Predicting and Preventing Child Abuse and Neglect', in K. Browne, C. Davies and P. Stratton (eds), *Early Prediction and Prevention of Child Abuse*, Chichester: J. Wiley and Sons.

Van As, N.M.C. and Janssens, J.M.A.M. (2002), 'Relationships between Child Behaviour Problems and Family Functioning: A Literature Review', *International Journal of Child and Family Welfare*, No. 5, March, pp. 1–2.

Vorria, P. (1994), 'The Effect of Long-term Institutionalization on Children's Social Behaviour', in *Growing up in an Institution*, Greek Society of Mental Hygiene and Child Neuropsychology, Athens (in Greek).

Chapter 13

The Rights and Wrongs of Ethnographic Research in a Youth Residential Setting

Tarja Pösö

Introduction

The complexities of residential life pose a challenge to the analytic tools of the researcher. If the researcher is involved in studying any qualitative aspects of residential life, then the issues of reflective and ethically sound research approaches make the challenge even more acute. According to David Berridge and Isabelle Brodie (1998, p. 25), in-depth studies of children's homes must be among the most sensitive and potentially threatening areas of social inquiry. Therefore, the research should be fair to the people involved, especially the most vulnerable ones, most often the residents, so as not to harm them any more than life has harmed them already so far. Being humanistic – or critical humanistic (Plummer, 2001) – is not, however, very straightforward.

This chapter discusses the ethical dilemmas encountered in a research project looking into the experiences of residential life (Pösö, 2003). The study aimed to learn about young people's experiences of residential life in Finnish reformatory schools, that is state-run institutions aimed at the youth seen as 'the most problematic'. The initiative for the study came from the Research and Development Centre of Social Welfare and Health which is in charge of those institutions. The aim set for the study was to learn about the experiences and identities the residential space made possible, and to understand them in relation to the biographies of the adolescents.

To carry out the research, ethnographic approach was chosen. In practical terms it meant that the researcher lived in two institutions for a longer period of time so as to be able to talk with the residents in semi-structured interviews as well as in naturally occurring discussions. The young people were also given cameras in order to give them an opportunity to communicate about residential life in the form of photographs. Staff interviews, case notes and participation in residential life were also included. Additionally, some group interviews were carried out in order to discuss the concept and meaning of violence as a separate study (Honkatukia, Nyqvist and Pösö, 2003).

The material is rich, as was the involvement of the researcher in the residential life. The research should not, however, be assessed only in terms of the quantity or quality of the data, but also in terms of the social, personal and ethical processes it brought about and how they were handled. A majority of those issues are of ethical nature. Most of them can be categorised as dilemmas as it is not evident whether the research process is having an adverse affect on the youth involved or whether it is giving a voice to the young residents who often are excluded from research (e.g. O'Neill, 2001, p. 12). The traditional criteria for solving these dilemmas (e.g. Kvale, 1996, pp. 109–23) have to be negotiated from within the peculiarities of the residential setting as will be shown later.

Voluntary Participation as a Complicated Code

The ethnographic approach means that most of the research data is created in face-to-face interaction. Ethnography is merely an approach or methodology for study rather than a set of tools as such (e.g. Pink, 2001). The method and the data are very much tuned by the roles, interpersonal skills and interpretations of the researcher. The strength is that the approach can, if successful, touch issues which would not otherwise be brought into being by questionnaires or structured interviews. It does not, however, possess any magic power which would overcome the barriers the actors set for their privacy (such as their experiences of residential life and biographies) or human beings have in understanding each other.

In a residential setting, the residents only have a limited number of ways to control their lives in the institution. The staff and the residential rules create a frame for everyday life. That frame is to be followed by the residents as well as by the researcher who enters the institution as an outsider. The researcher is dependent on the good-will of the staff even after formal research permission has been granted. The staff, in practice, sets the limits and arenas for the researcher to communicate with the adolescents. In order to keep up good relations with the staff, the researcher has to convince the staff that the intentions of the research are not to harm the image of the institution nor to function as a tool of external control, among many other things.

In this particular research, the involvement of the young residents in the research was based on voluntary participation as is done so often. It was made easy for the residents to say 'no' when the research was introduced. However, most of the adolescents participated in one way or another and only a couple did not want to be involved. The reasons for participating could be that:

- some youngster wished to have a change to their residential routine. The interviews, pictures, chatting with the researcher, meant a change to the routines;
- some youngsters wished to have a listening ear;
- some adolescents wished to tell about their views and experiences as they found the prospect of telling therapeutic;
- some of them viewed the research and the researcher as advocates, that is as tools to make their experiences of poor practices heard in order to effect a change in the practices;
- some adolescents wished to do the same as their fellow residents which meant participating in the research;
- some adolescents wished to please the staff members who were in favour of the research.

There might also be a variety of other reasons. The statement here is, however, that the actual fact of the adolescents staying in a closed institution had a strong impact on the decision whether to participate in the research or not. The interdependency which is so typical of any aspect of residential life was included in the research participation as well (Honkatukia, Nyqvist and Pösö, 2003).

The very idea of participating in research could also have been poorly informed. The custom in this research was that the researcher explained the background and process of the research in detail before asking about the willingness to participate. Even a written text about the research and the researcher was given. However, to some adolescents, the idea of the research remained obscure. A book? What for? Who will read it? Why should people know about my views? What will it change? They are critical questions which cannot be easily answered. Can a researcher honestly say that the book will have some influence on residential life or on an adolescent's life and that in that sense, it would make sense to participate? In this case, it was not possible to say, as is often the case, that the research is a part of the researcher's studies and therefore required for personal reasons. The answers about the actual role and impacts of the research remained vague. Nevertheless, the residents were ready to participate.

An approach which means close face-to-face contact intervenes in residential life in many ways. At least four ways or levels can be mentioned

(Honkatukia, Nyqvist and Pösö, 2003). Firstly, the actual act of researching meant an intervention in the residential life as the researcher entered the residential institution with tasks outside the daily running of the institution. As the institutions are situated in the countryside far from the towns, the research period meant concretely living – sleeping, eating, exercising etc. – in the institutions sharing some living space with the residents and the staff. Secondly, the research meant an intervention in the identities of the residents: their opinions and experiences became important but the research also gave them an opportunity to build up, to test and to practise quite a variety of roles. Thirdly, the researcher intervened in the group dynamics of the residents as well as of the staff. Fourthly, and most importantly, the research participated in a process where the views and experiences of the residents were made important. The research was involved in reconstructing the residential experience as the themes and questions of the researcher are not neutral: they make some issues important, worth paying a lot of attention to, sometimes in very different ways to those in residential culture. Also, the stories told to an outsider are most likely different from those ones told and known in professional relationships. More important than arguing which story is more valid or true, is the point that with the researcher, the residents tell a story which may otherwise not have been told. None of the levels is such that residents could withdraw from them if they wanted.

The role of research participation in residential setting is, as described above, very strongly coloured by residential life and its interpersonal relations. My concern here is not the position of those residents who refused to participate but the impact of residential life on those who participated and on the stories told. The issue is not only about voluntary participation but the participation and the very idea of informed consent which are so strongly (and unavoidably) influenced by the context.

Confidentiality Challenged

A closed institution violates the privacy of the residents in many ways. For example, under some conditions, letters can be read or phone calls and personal belongings monitored if the staff has a reason to suspect something. The confidentiality code of the research is located in this agenda of continuous (possible) doubts and threats to one's privacy.

In principle, the confidential nature of research relationships can be maintained also in a residential setting as long as the researcher may stay an outsider on his/her own conditions to residential life. The code, however, can be also very strongly challenged as will be described in the following example about one field work period.

During a period of several weeks, violent encounters became daily issues in one of the institutions. The residents attacked the staff in a violent manner and sometimes the response of the staff was abusive as well. The police became involved due to some violent conflicts. The general atmosphere was highly tense. As I was talking to the adolescents, some of them explained to me that they felt utterly powerless in the institution and in their lives generally. It was always other people (adults, especially social welfare practitioners) who made decisions about them and that left them excluded from their own lives. In the institutions they had to follow the rules set by other people and were not given any right to express their own points of view and needs. Their experience was that they did not have any tools to have an influence on residential life apart from violence. Violence had become a tool for them to be heard, to be seen and to have a say in residential life.

I was involved in one violent encounter between the residents and the staff which horrified me. However, one of the boys left the scene winking at me. Afterwards he came to explain to me that he had demonstrated to me what he had meant by saying that violence was his tool: by using the tool he made the staff afraid and when they were frightened they might listen to him. A couple of other residents joined the discussion. They had a more pessimistic view on the role of violence. They expressed the view that in order to be heard and to be taken seriously they had only one tool to use – that was to kill someone. Only if they killed someone in the institution, would people believe that they were very serious about their unfair treatment.

What is the role of the researcher in this kind of situation? How far does the confidentiality code take the researcher? In this episode, it was not only listening but being aware of their plans which confused me deeply as the plans were beyond the moral codes I could share. As I have previously done research in prison and in the institutions in question as well, encountering the destructive messages from within institutional life was not a totally new experience. The depth of commitment and emotions in the boys' expressions, however, shocked me. I did feel that I had to present some counter-arguments to make them see the ultimate wrongness of their plan but I felt totally silly and wordless. Whatever I said was something they had already thought of. The deep feeling of being excluded from their own lives gave the legitimation for the use of violence and I did not have any tools to break that interpretation.

After one sleepless night occupied by thoughts as to whether I should take the plans as 'real' or as ' just talk', I decided to take them as 'real' (as talking makes things real to some extent). I also decided that it was not right to treat the previous episode only as a piece of research data but also as an important piece of ongoing residential life which I had no right to keep to myself. Therefore I met the head of the institution – whom I had learnt to know as a very experienced, skilful and caring manager – the day after. I did not give him a report about the episode the previous evening or about the boys who were talking about killing nor the names of the staff members who were mentioned as targets. Instead, I told him about the deep, continuous theme of voicelessness, powerlessness, exclusion and lack of individuality which the residents had told from one interview to another. And that those feelings are so strong that they seem to give legitimation to violence as a method to obtain a voice. The themes as such did not surprise him as he had been very concerned about the abusive atmosphere in the institution but the strength with which they were expressed and experienced did.

Did I break the code of confidentiality? My answer is yes. Despite the fact that I did not give any names of persons, it was possible for the head of the institution to link the information given to the residents in his institution thereby undermining one of the reasons for doing research in two institutions, namely to make it difficult to identify the institution and the residents. I also functioned as a feedback mechanism from the residents to the management of the institution and not as a researcher writing to a non-residential audience. However, I felt very uneasy with the thought of not having told anything about the talk about violence as a legitimated tool during the field work as the ongoing processes seem to harm so many of the people involved.

The same type of dilemmas might be typical for any researcher of residential life. Often the residents regulate the themes they let the researcher share with them and that distance keeps the researcher safe from confidentiality dilemmas. What should the researcher do if she or he is told about the drug dealing practices within an institution? Or about the plans to organise a joint escape or to start a fire? The collective abuse of a newcomer? A staff member abusing residents? The residential stories told about such issues may make the report an exciting piece to read but the excitement of the report should not be the thing that only counts. The report is written about very vulnerable people in very vulnerable situations and the researcher gets involved in their lives for a short period of life. Surely the researcher should have an obligation to stop any more harm from happening, shouldn't s/he?

The Powerful Choices of Analysis

Doing empirical research is not only 'collecting data' but interpreting, presenting and reporting it. In ethnography, the processes of creating, interpreting, analysing and presenting often become interwoven. Sarah Pink (2001, p. 18) writes that:

> Rather than being a method for the collection of 'data', ethnography is a process of creating and representing knowledge (about society, culture and individuals) that is based on ethnographers' own experiences. It does not claim to produce an objective or 'truthful' account of reality, but should aim to offer versions of ethnographers' experiences of reality that are as loyal as possible to the context, negotiations and intersubjectivities through which the knowledge was produced.

According to Pink, being as loyal as possible to the context, negotiations and intersubjectivities through which the knowledge was produced is one essential principle in ethnography. Loyalty becomes an issue instead of validity and reliability emphasising the social and human nature of ethnography She also recognizes (2001, p. 18) that ethnography should engage with issues of representation that question the right of the researcher to represent 'other' people, recognize the impossibility of 'knowing other minds' and acknowledge that the sense we make of informants' words and actions is 'an expression of our own consciousness'.

In ethnography about residential life, the issues of interpreting, analysing and (re)presenting are complicated as residential life itself is fundamentally complicated. The researcher has a lot of power in choosing what to tell about and how to relate his/her experiences of residential life. The fact, however, is that the story told by the researcher is always only very limited (and personal). Whatever period the researcher has spent in the institutions, her/his experiences are time-bound. If the combination of residents and/or staff changed, some of the researcher's experiences would change as well. In my research, for example, the abusive period with a lot of violent encounters was unique in its intensity. That period was very 'true' and real but to describe residential life as so strongly violent would mean that other periods, more harmonious or differently problematic, would be overlooked. Residential units vary as well. To study one or two institution does not entitle the researcher to speak as if s/he was familiar with residential institutions in general. Even more importantly, the intersubjective nature of ethnographic knowledge cannot (should not) be hidden away by any formal analysis or writing approach.

One of the most powerful contributions to our understanding of residential life, Erving Goffman's *Asylum* (1961/87) is not informative about how the writer reached his analysis (Drew and Wootton, 1988). Doing qualitative research on residential life does not obviously challenge the researchers to reflect how the analytic assumptions have been made and how the researcher's story is to be told. This might be linked with the thin traditions of doing research on residential institutions (e.g. Curry, 1995; Berridge and Brodie, 1998). However, the researcher's power is very strong when deciding how to convince the reader about the analytic value of the researcher's notions.

In very mundane terms, the researcher may choose what to tell and what to exclude from the main corpus of the story and how to make sense of the stories told. Should the plans of the boys, described above, to kill a staff member be included in the main analysis and told to outsiders if the researcher is of the understanding that the episode was situationally unique, and therefore might give an unfair idea about residential life? Does the researcher have the right to decide that the residents' stories about voicelessness are more important and of more analytic value than the plan to kill?

The most confusing choice experienced in this research was how to treat conflicting information from different sources. In residential research (e.g. Kelly, 1992; Levin, 1998; Strömpl, 2002) this has often been treated as a conflict between rhetoric and practice which did not satisfy me as an interpretation. The young residents, whose experiences and views were the main focus of the study, told over and over again how they could not trust any member of the staff during their residential stay. Some staff were just anxious to maintain good order and did not permit any closer relationships to develop. Some of them were so full of doubts that they did not trust anything they were told which made it pointless for the young people to develop a trusting relationship. The main problem was that the staff did not understand what the young residents tried to tell them. The residents experienced that their points were not taken as they were and so their confidentiality and privacy were threatened. However, when talking to the staff, several of them told about very caring and close relationships they had with residents. Some relationships continued after the residential period and so it was not atypical that ex-residents visited the institution to meet their old staff. In participating in the daily life of the institutions, I also came across many episodes where mutual closeness, caring and respect seemed to characterise the encounters between the residents and staff. How should one understand the accounts given by the residents about the distant and cool relationships and their pessimism about trusting relationships?

In the analysis, to my understanding, I did not have any right to overlook the residents' descriptions of the lack and impossibility of caring relationships. However, my confusion is whether residential life as the context for the giving of these accounts had an impact on the accounts themselves. As residential life is so full of doubts, tensions and intersubjective and overgenerational conflicts, only certain types of stories were easily told. The ways how residential life was (re)presented in the research interviews followed the general line of residential life. It does not render meaningless the other types of encounters experienced in the institutions but it demonstrates the contextual nature of verbalising residential experiences. In the analysis, the contradictory accounts give a resource but also a reminder of the limitations of research knowledge. The judgement of the researcher of how the context and non-verbal communication should be taken into consideration has a powerful impact on what is to be known as 'research results'.

In a residential setting, it is not easy for the researcher to reflect her/his analytic notions with the residential people, as is often done in qualitative research, in order to give the informants a chance to validate (in a way or another) the researcher's interpretations. In the case of this research, the staff did not wish me to go back to meet the young residents to talk about the 'results' grounded in the field work periods. They were worried about the impact of such discussions: as one of the units was going through a difficult period with a lot of restlessness, extra input from the researcher was not welcome. Additionally, the staff did not assume the adolescents to be interested in the results. I did manage, however, to leave a note to the residents expressing my thanks and gratefulness for the interviews and other forms of participation. No one contacted me afterwards based on the contact information given (which is hardly surprising as phoning, e-mailing or letter writing is not free in the residential setting). That experience makes me wonder how easy it would be to develop any collaborative or reflective research approaches (e.g. Humphries et al., 2000) with the residents as it is, after, all, the staff who regulates the forms of social inquiry.

The first draft of the report was given to the staff of both institutions studied for their comments. I will return to the comments later. The role of the comments of those people involved in the study is not solely to rule out the interpretative misunderstandings or faults but to make the researcher aware of the issues or viewpoint s/he never learnt about. It is, of course, up to the researcher to decide how to deal with those comments.

The Vulnerability of the Researcher

Side-by-side with verbal knowledge, other sources of knowledge from seeing to feeling play a role in residential life. For example, space, the main tool of residential placement as such, is experienced bodily. The researcher experiences residential life in many other ways as well: the anxiety created by closed units, the continuous surveillance of one's movement in the residential grounds, the moments of physical violence or the tears on the young residents' face mark the researcher in ways which are not always easy to verbalize. The experiences might also take place on a very personal level, not always even known to the researcher.

The subjective feelings are discussed to some extent in ethnographic literature, whereas the literature around residential research touches upon this issue only occasionally. There are notions about the sensitive nature of research on residential care (e.g. Berridge and Brodie, 1998) but very often the researcher's own experiences, feelings, concerns or doubts are excluded from the written agenda of the research. The position given to the researcher is such as if s/he was untouched by the grief and conflicts experienced in residential life. I claim, however, that research on residential life leaves a mark on the researcher as well. The marks are not only personal but also part of the research knowledge.

Personally, the first visit to the reformatory schools after an absence of ten years (since my previous study of those institutions) was emotionally upsetting: the joy of revisiting the institution and its people was coloured by the deep worry the staff expressed in the very first discussions. They told about the decreasing age of the residents, the abusive and neglectful parents with whom family-centred work – so topical ten years ago – was impossible, the adolescents' exclusion experiences from school, new problems of literacy and multicultural tensions, among other things. The messages were very serious and reported residential care to be even more difficult than ten years ago. When I started talking with the residents, the stories became even richer in problems – loneliness, anxiety, unfairness and hopelessness. What happened to me? I started crying. The experienced researcher of social work, approaching middle-age, withdrew to the privacy of her own room to cry over the sadness and unfairness of the young people's stories. It was not only once but several times; and it was not only crying but the deep commitment to listen to the stories as fairly as possible. It was also the question of becoming partial – to stand on the young residents' side even though I knew that I had no easy access to know what their 'side' really was and that naivety is always lurking round the corner when one becomes emotionally involved.

The subjective involvement of the researcher is often seen as a threat to objectivity. In social work research, however, objectivity can mean an inhuman approach to the issues studied. Humiliation, exploitation, abandonment and grief are not only themes to discuss in a research interview but themes which both the researcher and the researched share as human beings as part of the social world (e.g. Harre, 1998; Liebling and Stanko, 2001). Being the same and different is one of the notions which has to be taken into account when doing research on difficult social issues. It cannot only be solved by excluding the subjective experiences of the researcher, nor by focusing only on the researcher's experiences. The vulnerability of the researcher is an issue which should be taken into account in a greater variety of ways than has been done so far.

The Research Report as Risk

Qualitative, especially ethnographic research reports on special groups of people, such as residents, can be read in many different ways. They can inform the reader about the otherwise unknown life styles and living conditions and they might promote some sympathy towards the people involved. The style of the reports might be close to any form of art, especially literature, as they impress and convince people instead of presenting 'plain truths' and often the researcher is balancing between writing fiction and doing qualitative analysis (Lofland, 1971; van Maanen, 1995), sometimes leaving the reader in doubt about the style. However, due to the easiness of the style, qualitative research reports might be read by a large variety of people, not only by academics. Being rich in giving accounts about mundane practices, the reports can be read also as control reports by the people in charge of those activities. The writer might carry in her/his mind all the possible readers and their reading styles when writing the report. However, the reader does not own the text and therefore it can be read and used in many ways.

When studying vulnerable adolescents in vulnerable conditions, the concern is strong. Could the report harm the people involved, not only personally but as a group (as residential youth)? Does the research repeat the same exclusive practices which so many adolescents in the reformatory schools had experienced many times in their lives?

The possible harm which the research report might cause was the main concern of the staff who read the first manuscript of the research discussed in this chapter. As residential care has been under continuous scrutiny for decades, staff may see a risk of the report being used against the institution's interests. As the report described the residents' experiences, quite a high number of critical remarks were to be found in the report. Especially the residents' accounts (represented by me through the analysis) about the surveillance practices concerning drugs when returning to the institution after a break and the regulation about dressing styles upset the staff readers. They did not argue that those statements were wrong but worried that they could be easily misunderstood by outside readers. They therefore tried to persuade me to write them differently so that their intentions behind the restrictive practices would be presented side by side with the residents' accounts. And that was what I did. I did not change any of the analysis based on the residents' accounts or practices I came across but I added more background information about the residential practices in order to avoid any clashes with the reformatory schools.

That decision to change the report can be criticized from different points of view. I argue, however, that it was socially and ethically right to do so if any future collaboration with the reformatory schools is seen as an important argument. Also, I trust the fair judgement of the residential staff about the possible harms and threats certain type of publicity could bring them. However, the question remains what possible changes the young residents would have wished to suggest if they had been given the chance. I had wished to be on the side of the residents, but was liaising with the staff, which was one of the social and ethical dilemmas.

Concluding Remarks

On the one hand, it is important to give the youngsters the chance to speak and to tell about their experiences in research. A research interview might offer a secure and confidential opportunity to speak about issues which have possibly not been given enough – or any – attention before. The research may function as a catalyst, possibly empowering the residents to see, among other things, as they learn that their personal views are of interest.

On the other hand, the research may objectify the adolescents when, for example, presenting the results of the analysis. The research results may be used against them (within the institution or in public debates). The problems are always there when doing qualitative research: the researcher might get so much and so rich information that its misuse is possible as well.

Michael Bloor (1997) discusses the engineering, empowering and critical aspects of social inquiry. Some of his examples come from residential settings. According to him, empowering and critical aspects of qualitative research can offer, for example, a source for reflection for practitioners to evaluate their practices. Research in residential setting can include all those aspects but my experience has been that there is always the possibility of harming and hurting as well.

The residential setting is very vulnerable, as the different actors it contains. What I suggest here is that the very nature of the residential setting is to be taken into account when conducting or judging research in residential institutions. As shown above, the residential setting is interwoven into many processes and dimensions of research. I also suggest that the ethical issues should be revisited over and over again and that they should not be excluded as a separate issue to discuss at the end of the report but that they actually make a fundamental cornerstone of knowledge production. What I experienced in this study most personally, was that there did not seem to be any way to make right decisions in order to avoid the wrong ones. Whatever I did, was partially right (to some), partially wrong (to the others). The lesson learnt might be that ambivalence belongs to research on residential life as well as to residential life itself. That should not, however, be any excuse to exclude the social, emotional, personal and ethical issues from the agenda on qualitative residential research.

References

Berridge, D. and Brodie, I. (1998), *Children's Homes Revisited*, London and Philadelphia: Jessica Kingsley Publishers.

Bloor, M. (1997), 'Addressing Social Problems through Qualitative Research', in D. Silverman (ed.), *Qualitative Research. Theory, Method and Practice*, London and Thousand Oaks and New Delhi: Sage, pp. 221–38.

Curry, J.F. (1995), 'The Current Status of Research in Residential Treatment', *Residential Treatment for Children and Youth*, Vol. 3 (12), pp. 1–15.

Drew, P. and Wootton, A. (eds) (1988), *Erving Goffman: Exploring the Interaction Order*, Cambridge: Polity Press.

Goffman, E. (1961/87), *Asylums. Essays on the Social Situation of Mental Patients and Other Inmates*, London: Penguin Books.

Harre, Rom (1998), 'When the Knower is also the Known', in T. May and M. Williams (eds), *Knowing the Social World*, Buckingham and Philadelphia: Open University Press.

Honkatukia, P., Nyqvist, L. and Pösö, T. (2003, forthcoming), *Sensitive Issues in vulnerable Conditions – Studying Violence in Youth Residential Care*, Young.

Humphries, B. (2000), *Research in Social Care and Social Welfare*, London: Jessica Kingsley Publishers.

Kelly, B. (1992), *Children Inside. Rhetoric and Practic in a Locked Institution for Children*, London and New York: Routledge.

Kvale, S. (1996), *InterViews. An Introduction to Qualitative Research Interviewing*, Thousand Oaks and London and New Delhi: Sage.

Levin, C. (1998), *Uppfostringsanstalten. Om tvång I föräldrars ställe*, Arkiv: Lund.

Liebling, A. and Stanko, B. (2001), 'Allegiance and Ambivallence. Some Dilemmas in Resarching Disorder and Violence', *British Journal of Criminology*, No. 41, pp. 421–30.

Lofland, J. (1971), *Analyzing Social Settings. A Guide to Qualitative Observation and Analysis*, Belmont: Wadsworth Publishing Company.

O'Neill, T. (2001), *Children in Secure Accomodation*, London: Jessica Kingsley.

Pink, S. (2001), *Doing Visual Ethnography*, London and Thousand Oaks and New Delhi: Sage.

Plummer, K. (2001), *Documents of Life 2. An Invitation to a Critical Humanism*, London and Thousand Oaks and New Delhi: Sage.

Pösö, T. (2003, forthcoming), *Vakavat silmät ja muita kokemuksia koulukodista* (*Solemn Eyes and Other Experiences from the Reformatory Schools*).

Strömpl, J. (2002), *The K. School. Residential Management of Troublesome Girls in Transition-time Estonia*, Tartu: Tartu University Press.

Van Maanen, J. (ed.) (1995), *Representation in Ethnography*, London: Sage.

Index